VOLUME ONE

A COUNTERINTELLIGENCE READER

AMERICAN REVOLUTION TO WORLD WAR II

FRANK J. RAFALKO (EDITOR)
NATIONAL COUNTERINTELLIGENCE CENTER

Published by Books Express Publishing
Copyright © Books Express, 2011
ISBN 978-1-78039-535-7

Books Express publications are available from all good retail and online booksellers. For publishing proposals and direct ordering please contact us at: info@books-express.com

PREFACE

After the National Counterintelligence Center designed and conducted several iterations of a seminar on *The Evolution of American Counterintelligence*, it became apparent that a well-thought out reader would be ideal to complement the lectures. We concluded that the great abundance of literature on counterintelligence and intelligence is, ironically, one of the main obstacles to understanding our discipline. Most of the current books and articles concern the numerous espionage cases that have plagued our profession over the past few years. The more famous, or infamous, the spy, the more books written. Only a few books endeavored to scrutinize counterintelligence but the treatment was uneven.

Our reader's three volumes cover counterintelligence's past and present. Nevertheless they form a whole: the first volume provides material elucidating counterintelligence's antecedents from the American Revolution to World War II. Volume two focuses on World War II while volume three begins with the Atom Bomb spies and concludes with the latest espionage cases. History is more than background; it is the framework of the present.

We have taken material from official government documents, indictments from several espionage cases, and articles written by professors, scholars and counterintelligence officers. We have abridged some selections while trying not to change the sense of the original but we have not altered the original usage of the English language.

Each chapter in the three volumes has an introduction, which sketches out the main trends and characteristics of the period in question. There is a chronology with each chapter for volumes one and three, but volume two only has one chronology to cover the entire period. At the end of each chapter is a selected bibliography. We hope this will help you get a sense of the period as a whole. The reader is not all-inclusive and people may disagree with our selections, but at least we hope to have provided sufficient material to entice our colleagues to do further research.

Counterintelligence is a fascinating and challenging discipline. Our response to these challenges is determined, not by the requisites of the immediate situation but by our historical legacy. Thus we urge that the materials presented in the three volumes be read, not as background to the present, but as part of the present itself.

TABLE OF CONTENTS

Chapter 1–*The American Revolution And The Post Revolutionary Era: A Historical Legacy* 1
    Introduction 1
Counterintelligence 2
    Paul Revere and the Mechanics 2
    Benjamin Church 3
    West and Gerry-Porter Letter Translation 8
Incercepting Communications 9
Deception Operations 9
The Hickory Plot 10
Minutes of the Committee For Detecting Conspiracies 11
Enoch Crosby Describes His Career As A Spy 12
Benedict Arnold 17
    The "Enabling" Causes 17
    The "Precipitating" Causes 19
    Implications for US Counterintelligence Today 20
    Epilogue for a Spy 21
Dr. Edward Bancroft 21
Secret Writing 24
Other Spies 24
    To Joseph Reed or Colonel Cornelius Cox– *April 7, 1777* 24
    To Governor William Livingston–*January 20, 1778* 25
    To Governor William Livingston–*March 25, 1778* 25
    To Colonel Stephen Moylan–*April 3, 1778* 25
    To Governor William Livingston–*June 1, 1778* 26
    To Brigadier General William Swallowed–*June 1, 1778* 26
    To The Board Of General Officers–*June 2, 1778* 26
    General Orders–*September 14, 1778* 26
    To Major General Alexander McDougall–*March 25, 1779* 27
    To Major General Alexander McDougall–*March 28, 1779* 27
    Joseph Hyson 27
    Lydia Darragh 28
    James Armistead 29
    John Honeyman 29
    Daniel Bissell 29
    David Gray 30
The XYZ Affair 30
The Burr Conspiracy 31
The Alien And Sedition Acts–1798 33
    The Naturalization Act–*June 18, 1798* 33
    The Alien Act *June 25, 1798*–An Act Concerning Aliens 34

  The Alien Enemies Act *July 6, 1798*–An Act respecting Alien Enemies 34
  The Sedition Act *July 14, 1798* 35
American Revolution Bibliography 36
American Revolution Chronology 38
American Revolution End Notes 186

Chapter 2–*The Civil War: Lack Of A Centralized Direction* 43
 Introduction 43
William H. Seward 44
Allan Pinkerton 45
 Pinkerton Letter 47
Layfayette Baker 49
Henry Beebee Carrington 56
 Stanton's Letter–*May 2, 1863* 58
Spies 59
 Belle Boyd 59
 Spencer Kellogg Brown 59
 Rose O'Neil Greenhow 60
 C. Lorain Ruggles 61
 Henry Bascom Smith 61
 Felix Grundy Stidger 61
 Benjamin Franklin Stringfellow 62
 Elizabeth Van Lew 62
Civil War Bibliography 64
Civil War Chronology 68
Civil War End Notes 188

Chapter 3–*Post Civil War To World War I* 69
 Introduction 69
The Office Of Naval Intelligence: A Proud Tradition Of Service 71
 General Order No. 292 71
 The War Years 72
 The Lean Years 73
A Tardy Awakening 74
The Underside Of The Mexican Revolution: El Paso 1912 83
Imperial Germany's Sabotage Operations In The U.S. 89
 Heinrich Friedrich Albert 94
 Paul Koenig 96
 Franz von Rinelen 97
 Black Tom Island 101
 The Kingsland Site 102
Department Of State And Counterintelligence 102
From Robert Lansing, With Enclosure 104

From Robert Lansing 106
From Walter Hines Page 106
Counterintelligence: Pre-World War I 108
A Navy Spy 108
The American Protective League 110
Counterintelligence In World War I 111
War Department General Order 113
    26 August 1918 113
From Albert Sidney Burleson 113
From Newton Diehl Baker 114
The Witzke Affair: German Intrigue On The Mexican Border, 1917-18 114
The Espionage Act May 16, 1918 122
From Edward Mandell House 122
The Red Scare Period 123
Military Intelligence Division 127
    Neglect of Military Intelligence 1919 127
    Organization of Military Intelligence Division 127
        The Negative Branch 129
Post Civil War Bibliography 133
Post Civil War Chronology 135
Post Civil War End Notes 190

Chapter 4–*Counterintelligence Between The Wars* 143
    Introduction 143
The Corps Of Intelligence Policy From 1917 To World War II 145
    Memo To Director Of Naval Intelligence 147
ONI Message 156
Attorney General Harlan Stone's Reforms 157
    Letter Hoover To Lang 159
    Navy Department Memo 160
Special Committee To Investigate Un-American Activities 160
The FBI Intelligence Program, 1936-1938 161
The Search For Japanese Spies 163
Special House Committee For The Investigation Of Un-American Activities 166
Defectors 166
    Alexander Gregory Barmine 166
    Ignace Reiss 167
    Walter G. Krivitsky 168
    Aleksandr Orlov 168
FBI Intelligence Authority And Sbbversion 169
    Presidential Directive–*June 26, 1939* 173

Letters To/From ONI 174
    H.G. Dohrman to Ellis–*April seventh 1934* 174
    Ellis to Dohrman–*Apr 12, 1934* 175
    Dohrman to Ellis–*April twentieth 1934* 175
    Dohrman to Ellis–*April twenty seventh, 1934* 176
    Dohrman to Ellis–*April thirteth 1934* 176
    Hoover to Ellis–*May 21, 1934* 177
Presidential Directive Of *September 6, 1939* 177
    Police Cooperation 177
The Scope Of FBI Domestic Intelligence 178
Counterintelligence Between The World Wars Bibliography 182
Counterintelligence Between The World Wars Chronology 184
Counterintelligence Between The World Wars End Notes 198

v

CHAPTER 1

CHAPTER 1

The American Revolution and the Post-Revolutionary Era: A Historical Legacy

Introduction

From 1774 to 1783, the British government and its upstart American colony became locked in an increasingly bitter struggle as the Americans moved from violent protest over British colonial policies to independence. As this scenario developed, intelligence and counterintelligence played important roles in America's fight for freedom and British efforts to save its empire.

It is apparent that British General Thomas Gage, commander of the British forces in North America since 1763, had good intelligence on the growing rebel movement in the Massachusetts colony prior to the Battles of Lexington and Concord. His highest paid spy, Dr. Benjamin Church, sat in the inner circle of the small group of men plotting against the British. Gage failed miserably, however, in the covert action and counterintelligence fields. Gage's successor, General Howe, shunned the use of intelligence assets, which impacted significantly on the British efforts. General Clinton, who replaced Howe, built an admirable espionage network but by then it was too late to prevent the American colonies from achieving their independence.

On the other hand, George Washington was a first class intelligence officer who placed great reliance on intelligence and kept a very personal hand on his intelligence operations. Washington also made excellent use of offensive counterintelligence operations but never created a unit or organization to conduct defensive counterintelligence or to coordinate its activity. This he left to his commanders and to committees established in the colonies.

When the Revolution was over and a new nation emerged, there continued to be ample opportunities to create a counterintelligence service. Spy scares, conspiracies and European meddling occurred repeatedly. But it isn't until the Civil War period that an effort is made to create a federal agency to conduct counterintelligence.

This chapter provides the legacy for America's use of counterintelligence in future years.

Counterintelligence

Probably the first patriot organization created for counterintelligence purposes was the Committee (later called a Commission) for Detecting and Defeating Conspiracies. It was made up of a series of groups established in New York between June of 1776 and January of 1778 to collect intelligence, apprehend British spies and couriers, and examine suspected British sympathizers. In effect, there was created a "special service" for New York which had the power to arrest, to convict, to grant bail or parole, and to jail or to deport. A company of militia was placed under its command to implement its broader charter. John Jay has been called the first chief of American counterintelligence because of his role in directing this Committee's work.

Nathaniel Sackett and Colonel William Duer were particularly successful in ferreting out British agents, but found their greatest success in the missions of one of the dozen or so agents of their own, Enoch Crosby. Crosby, a veteran of the Continental Army, had been mistaken by a Westchester County Tory as being someone who shared his views. He confided to Crosby that a secret Tory military company was being formed and introduced him to the group. Crosby reported the plot to the committee and was "captured" with the group. He managed to "escape" and, at Committee direction, infiltrated another secret Tory unit. This unit, including Crosby, was also taken and he "escaped" once more. He repeated the operation at least two more times before Tory suspicions made it necessary for him to retire from counterintelligence work.

Another successful American agent was Captain David Gray of Massachusetts. Posing as a deserter, Gray entered the service of Colonel Beverly Robinson, a Tory intelligence officer, and became Robinson's courier. As a result, the contents of each of Robinson's dispatches were read by the Americans before their delivery. Gray eventually became the courier for Major Oliver DeLancey, Jr., the head of the British secret service in New York. For two years, Gray, as DeLancey's courier to Canada, successfully penetrated the principal communications link of the British secret service. Upon completing his assignment, Gray returned to the ranks of the Continental Army and his name was struck from the deserter list, where George Washington placed it at the beginning of the operation.

Colonel Benjamin Tallmadge, a senior intelligence officer under Washington, is credited with the capture of Major John Andre, who preceded DeLancey as chief of the British secret service in New York. Although Tallmadge declined to discuss the episode in his memoirs, it is said that one of his agents had reported to him that Major Andre was in contact with a "John Anderson" who was expecting the surrender of a major patriot installation. Learning that a "John Anderson" had passed through the lines "en route to" General Benedict Arnold, the commander at West Point, Tallmadge had Anderson apprehended and returned for interrogation. "Anderson" admitted to his true identity—he was Major Andre—and was tried, convicted and executed as a spy. Arnold, learning that Andre had been taken and that his own traitorous role no doubt was exposed, fled West Point before he could be captured, and joined the British forces.

General Washington demanded effective counterintelligence work from his subordinates. On March 24, 1776, for example, he wrote: "There is one evil I dread, and that is, their spies. I could wish, therefore, the most attentive watch be kept ... I wish a dozen or more of honest sensible and diligent men, were employed...in order to question, cross question etc., all such persons as are unknown, and cannot give an account of themselves in a straight and satisfactory manner ... I think it is a matter of importance to prevent them obtaining intelligence of our situation."

Paul Revere and the Mechanics

The first patriot intelligence network on record was a secret group in Boston known as the "mechanics." The group apparently grew out of the old "Sons of

Liberty" organization that had successfully opposed the hated Stamp Act. The "mechanics" organized resistance to British authority and gathered intelligence. In the words of one of its members, Paul Revere, "In the Fall of 1774 and winter of 1775, I was one of the upwards of thirty, chiefly mechanics, who formed ourselves into a Committee for the purpose of watching British soldiers and gaining every intelligence on the movements of the Tories." According to Revere, "We frequently took turns, two and two, to watch the (British) soldiers by patrolling the streets at night."

Through a number of their intelligence sources, the "mechanics" were able to see through the cover story the British had devised to mask their march on Lexington and Concord. Dr. Joseph Warren, chairman of the Committee of Safety, charged Revere with the task of warning John Adams and John Hancock at Lexington that they were the probably targets of the enemy operation. Revere arranged for the warning lanterns to be placed in the Old North Church to alert patriot forces at Charleston, and then set off on his famous ride. He completed his primary mission of notifying Adams and Hancock. Then Revere, along with Dr. Samuel Prescott and William Dawes, rode on to alert Concord, only to be apprehended by the British en route. Dawes got away, and Dr. Prescott managed to escape soon afterward and to alert the patriots at Concord. Revere was interrogated and subsequently released, after which he returned to Lexington to warn Hancock and Adams of the proximity of British forces. Revere then turned to still another mission, retrieving from the local tavern a trunk belonging to Hancock and filled with incriminating papers. With John Lowell, Revere went to the tavern and, as he put, during a "continual roar of Musquetry . . . we made off with the Trunk."

Fortunately, when interrogated by the British, Revere did not have his travel orders from Dr. Warren; the authorization was not issued to him until two weeks later. And when Paul Revere filed a travel voucher for his famous ride, it was not until August, some four months later, that it was approved—and when it was approved, his per diem payment was reduced from five shillings a day to four.

Paul Revere had served as a courier prior to his famous "midnight ride," and continued to do so during the early years of the war. One of his earlier missions was perhaps as important as the Lexington ride. In December of 1774, Revere rode to the Oyster River with the intelligence report that the British, under General Gage, intended to seize Fort William and Mary. Armed with this intelligence, Major John Sullivan of the colonial militia led a force of four hundred men—all in civilian clothing rather than militia uniform—in an attack on the fort. The one hundred barrels of gunpowder taken in the raid were ultimately used by the patriots to cover their retreat from Bunker Hill.

Benjamin Church[1]

In late 1768, British troops commanded by General Thomas Gage occupied Boston, Massachusetts to curb the widely separated incidents of mob disorder that troubled the city following the enactment of the Townsend Acts. The Acts, which levied custom duties on the import of glass, lead, paints, paper and tea, was the latest in a series of burdensome taxation measures the British Parliament tried to impose on the colonies. Skirmishes occurred between Gage's troops and the civilian population in opposition to the tax. On 5 March, 1770, five men, "the first to defy and the first to die," were felled by British gunfire in what is termed the "Boston Massacre." From that moment, wrote Daniel Webster, "we date the serverence of the British empire."

Benjamin Church

Paul Revere's now famous engraving of the incident stirred emotion of protest in the hearts of the colonists, and Samuel Adams' well-orchestrated propaganda effort made the men martyrs and a symbol of the patriot cause. In response to the growing anger, General Gage strengthened the Boston garrison. When 1775 began, Gage had almost forty-five hundred soldiers in the city. The patriots were not idle during this time frame. They raised and drilled additional militia units throughout Massachusetts and continued to gather arms, ammunition and other military supplies which they cached at secret storehouses in the countryside.

Gage was aware that continued flare-ups between the British and the colonists could ignite into a war and he wanted to avoid precipitating such action. He also knew that to avoid a fight he needed military intelligence on the militia units within Massachusetts. Gage, who also served as colonial governor of Massachusetts, established a network of spies among the patriots. These spies provided information, sometimes in great detail, on the military preparations of the patriots. For example, in March 1774, one of his secret agents reported the patriots had stockpiled weapons and ammunition at Cambridge. On 1 September that year, the British successfully raided the Cambridge warehouse. The patriots, knowing that they needed information to avoid losing their munitions, created a small surveillance committee within the Sons of Liberty in Boston. The Sons of Liberty were secret organizations within the colonies, started in 1765, to organize opposition to the Stamp Act.

During the winter of 1774-75, the 30 members of the surveillance committee met regularly at the Green Dragon Tavern on Union Street in Boston. Members of the group regularly patrolled Boston's streets at night to detect British military preparations and other activity. They constituted an early warning system for the patriots by identifying possible British raids into the countryside which would allow their colleagues to move their military stores to new secret locations before British troops arrived. For example, in December 1774, the committee acquired intelligence that General Gage arranged to fortify a British arsenal at Portsmouth, New Hampshire with two regiments, intelligence that drove the Sons of Liberty to raid the installation before the British arrived and haul off about a hundred barrels of gunpowder and several cannons.

The leadership of the Mechanics, as the Green Dragon group is now sometimes called, consisted of Dr. Joseph Warren, Samuel Adams, John Hancock, Paul Revere, Dr. Benjamin Church, and one or two others. It is believed that Warren, a prominent Boston physician and later a major general who was killed at Bunker Hill, was leader of the group. Church, another physician and political leader, was also a member of the Boston Committee of Correspondence and Safety, the latter body responsible for control of the militia. A minor poet as well as a medical man, Church was a prolific author of Patriot propaganda and was famous for the oration he delivered in commemoration of the Boston Massacre on the third anniversary of that event.

Dr. Church was also one of General Gage's informers, a British double agent and probably the most valuable spy the British had in America at the time. Church was a native of Newport, Rhode Island. He graduated from Harvard in 1754 and went to England to study medicine at the London Medical College. Possibly in 1768, he returned to America with an English wife and began practicing medicine in Raynham, Massachusetts. Still accustomed to living a life of indulgence, which he acquired in London, Church kept a mistress and built an elaborate summer home. His penchant for free spending did not match his income from his medical practice. To compensate and obtain additional money, Church added spying to his professional resume.

No one knows when Church began his double agent career. "Whether he was driven by his debt or by doubt that the patriots could win, Church had apparently begun spying in 1771, while Samuel Adams was struggling to keep the cause alive. The next year, Thomas Hutchinson[2] had passed along gratifying news to Francis Bernard[3] in London that the man[4] who had written insultingly against Bernard had come over to the government's side."[5] Another writer states "It is not possible to pinpoint the exact date that Church began his spying for Gage, but a reasonable guess is 1774. In that year, Paul Revere was aware that the activities of his secret group, of which Church was a part, were known to General Gage. According to Dr. Savage of Barnstable, Massachusetts, who was training with Church at the same time, the latter's finances suddenly improved. Previously, Church had been financially pressed, built a mansion in Raynham which appeared beyond his means and acquired a mistress; classic indicators for counterintelligence."[6]

Paul Revere, who had his own spies within General Gage's command, knew that the Mechanics had been penetrated. Revere received information in November 1774 from his source that the proceedings of at least one meeting at the Green Dragon were known to Gage within 24 hours after the meeting. The only problem was the source could not provide Revere with the identity of the traitor. "We did not then distrust Dr. Church," he later remembered, "but supposed it must be some one among us." The only security measure the Mechanics adopted was to have each member swear on a Bible at every meeting at the Green Dragon that he would not divulge the group's secrets; an admirable procedure but hardly counterintelligence.

On April 14, 1775, Lord Dartmouth, British secretary for the colonies, sent secret instructions to Gage pressing him to take some forceful action against the patriots, such as arresting their leaders, before the situation in Massachusetts reached "A riper state of Rebellion." Gage ignored Lord Dartmouth's direction. Instead, Gage decided to capture the patriot military stockpile that Dr. Church and several other agents reported were located in Concord. In fact, the General's intelligence was so comprehensive he knew the exact location of the military stockpile within the town. Gage issued secret orders to Lt. Col. Francis Smith to proceed with a 700-man force to destroy the patriot ammunition and supply stores.

The surveillance committee obtained information on the destiny of the troops and sent Paul Revere and William Dawes to alert the patriots. They were later joined by Dr. Samuel Prescott. On the way to Concord, they encountered a mounted British patrol. Dawes escaped but had to return to Boston, Revere was captured and taken to Lexington where he told the British everything and then was released. Prescott managed to evade the patrol and get the message to Concord.

When Col. Smith and his troops arrived at Concord, he found 70 Minute Men waiting for him on the Common. Ordered repeatedly to leave the Common area, the Minute Men began to leave but ignored a British order to leave their weapons behind. A shot was fire from within the British ranks, followed by a volley from the British platoons. The gunshots killed eight patriots and wounded 10 others. Only one British soldier was wounded in the return fire. Smith destroyed a few military supplies in Concord and then began his return to Boston.

On his way back, he encountered patriot militiamen who continually assaulted his troops. British reinforcements at Lexington saved Smith and his troops from a complete disaster but it wasn't until all the British troops arrived in Charlestown, where British men-of-war were in the harbor, that Smith could feel comfortable. The British lost 73 killed, 174 wounded and 26 were missing while the American militia suffered 93 dead, wounded or missing. Following the battles of Lexington and Concord, the American militia men surrounded Boston and began a siege, which lasted until March 1776.

On April 21, 1775, after the patriots had driven the British troops back into Boston, Church crossed the patriot lines at Cambridge and entered the besieged city to meet with Gage. It is probable that Church ignored the security risks to his espionage role for Gage because he was more concerned about maintaining contact and getting paid. Paul Revere recalled 23 years after this happened that Church told the Committee of Safety that he was going into Boston. Dr. Warren, the president of the committee, told Church that the British would hang him if he was caught but Church was adamant about going. Warren then told Church that he needed to have a cover story for being in Boston and both men devised the story that Church was there to obtain needed medicines.

According to Revere, Church returned in a few days to Cambridge. He told the committee he had been arrested, taken before Gage, and then held for several days for interrogation but set free. Revere said that after Church's arrest later by Washington, Revere met with Deacon Caleb Davis and the two of them began to discuss Church. Revere said that "He (Davis) received a Bilet for General Gage-(he then did not know that Church was in Town)-when he got to the General's House, he was told the General could not be spoke with, that He was in private with a gentleman; that He waited near half an Hour, when General Gage & Dr. Church came out of a room, discoursing together, like persons who had been long acquainted." Davis further added that Church "went where he pleased, while in Boston, only a Major Caine, one of Gage's Aids, went with him." Revere also said that he "was told by another person, whom I could depend upon, that he saw Church go into General Gage's House, at the above time; that He gout out of the Chaise and went up the steps more like a man that was acquainted than a prisoner."[7]

On May 24, 1775, Dr. Church wrote to Gage advising him that the Massachusetts Provincial Congress was sending him to consult with the Continental Congress in Philadelphia. His mission was to appeal to the Congress to embody the various New England militias, currently laying siege to Boston, as its own army. Neither Gage nor Dr. Church saw the opportunities presented by having a British double agent handle such an important and sensitive assignment. Church was in a unique position to spread havoc within the patriot ranks by feeding false or misleading information to the Continental Congress and/or working to defeat the assignment. The only thing Church complained about to Gage was that he would be prevented from reporting to Gage for some time.

Church's handling of the Provincial Congress was so successful that soon after his return to Cambridge, the Massachusetts militias laying siege to Boston were converted into the Continental army under the command of George Washington. So impressive was Church that the Continental Congress appointed him director general of the army's hospital at Cambridge and chief physician of the Continental army at a salary of four dollars per day and granted him the authority to hire four surgeons and other medical staff.

In espionage and counterespionage, luck plays an important role. For Church his luck began to run out when he received a letter in cipher from his brother-in-law, John Fleming, a Boston printer and bookseller. In his letter, Fleming urged Church to repent his rebellion against the British government and return to Boston, where Fleming believed Church would be pardoned for his crime. Fleming told Church to reply no matter what his decision and to write his response in cipher, addressing the letter in care of Major Cane (one of General Gage's aides) and send it via Captain Wallace[8] of the H.M.S. Rose, a British warship then stationed near Newport, Rhode Island.

Church replied, but it is not clear whether he believed he was writing to his brother-in-law or to General Gage. Since all communications between Church and Gage ceased when Church departed for Philadelphia, it is possible Church saw Fleming's method of communication as a secure means of resuming his profitable espionage role with the British commander-in chief. In his response to Fleming, Church provided some exaggerated information on American military strength and some inaccurate reports of military plans, all framed within an impassioned plea to the British to adopt a more reasonable colonial policy.

Unable to take the letter directly to Newport, Church asked his mistress to take it there. Church told her to deliver the letter to Captain Wallace of the H.M.S. Rose, or to the Royal Collector, Charles Dudley. If neither of these men were available, she was instructed to give it to George Rome, a known Tory and a rich merchant and ship owner. Not familiar with the Newport environs, the mistress went to Godfrey Wainwood,[9] a local baker, whom she had known in Boston and believed to be a Tory.

She asked Wainwood to take her to any of the three individuals but he made an excuse not to do so. Exasperated, she then asked Wainwood to deliver the letter for her. Wainwood agreed but deposited the letter on a shelf and forgot about it until late September 1775, when he received a pressing inquiry from the woman expressing her concerned that "you never Sent wot yo promest to send." Realizing that only the British could have known that the letter was not delivered, Wainwood became suspicious.

Some historians claimed that part of Wainwood's suspicions is based on the fact that the letter was in cipher, but cipher was used by many people, including Thomas Jefferson for personal letters during the colonial days. What caused Wainwood's suspicions is the British officer as the recipient of the letter. Instead of doing as the woman requested,

Wainwood took the letter to Henry Ward, Secretary of the Colony, who wrote a letter of introduction and sent Wainwood with Church's letter to General Nathaniel Green, commander of the Rhode Island contingent of the Continental army. Greene, accompanied by Wainwood, went to see General Washington.

When Washington examined the letter he saw that it was dated July 22, (1775) on the outside and when unfolded showed it addressed to Major Cane in Boston. The ciphered contents were unreadable. Wainwood explained that before the outbreak of hostilities between the British and the Americans, he had fraternized with the woman, who was of easy virtue. Upon Washington's orders, the woman was seized and brought to Washington's Headquarters.

"I immediately secured the Woman," Washington reported in a letter to the president of the Continental Congress, "but for a long time she was proof against every threat and persuasion to discover the Author, however at length she was brought to a confession and named Dr. Church."[10] Washington told James Warren and Major Joseph Hawley the details of the woman's story and ordered them to go to Cambridge to arrest Church and get his papers.

In a few hours, Church appeared under guard and submitted to questioning. According to Washington's letter, he "readily acknowledged the Letter. Said it was designed for his Brother Fleming and when deciphered wou'd be found to contain nothing Criminal." Church offered no justification why he tried to send the letter to Boston by way of a British warship off Rhode Island when he have easily sent it under a flag of truce into the city from Cambridge. He also could not explain why he wrote it in cipher and refused to provide the key to decipher the message.

Washington informed the Continental Congress that a search of Church's papers failed to find the cipher key or any other incriminating evidence, but added that he was told that a confident of Church had been to Church's home and probably removed all the incriminating items before Washington's men arrived to conduct the search. Washington then turned his attention to finding the key to the cipher letter.

An amateur cryptanalyst stepped forward in the person of Reverend Samuel West, who happened to have been a Harvard classmate of Church. A second person, Elbridge Gerry, a member of the Massachusetts Provincial Congress and the Committee of Safety, who would later be the fifth vice-president of the United States, teamed with Colonel Elisha Porter, a colonel in the Massachusetts militia, to conduct a separate cryptanalytic attack on the cipher.

Church had used a type of cipher known as a monoalphabetic substitution, one of the easiest ciphers to solve (Edgar Allen Poe explains the technique in his short story *The Gold Bug*). Both West and the Gerry-Porter team provided Washington with identical translations of the letter: (see insert entiled *West and Gerry-Porter Letter Translation*).

Washington confronted Church with the deciphered text. In response, Church said he only sought to impress the British with the strength and determination of the Patriots and wanted to discourage General Gage from carrying on further military action. He asserted the letter was not an intelligence report. General Washington was not persuaded by his explanation, particularly since the last line read "Make use of every precaution, or I perish."

Washington convened his officers to discuss what to do with Church. They all agreed that the issue should be presented to the Continental Congress. Washington noted in his letter that he wanted Congress to review the 28th article of war to determine if it applied to Church."[11] On orders of the Continental Congress, Church was confined at Norwich, Connecticut.[12] Within a year or two-there is some confusion over the date in the record-he was released and permitted to depart on a schooner for the West Indies. Neither the ship nor the doctor was heard from again. Presumable both were lost at sea.

The full extent of Church's espionage activities on behalf of the British remained a mystery to Washington and the other patriot leaders. The only evidence they had was the intercepted letter. From the letter they could surmise that Church had previously provided intelligence to Gage but they did not know how much or on what topics. It was only when historians found Church's earlier reports among General Gage's papers did Church's double agent role become clear.

WEST AND GERRY-PORTER LETTER TRANSLATION

To Major Crane in Boston, on his Magisty's Service

I hope this will reach you; three attempts have I made without success. In effecting the last, the man was discovered in attempting his escape, but fortunately my letter was sewed in the waistband of his breeches. He was confined a few days during which time you may have guess my feelings. But a little art and a little cash settled the matter.

Tis a month since my return from Philadelphia. I went by the way of Providence to visit mother. The committee for Warlike Stores made me a formal tender of 12 pieces of cannon, 18 and 24 pounders, they having to a previous resolution to make the offer to General Ward. To make a merit of my services, I sent them down and when they received them they sent them to Stoughton to be out of danger, even tho' they had formed the Resolution as I before hinted of fortifying Bunker's Hill, which together with the cowardice of the clusmy Col Gerrish and Col Scammon, were the lucky occasion of their defeat. This affair happened before my return from Philadelphia. We lost 165 killed then and since dead of their wounds, 120 now lie wounded. The chief will recover,. They boast you have lost 1500, I suppose, with equal truth.

The people of Connecticut are raving in the cause of Liberty. A number from this colony, from the town of Stanford, robbed the King's stores at New York with some small assistance the New Yorkers lent them. These were growing turbulent. I counted 280 pieces of Cannon from 24 to 3 pounders at King's Bridge which the committee had secured for the use of the colonies. The Jersies are not a whit behind Connecticut in zeal. The Philadelphians exceed them both. I saw 2200 men in review there by General Lee, consisting of Quakers and other inhabitants in uniform, with 1000 riffle men and horse who together made a most warlike appearance. I mingled freely and frequently with the members of the Continental Congress. They were, united, determined in opposition, and appeared assured of success. Now to come home; the opposition is become formidable; 18 thousand men brave and determined with Washington and Lee at their head are no contemptible enemy. Adjutant General Gates in indefatigable in arranging the army. Provisions are very plenty. Cloaths (sic) are manufacturing in almost every town for the soldiers. Twenty tons of powder lately arrived at Philadelphia, Connecticut and Providence. Upwards of 20 tons are now in Camp. Salt Petre is made in every colony. Powder Mills are erected and constantly employed in Philadelphia and New York. Volunteers of the first fortunes are daily flocking to camp. One thousand riffle men in 2 or 3 days recruits are now levying to augment the army to 22 thousand men. Ten thousand militia are now appointed in this government to appear on the first summons.

The bills of all the colonies circulate freely and are readily exchanged for cash. Add to this that, unless some plan of accommodation takes place immediately, these harbours will swarm with privateers. An army will be raised in the middle Provinces to take possession of Canada. For the sake of the miserable convulsed empire, solicit peace, repeal the acts or Britain is undone. This advice is the result of warm affection to my king and to the realm. Remember, I never deceived you. Every article here sent you is sacredly true.

The papers will announce to you that I am again a member for Boston. You will there see our motley council. A general arrangement of offices will take place, except the chief which will be suspended buy for a little while to see what part Britain takes in consequence of the late continental petition. A view to independence grows more and more general. Should Britain declare war against the colonies, they are lost forever. Should Spain declare against England, the colonies will declare a neutrality which will doubtless produce an offensive and defensive league between them. For God's sake prevent it by a speedy accommodation.

Writing this has employed a day. I have been to Salem to reconnoitre, but could not escape the geese of the Capital. Tomorrow, I set out for Newport on purpose to send you this. I write you fully, it being scarcely possible to escape discovery. I am out of place here by choice; and therefore, out of pay, and determined to be so unless something is offered my way. I wish you could contrive to write me largely in cipher, by the way of Newport, addressed to Thomas Richards, Merchant. Inclose it in a cover to me, intimating that I am a perfect stranger to you, but being recommended to you as a gentlemen of honour, you took the liberty to inclose that letter, intreating me to deliver it as directed, the person, as you are informed, being at Cambridge. Sign some fictional name. This you may send to some confidential friend in Newport, to be delivered to me at Watertown. Make use of every precaution or I perish.

It appears Church may have been a volunteer walk-in or a defector-in-place, not a well-planned recruitment operation by Gage. Fortunately for the patriot's cause, Gage was mainly interested in the military intelligence Church provided. Gage failed to see the political importance Church offered to the British. For in Church, Gage had a penetration of the Patriot's inner circle in Massachusetts, a spy who sat at the secret meetings of the Committee of Correspondence and Safety, who was a trusted member of the Mechanics, and who even served briefly as liaison with the Continental Congress, but was never exploited for his political reporting or used to conduct political sabotage. It was a major shortsightedness of Gage. Church's espionage did have one positive benefit for counterintelligence, it lead to the enactment of the first espionage law in the colonies.

Intercepting Communications

The Continental Congress regularly received quantities of intercepted British and Tory mail. On November 20, 1775, it received some intercepted letters from Cork, Ireland, and appointed a committee made up of John Adams, Benjamin Franklin, Thomas Johnson, Robert Livingston, Edward Rutledge, James Wilson and George Wythe "to select such parts of them as may be proper to publish." The Congress later ordered a thousand copies of the portions selected by the Committee to be printed and distributed. A month later, when another batch of intercepted mail was received, a second committee was appointed to examine it. On the basis of its report, the Congress resolved that "the contents of the intercepted letters this day read, and the steps which Congress may taken in consequence of said intelligence thereby given, be kept secret until further orders..." By early 1776, abuses were noted in the practice, and Congress resolved that only the councils or committees of safety of each colony, and their designees, could henceforth open the mail or detain any letters from the post.

James Lovell is credited with breaking British ciphers, but perhaps the first to do so was the team of Elbridge Gerry, Elisha Porter and the Rev. Samuel West who successfully decoded the intercepted intelligence reports written to the British by Dr. Benjamin Church, the Director General of Hospitals for the Continental army.

When Moses Harris reported that the British had recruited him as a courier to carry messages for their Secret Service, General Washington proposed that General Schuyler "contrive a means of opening them without breaking the seals, take copies of the contents, and then let them go on. By these means we should become masters of the whole plot..." From that point on, Washington was privy to British intelligence pouches between New York and Canada.

Deception Operations

To offset British superiority in firepower and troops, General Washington made frequent use of deception operations. He allowed fabricated documents to fall in the hands of enemy agents or to be discussed in their presence. He allowed his couriers—carrying bogus information-to be captured by the British, and inserted forged documents in intercepted British pouches that were then permitted to go on to their destination. Washington even had fake military facilities built. He managed to make the British believe that his three thousand man army was outside Philadelphia was 40,000 strong! With elaborate deception, Washington masked his movement toward Chesapeake Bay—and victory at Yorktown—by convincing the British that he was moving on New York.

At Yorktown, James Armistead, a slave who joined Lafayette's service with his master's permission, crossed into Cornwallis' lines in the guise of an escaped slave, and was recruited by Cornwallis to return to American lines as a spy. Lafayette gave him a fabricated order that supposedly was destined for a large number of patriot replacements—a force that did not exist. Armistead delivered the bogus order in crumpled dirty condition to Cornwallis, claiming to have found it along the road during his spy mission. Cornwallis believed him and did not want to believe he had been tricked until after the battle of Yorktown. Armistead was granted his freedom by the Virginia legislature as a result of this and other intelligence services.

Another deception operation at Yorktown found Charles Morgan entering Cornwallis' camp as a deserter. When debriefed by the British, he convinced them that Lafayette had sufficient boats to move his troops against the British in one landing operation. Cornwallis was duped by the operation and dug in rather than march out of Yorktown. Morgan in turn escaped in a British uniform and returned to American lines with five British deserters and a prisoner!

The Hickey Plot[13]

On 21 June 1776, General George Washington authorized and requested the Committee to Detect Conspiracies to arrest David Matthews, the Tory mayor of New York City, and confiscate his papers. Matthews, accused of distributing money to enlist men and purchase arms for the British cause and corrupting American soldiers, was residing at Flatbush, on Long Island, near General Greene's encampment. Washington transmitted the warrant drawn by the Committee to General Greene on the 21st with directions that it should be executed with precision exactly at one o'clock of the ensuing morning by a careful officer. Greene dispatched a detachment of men who took Matthews into custody but found no incriminating papers.

Matthews' arrest was the result of hearings conducted from 19 to 21 June 1776 by the Committee to Detect Conspiracies under the able leadership of John Jay. Until Jay was appointed to head the Committee, it had put off real efforts to uncover any information concerning activities or persons still loyal to the king.

During the hearings, conducted at Scott's Tavern on Wall Street, the Committee first heard testimony from Isaac Ketchum, a counterfeiter who had been arrested and was incarcerated in the City Hall jail. Ketchum wanted to work a deal with the Committee; in exchange for his information he wanted to be set free. The Committee agreed.

According to Ketchum, two prisoners by the name of Thomas Hickey and Michael Lynch, who were in jail on suspicion of counterfeiting, attempted to recruit him for the British. Hickey and Lynch both said they abandoned the American cause and secretly joined the British side. They indicated that others had also secretly agreed to serve the British. Ketchum further told the Committee that Hickey and Lynch were recruited to the British cause by an individual name "Horbush." The Committee at first was unable to identify Horbush but soon realized that Ketchum probably meant "Forbush," which is a variant of the name Forbes. The Committee then quickly identified Forbes as Gilbert Forbes, a well-known gunsmith who owned "The Sign of the Sportsman" shop on Broadway. The Committee also determined that Hickey was a sergeant in Washington's personal guards.

Two days after Ketchum's testimony, the Committee heard from William Leary, a prominent local businessman. Leary told the American authorities that he was in the city hunting for a runaway indentured worker of his who had disappeared. Leary successfully found the worker but later lost him. As he was walking around the city, he accidentally met another former employee James Mason. Mason, believing that Leary had left the company, asked Leary if he was in New York to join the other men. Leary, not knowing what Mason was discussing, feigned agreement. Mason, joined by several others, began to recruit Mason into a conspiracy but suddenly stopped when they became suspicious of him.

The Committee interviewed Mason who provided additional details about the Loyalist plot. He informed the Committee that men were being recruited to join a special Tory corps and had received pay from Governor Tryon. A Sergeant Graham, an old soldier, formerly of the royal artillery, had been recruited by Tryon to prowl around and survey the grounds and works about the city and Long Island. Based on his information, a plan of action was conceived. Upon arrival of the fleet, a man-of-war would cannonade the battery at Red Hook. While doing so, a detachment of the army would land below the cannonade and by a circuitous route surprise and storm the works on Long Island. The ships would then divide with some sailing up the Hudson River and the others up the East River. Troops were to land above New York, secure the pass at King's Bridge and cut off all communications between the city and the country. Upon a signal, artillerymen who were conspirators were to turn their cannon on the

American troops, the ammo stores were to be blown up and King's Bridge was to be cut to prevent the Americans from escaping.

Under pressure of interrogation, Mason revealed the names of several of Washington's guards: Hickey, William Green (drummer), James Johnson (fifer), and a soldier named Barnes. Gilbert Forbes was the paymaster, giving the men ten shillings a week. Mason also said New York mayor Matthews contributed 100 British pounds to the plot. Mason also identified three taverns as favorite hangouts of the conspirators; The Sign of the Highlander, Lowrie's Tavern, and Corbie's Tavern. Corbie's Tavern, near Washington's quarters, was a rendezvous site for the conspirators. Thomas Hickey was supposedly recruited here. Hickey recruited Green the drummer and Johnson the fifer. According to a conversation overheard at Corbie's Tavern, Washington was to be assassinated when the British army landed, as part of a plan for a surprise attack on the core of the Continental Army.

The Committee halted further depositions and went to notify Washington. The information was sufficient for Washington to issue the warrant for Matthews' arrest. Since Hickey and Lynch had already been returned to Washington's Headquarters, they were arrested by Washington's troops. A Court-martial was convened on 24 June 1776 and Hickey was charged with "exciting and joining in a mutiny and sedition, and of treacherously corresponding with, enlisting among, and receiving pay from the enemies of the United Colonies." Hickey pleaded not guilty.

The army produced four witnesses to testify against Hickey. Greene confirmed that Hickey had accepted funds to enlist in the Loyalist plot. Gilbert Forbes also said that he gave Hickey money. Ketchum repeated the hearsay evidence he presented to the Committee and a fourth person, William Welch said that Hickey had tried to recruit him. The only defense Hickey offered was that he was trying to cheat the Tories out of their money. As to having his name placed on board the British warship, he said he agreed to it as a precaution should the British defeat the Americans and he was taken prisoner, then he would be safe.

After a short deliberation, the officers found Hickey guilty as charged and sentenced him to death. On 27 June, Washington and his Council of Officers met. They reviewed the transcript of the trial and agreed with the sentence. On 28 June 1776 Hickey was hanged. He was the only conspirator to be executed; 13 others were imprisoned. Matthews was held as a prisoner but escaped to London. After the war he testified he had formed a plan for taking Washington and his guard but it was never realized.

Minutes Of The Committee For Detecting Conspiracies

(Fishkill), December 23rd, 1776

Present: Leonard Gansevoort Esqr. Chairman; John Jay, Zephaniah Platt, Nathaniel Sacket, Esqrs.

Resolved that Enoch Crosby assuming the name of _____ do forthwith repair to Mount Ephraim and use his utmost art to discover the designs, places of resort, and route, of certain disaffected persons of that quarter, who have formed a design of joining the enemy, and that for that purpose the said Enoch be made acquainted with all the Information received by this Committee concerning this plan, and that he be furnished with such passes as will enable him to pass there without interruption, and with such others as will enable him to pass as an emissary of the enemy amongst persons disaffected to the American Cause.

Resolved that Enoch Crosby be furnished with a horse and the sum of 30 dollars in order to enable him to execute the above resolution.

Resolved that Mr. Nathaniel Sackett be requested to give such instructions to Enoch Crosby as he shall think best calculated to defeat the designs of the persons above mentioned.

Ordered that the Treasurer pay Enoch Crosby 30 dollars for secret services. . .

Resolved that Nathaniel Sacket Esqr. be requested to furnish Mr. Enoch Crosby with such clothing as he may stand in need of.

Enoch Crosby Describes His Career As A Spy

*Southeast, Putnam County,
15 October 1832*

In the latter part of the month of August in the year 1776, he enlisted into the regiment commanded by Col. Swortwaut[14] in Fredericksburgh now Carmel in the County of Putnam and started to join in the army at KingsBridge. The company had left Fredericksburgh before the declarent started, and he started along after his said enlistment and on his way at a place in Westchester County about two miles from Pines bridge he fell in company with a stranger, who accosted the deponent and asked him if he was going down.

The stranger then asked if declarent was not afraid to venture alone, and said there were many rebels below and he would meet with difficulty in getting down.

The declarent perceived from the observations of the stranger that he supposed the declarent intended to go to the British, and, willing to encourage that misapprehension and turn it to the best advantage, he asked if there was any mode which he the stranger could point out by which the declarent could get through safely. The stranger after being satisfied that declarent was wishing to join the British army, told him that there was a company raising in that vicinity to join the British army, and that it was nearly complete and in a few days would be ready to go down and that declarent had better join that company and go down with them.

The stranger finally gave to the declarent his name, it was Bunker, and told the declarent where and showed the house in which he lived and told him that Fowler[15] was to be the captain of the company then raising and Kipp[16] Lieutenant. After having learned this much from Bunker, the declarent told him that he was unwilling to wait until the company could be ready to march and would try to get through alone and parted from him on his way down and continued until night when he stopped at the house of a man who was called Esquire Young, and put up there for the night.

In the course of conversation with Esquire Young in the evening, the declarent learned that he was a member of the committee for safety for the county of Westchester and then communicated to him the information he had obtained from Mr. Bunker, Esqr. Young requested the declarent to accompany him the next morning to the White plains in Westchester County as the committee of safety for the County were on that day to meet at the Court house in that place.

The next morning the declarent in company with Esqr. Young went to the White plains and found the Committee there sitting. After Esqr. Young had an interview with the committee, the declarent was sent for, and went before the committee, then sitting in the Court room, and there communicated the information he had obtained from Bunker.

The Committee after learning the situation of declarent, that he was a soldier enlisted in Col. Swrotwaut's regiment and on his way to join it if he would consent to aid in the apprehension of the company then raising. It was by all thought best, that he should not join the regiment, but should act in a different character as he could thus be more useful to his country.

He was accordingly announced to Capt. Townsend who then was at the White plains commanding a company of rangers as a prisoner, and the Captain was directed to keep him until further orders. In the evening after was placed as a prisoner under Capt. Townsend, he made an excuse to go out and was accompanied by a soldier. His excuse led him over a fence into a field of corn then nearly or quite full grown. As soon as he was out of sight of the soldier he made the best of his way from the soldier and when the soldier hailed him to return he was almost beyond hearing. An alarm gun was fired but declarent was far from danger.

In the course of the night the declarent reached the house of said Bunker, who got up and let him in. The declarent then related to Bunker the circumstances of his having been taken prisoner, and his going before the Committee at the Court house, of being put under the charge of Capt. Townsend and of his escape, that he had concluded to avail himself of the protection of the company raising in his neighborhood to get down. The next morning Bunker went with declarent and introduced him as a good loyalist to several of the company. The declarent remained some days with different individuals of the company and until it was about to do down, when declarent went one night to the house of Esqr. Young to give information of the state and progress of the company. The distance was four or five miles from Bunkers.

At the house of Esqr. Young, the declarent found Capt. Townsend with a great part of his company and after giving the information he returned to the neighborhood of the Bunkers. That night the declarent and a great part of the company which was preparing to go down were made prisoners. The next day all of them, about 30, were marched to the White plains, and remained there several days, a part of the time locked up in jail with other prisoners, the residue of the time he was with the Committee. The prisoners were finally ordered to Fishkill in the County of Dutchess where the State Convention was then sitting. The declarent went as a prisoner to Fishkill. Capt. Townsend with his company of rangers took charge of the company.

At Fishkill a Committee for Detecting Conspiracies was sitting composed of John Jay, afterwards Governor of N York, Zerpeniah Platt afterwards first judge of Dutchess County, Colonel Duer of the County of Albany, & a Mr. Sackett. The declarent was called before that committee, who understood the character of declarent and the nature of his services, this the committee must have learned either from Capt. Townsend or from the Committee at White plains. The declarent was examined under oath and his examination reduced to writing. The prisoners with the declarent were kept whilst declarent remained at Fishkill in a building which had been occupied as a Hatters shop and they were guarded by a company of rangers commanded by Capt. Clark. The declarent remained about a week at Fishkill when he was bailed out by Jonathan Hopkins. This was done to cover the character in which declarent acted.

Before the declarent was bailed, the Fishkill Committee had requested him to continue in this service, and on declarent mentioning the fact of his having enlisted in Col. Swortwaut's company and the necessity there was of his joining it, he was informed that he should be indemnified from that enlistment, that they would write to the Colonel and inform him that declarent was in their service. The Committee then wished declarent to undertake a secret service over the river. He was furnished with a secret pass, which was a writing signed by the Committee which is now lost and directed to go to the house of Nicholas Brawer near the mouth of the Wappingers creek who would take him across the river, and then to proceed to the house of John Russell about 10 miles from the river, and make such inquiries & discoveries as he could.

He proceeded according to the directions to said Brawers, and then to John Russells, and there hired himself to said Russell to work for him but for no definite time. There was a neighborhood of Loyalists and it was expected that a company was there raising for the British army. The declarent remained about 10 days in Russells employment and during that time ascertained that a company was then raising but was not completed. Before the declarent left Fishkill on this service, a time was fixed for him to recross the river and given information to some one of the committee who was to meet him.

This time having arrived and the company not being completed, the declarent recrossed the river and met Zepeniah Platt, one of the Committee, and gave him all the information he had then obtained. The declarent was directed to recross the river to the neighborhood of Russells and on a time then fixed, again to meet the Committee on the east side of the river.

The declarent returned to Russells neighborhood, soon became intimate with the Loyalists, and was introduced to Capt. Robinson, said to be an English officer and who was to command the company then raising. Capt. Robinson occupied a cave in the mountains, and deponents—having agreed to go with the company—were invited and accepted of the invitation to lodge with Robinson in the cave. They slept together nearly a week in the cave and the time for the company to start having been fixed and the rout designated to pass Severns, to Bush Carricks where they were to stop the first night.

The time for starting having arrived before the appointed time to meet the Committee on the east side of the river, the declarent—in order to get an opportunity to convey information to Fishkill—recommended that each man should the night before they started sleep where he chose and that each should be by himself for if they should be discovered that night together all would be taken which would avoided if they were separated.

This proposition was acceded to, and when they separated declarent not having time to go to Fishkill, and as the only and as it appeared to him the best means of giving the information, as to go to a Mr. Purdy who was a stranger to declarent and all he knew of him was that the Tories called him a wicked rebel and said that he ought to die, declarent went and found Purdy, informed him of the situation of affairs, of the time the company was to start and the place at which they were to stop the first night, and requested him to go to Fishkill and give the information to the Committee. Purdy assured the declarent that the information should be given. Declarent returned to Russells and lodged in his house.

The following evening the company assembled consisting of about thirty men and started from Russell's house which was in the Town of Marlborough and County of Ulster for New York and in the course of the night arrived at Bush Carricks and went into the barn to lodge after taking refreshments.

Before morning the barn was surrounded by American troops and the whole company including Capt. Robinson were made prisoners. The troops who took the company prisoners were commanded by Capt. Melancton Smith, who commanded a company of rangers at Fishkill. His company crossed the river to perform this service.

Col. Duer was with Capt. Smith's Company on this expedition. The prisoners including the declarent were marched to Fishkill and confined in the stone church in which there was near two hundred prisoners, after remaining one night in the church the Committee sent for declarent and told him that it was unsafe for him to remain with the prisoners, as the least suspicion of the course he had pursued would prove fatal to him, and advised him to leave the village of Fishkill but to remain where they could call upon him if his services should be wanted.

Declarent went to the house of a Dutchman a farmer whose name is forgotten about five miles from the Village of Fishkill and there went to work at making shoes. After declarent had made arrangements for working at shoes he informed Mr. Sacket one of the Committee where he could be found if he should be wanted.

In about a week declarent received a letter form the Committee requesting him to meet some one of the Committee at the house of Doct. Osborn about one mile from Fishkill. Declarent according to the request went to the house of Doct. Osborn and soon after John Jay came there, inquired for the Doctor–who was absent, inquired for medicine but found none that he wanted, he came out of the house and went to his horse near which declarent stood and as he passed he said in a low voice it won't do, there are too many around, return to your work. Declarent went back and went to work at shoes but within a day or two was again notified and a horse sent to him, requiring him to go to Bennington in Vermont and from thence westerly to a place called Maloonscack, and there call on one Hazard Wilcox, a Tory of much notoriety and ascertain if anything was going on there injurious to the American cause.

Declarent followed this instructions, found Wilcox but could not learn that any secret measure was then projected against the interest of the county at the place, but learned from Wilcox a list of persons friendly to the British cause who could be safely trusted, from that place quite down to the south part of Dutchess County, declarent followed the directions of said Wilcox and called on the different individuals by him mentioned but could discover nothing of importance until he reached the town of Pawling in Duchess County where he called upon a Doctor, whose name he thinks was Prosser, and informed him that he wished to go below, but was fearful of some trouble.

The Doctor informed him that there was a company raising in that vicinity to go to New York to join the British Army, that the Captains name was Shelden that he had been down and got a commission, that the Prosser was doctoring the Lieutenant, whose name was Chase, that if declarent would wait a few days he could safely go down with that company, that he could stay about the neighborhood, and should be informed when the company was ready. That declarent remained in that vicinity, became acquainted with several of the persons who were going with that company, was acquainted with the Lieutenant Chase, but never saw the Captain to form any acquaintance with him.

The season had got so far advanced that the company were about to start to join the enemy to be ready for an early commencement of the campaign in 1777. It was about the last of February of that year, when a place was fixed and also a time for meeting. It was at a house situated half a mile from the road and about three miles from a house then occupied by Col. Morehause a militia Colonel. After the time was fixed for the marching of Capt. Sheldens company the deponent went in the night to Col. Morehause and informed him of the situation of the company of the time appointed for meeting of the place and Morehause informed declarent that they should be attended to.

The declarent remained about one month in the neighborhood, and once in the time met Mr. Sackett one of the Committee at Col. Ludingtons, and apprised him of what was then going on, and was to have given the Committee intelligence when the company was to march but the shortness of the time between the final arrangement and the time of starting was that declarent was obliged to give the information to Col. Morehause.

The company consisting of about thirty met at the time and place appointed and after they had been there an hour or two; two young men of the company came in and said there was a gathering under arms at old Morehauses, the inquiry became general, what could it mean, was there any traitors in the company. The captain soon called one or two of the company out the door for the purpose of private conversation about the situation, and very soon declarent heard the cry of stand, stand.

Those out the door ran but were soon met by a company coming from a different direction, they were taken in the house surrounded and the company all made prisoners. The Col. then ordered them to be tied together, two and two, they came to declarent and he begged to be excused from going as he was lame and could not travel, the Col. replied, you shall go dead or alive and if in no other way you shall be carried on the horse with me, the rest were marched off and declarent put onto the horse with Col. Morehause, all went to the house of Col. Morehause and when the prisoners were marched into the house declarent with the permission of Morehause left them and made the best of his way to Col. Ludingtons and there informed him of the operations of the night, he reached Col. Ludingtons about day light in the morning, from thence he went to Fishkill to the house of Doct. Van Wyck where John Jay boarded and there informed him of all the occurrences on that northern expedition.

Said Jay requested the declarent to come before the Committee the next night when they would be ready to receive him he accordingly went before the Committee where he declared under his oath all that had occurred since he had seen them. The Committee then directed him to go to the house of Col. Van Ness in Albany County and there take directions from him. He went to Van Ness house and was directed by him to go to the north but declarent cannot tell the place the duty was performed, but nothing material discovered, further that the confiscation of the personal property of the Tories and leasing of their lands had a great tendency to discourage them from joining the British Army, declarent then returned to Pokeepsie, where Egbert Benson and Melancton Smith acted in the room of the Fishkill Committee.

There was no more business at that time in which they wished to employ declarent, and he being somewhat apprehensive that a longer continuance in that employment would be dangerous, and the time for which he enlisted in Col. Swortwauts regiment having expired he came home with the approbation of the Committee. This was about the last of May 1777, and in the course of the fall after, the declarent saw Col. Swortwaut at his house in Fishkill and there talked over the subject of the employment of the declarent by the Committee and the Col. told declarent that he had drawn his pay the same as if he had been with the regiment, that the Paymaster of the Regiment lived in the town of Hurley in Ulster

American Revolution

County. Declarent went to the paymaster and received his pay for nine months service or for the term for which the regiment was raised. The declarent was employed in the secret service for a period of full nine months.

This declarent further says that in the year 1779 in the month of May he enlisted into a company commanded by Capt. Johah Hallett for six months declarent enlisted as a sergint in said Hallets company. The term of enlistment was performed on the lines in the County of Westchester, moving from place to place to guard the country and detect Tories, that the company continued in this service until after Stony Point was taken by Gen. Wayne and abandoned and also reoccupied and abandoned by the English troops.

When this company was ordered over the river and joined the regiment at Stony Point and continued there in making preparations for building a block house until the time of the expiration of the service when the company was ordered to march to Pokeepsie to be discharged by the Governor. When they arrived, the Governor was absent the company was billetted out and the declarent was billetted upon the family of Doct. Tappen.

After remaining a day or two and the Governor not arriving, they were discharged. During this service in Westchester County the following occurrence took place a British vessel of war lay at anchor near Tellers Point and a party of sailors or marines cam eon shore and wandered a short distance from the water when a party of our men got between them and the river and made them prisoners. They were marched to the place when the company then lay, a little east of Tellers point, the number of prisoners declarent thinks was twelve and the captors six. The prisoners were afterwards sent to Pokeepsie.

This declarent further says that in the month of May in the year 1780 he again enlisted for six months in a company commanded by Capt. Livingston in Col. Benschautens Regiment. He enlisted as a sergent in the Town of Fredericksburgh now the town of Kent in Putnam County. The Regiment assembled at Fishkill and marched to Westpoint and remained there a few days some ten or fifteen, a call was made for troops to fill up the Brigade or Brigades under the command of Gen. De La Fayettes, and they were to be raised by drafts or volunteers, a call first was made for volunteers and the declarent with others volunteered and made a company which was put under the care and charge of Capt. Daniel Delavan.

The declarent continued to be a sergent in Delavans company. Col. Phillip Van Cortland commanded the regiment to which Captain Delavans company was attached, soon after the company was formed they crossed the river from West Point and marched to Peekskill where they remained one night. The next day marched to Verplanks point and crossed over to Stony Point and from thence made the best of their way to New Jersey where they remained until late in the fall when the time of enlistment having expired they were discharged, after having fully and faithfully performed the service of six months for which he enlisted.

During this campaign in New Jersey. Major Andre was arrested, condemned and executed several of the soldiers of Capt. Delavan's company went to see him executed. This declarent was sergent of the guard that day and could not go to see the execution.

The declarent further says that he has no documentary evidence of his service, and that he knows of no person who can testify to his services other than those whose depositions are hereto annexed.

Enoch Crosby

The declarent hereby relinquishes every claim whatever to a pension or annuity except the present and declares that his name is not on the pension roll agency of any state.

The declarent has a record of his age.

The declarent was living in the town of Danbury in the state of Connecticut when he enlisted into the service, that since the revolutionary war the declarent has resided in the State of New York, in what is now the County of Putnam formerly the County of Duchess, and now lives in the same county and on the same farm where he has lived for the last fifty years. The declarent always volunteered in every enlistment and to perform all the services which he performed as detailed in this declaration.

That the declarent was acquainted with the following officers who were with the troops where he served. General Schuyler, Gen. Montgomery, General Wooster, Col. Waterbury, Col. Holmes, Gen. DeLa Fayette, Gen. Poor, Col Van Coretlandt, Col. Benschauten, Col. Ludington.

The declarent never received any written discharge, and if he ever received a sergents warrant it is through time and accident lost or destroyed.

This declarent is known to Samuel Washburn a Judge of the Court of Common Pleas of the County of Putman, Benaiah Y. Morse a clergyman in his neighborhood and who he believes can testify to his character for veracity and good behaviour and thus belief of his services as a soldier of the revolution.

/S/ Enoch Crosby

Benedict Arnold[17]

"bold, crafty, unscrupulous, unrepentant: the Iago of traitors"[18]

The US public prefers to dismiss Benedict Arnold as simply "a despicable traitor." To today's US counterintelligence (CI) specialists, however, he offers a valuable case study—the classic example of a "high performer" and "trusted insider" who (for complex and unpredictable reasons) decided to become an espionage "volunteer." What were Arnold's motivations, and what were the enabling and precipitating causes of his decision to go over to the enemy? More importantly, what changes in Arnold's behavior and activities should have raised "CI flags" in the minds of his friends and fellow officers?

The "Enabling" Causes:

Several personal and historical factors combined to make it possible for Benedict Arnold to eventually make the decision to become a traitor. These factors included:

1). Arnold was a "self-made man" in the truest sense of these words. Born into a poor but respectable New England family (his great-grandfather had been a colonial Governor of Rhode Island) he received the 18th Century equivalent of a high school education and was apprenticed to a pharmacist. Arnold learned the "military arts" by serving with (and—in a premonition of things to come—deserting from) several New York militia units in the late 1750s. During the next two decades he became a successful merchant, sea trader/smuggler (he sailed his own ships between Canada and the West Indies), and family man in Connecticut and Massachusetts.

From the outset, however, Arnold's personality demonstrated certain excesses which made him ill-suited for public service or other cooperative enterprises. These included: extreme personal ambition, ruthlessness in business dealings, opportunism, and a willingness to take risks and manipulate situations to his own advantage. By the time he joined the Continental Army in 1775, Arnold had established a reputation as a cranky and litigious "sharp trader" used to making his own rules and getting his own way. These personality characteristics were to remain constant throughout Arnold's life, and were often noted by those who dealt with him during his cooperation with the British authorities in 1779-1782 and throughout his subsequent career as a businessman in Canada and England.

2). Arnold's military career during the Revolutionary War was meteoric. Physically strong and apparently quite fearless in battle, he took part in a series of spectacular, high risk operations against the British (the capture of Fort Ticonderoga, the St. John's raid, the ill-fated invasion of Canada in the

American Revolution

Arnold tells Andre to hide West Point plans in his boots.

Andre is captured.

Andre on his way to the gallows.

Fall of 1775—during which he was severely wounded—and the Battle of Valcour Island) which boosted his reputation and self-confidence. Arnold's energy and valor ingratiated him to George Washington, who urged his promotion and supported him during a series of politically-motivated misconduct investigations. Although he was promoted to Brigadier in January, 1776, and Major General in May, 1777, Arnold resented the fact that some younger, less able men had been promoted ahead of him.

Carl Van Doren has described Arnold's "military persona" as follows:

"As a soldier he was original and audacious, quick in forming plans, quick in putting them into vigorous execution. He led his soldiers, not drove them, and won and held the devotion of the rank and file. He had a gift for command when the objective was clear and his imperious will could be fully bent upon it...But in the conflict of instructions and of other officers of rank equal or nearly equal to his, Arnold was restive and arrogant. He could not turn philosopher and patiently endure small irritations day by day."

"He was passionate and personal in almost all his judgments...At the same time, Arnold was a whirlwind hero who could not be bothered with keeping track of small expenses. Spend what had to be spent, and figure the amount up later." (It was these attitudes that got him into trouble with the Continental Congress.)

3). It is also important to remember the historical context within which Arnold acted. After four years of inconclusive combat operations, in the Spring of 1779 the final outcome of the "American War of Independence" remained uncertain. In purely military terms, the war had evolved into a stand-off, with the British unable to trap and destroy the Colonial armed forces, and the Continental Army incapable of driving the British from major ports and garrison cities. In addition, the Treaty of Alliance signed with France the previous year had yet to produce any successful joint military French-American operations (Admiral d'Estaing's fleet operations had failed repeatedly, and General Rochambeau's expeditionary force would not arrive until July, 1780).

Politically, things did not look much better. The British Government was still hanging tough on suppression of the colonial "rebellion," and hundreds of thousands of pro-British "Tories" or "loyalists" remained active in North America. Less than a third of the population of the thirteen colonies had actively supported the American revolutionary cause in the first place, and this base of support had eroded as the war progressed. By 1779, quite a few "Patriots of 1776" had begun to consider changing sides. Arnold was not alone in his growing cynicism and pessimism.

The "Precipitating" Causes

Seriously wounded in the same leg for a second time at the Battle of Saratoga, the partially disabled Arnold was placed in command of the Colonial forces in Philadelphia following the British evacuation of that city in June, 1778. Meanwhile, Congress had approved an adjustment in his date of rank, so that he now technically outranked his younger competitors. So, what was Arnold's motivation for committing treason a year later? What factors made it certain that he would finally choose to betray his country's cause? The following reasons come to mind:

1). He still nursed a long series of accumulated grievances against the Continental Congress, which he believed to be hopelessly incompetent and corrupt.

2). Arnold was a restless man of action—"driven and tremendously energetic," according to one biographer. Now less mobile because of a shortened leg, he saw his chances for a future field command slowly slipping away, and life as a garrison commander did not agree with him.

3). At the age of 38, the rough-cut war hero had just married beautiful and sophisticated 19-year-old Peggy Shippen (his first wife had died in 1775), the daughter of an old and wealthy Philadelphia family. Pro-British and socially ambitious, Peggy was a willing coconspirator in Arnold's espionage activities. He desperately wanted to live up to her expectations.

4). Arnold was essentially an arrogant, narcissistic opportunist who felt that his contributions to the Revolutionary cause had not been fully appreciated. His duty assignment in Philadelphia had given him a year to reflect upon his future prospects. By coincidence, in May, 1779 he found himself faced with an opportunity which was simply too good to pass up—the chance to make a fortune and (perhaps) end up on the winning side of what increasingly appeared to be a "war of attrition."

The "fortune" Arnold stood to make was not inconsequential. He first demanded 10,000 pounds for his services, but General Clinton demurred. The British became more cooperative after Arnold was put in charge of West Point, however, offering to pay 20,000 pounds, nearly $750,000 in today's money—if Arnold delivered West Point to them with its garrison and artillery intact. 20,000 pounds was a huge sum in the late 18th century, clearly sufficient to maintain Arnold and his family at a high standard of living anywhere in the world.

Implications for US Counterintelligence Today

What "CI indicators" or changes in Arnold's personality or behavior should his colleagues have noticed? Did any "CI anomalies" occur which should have been noted during the time that Arnold worked for the British? What steps could have been taken to anticipate, pre-empt, or prevent Arnold's treason?

Arnold's defection came as a complete surprise, both to his subordinates and George Washington's intelligence staff. This is remarkable, considering that Arnold remained "an agent in place" for sixteen months (from May, 1779 to September, 1780) after offering his services to the British. Under such circumstances, effective CI awareness and countermeasures should have detected Arnold's protracted negotiations and data sharing with the British Commander-in-Chief, General Henry Clinton. These exchanges made use of both verbal and written messages (some of which were in code). The communications were transmitted via loyalist intermediaries, Peggy Arnold, and Major John Andre, Clinton's aide-de-camp and intelligence coordinator. Much of this correspondence involved protracted bargaining over the terms of his "espionage contract"—a process which revealed Arnold's haggling skills and exaggerated self-esteem.

Arnold also was a valuable "reporting asset" during this period, warning Clinton of the impending arrival of French troops under Rochambeau and passing vital update information about the defenses of West Point and other Colonial strong points along the Hudson River. In addition, Arnold transmitted "bits and pieces of information" (via letters to Peggy Arnold which she passed to Andre) concerning the planning of what was to become the May-October, 1781 Yorktown campaign. Arnold had been asked to command part of the allied forces being prepared for that operation, and he remained "in the loop" until September, 1780—just eight months before US and French forces moved on Yorktown.

Most of the personal characteristics which made Arnold a dangerous spy also made him an effective military leader and a credible "Patriot." Arnold was certainly not the only arrogant and cantankerous field commander in the Continental Army, and probably no one but his new wife knew exactly what was going on in his mind when he decided to turn his coat. However, the fact that he had been embroiled in such a long series of courts-martial and Congressional investigations, should have raised some official eyebrows when Arnold began to lobby aggressively for command of the strategic Colonial garrison at West Point in May, 1780. Another "ignored" CI indicator was the fact that he also refused the offer of an attractive field command (the ring wing of Washington's army), claiming that he was disabled.

Arnold was an extremely resourceful and clever spy. After taking command of West Point, he used "profiteering" as a cover for his expanding contacts with local Tories whose homes provided opportunities for meetings with Major Andre. Even Arnold's closest aides—probably influenced by the General's past reputation as a smuggler— were taken in by this ploy. Arnold and the British used classic espionage tradecraft to cloak their conspiracy. These measures included the use of coded communications, clandestine signals, passwords, pseudonyms, safehouses, clandestine meetings, intermediaries, and—in an effort to distract Arnold's pursuers immediately following his defection—a diversion (a feigned "nervous breakdown") staged by his wife.

Arnold's activities apparently produced no "CI anomalies" that suggested the existence of a spy in the highest ranks of the Continental Army. This fact may be partly explained by the slow pace of communications in the late 1700's, as well as Clinton's understandable reluctance to jeopardize the security of his best-placed agent by acting precipitously on information that could only have been provided by someone at Arnold's level. In addition, the British military intelligence apparatus in North America was aggressive and resourceful, and was known to have intercepted and copied sensitive Continental Army documents in the past. For this reason, the British probably felt they did not have to mount a CI deception operation to "screen" Arnold's activities.

Epilogue for a Spy

Although he had failed to fulfill his "contract" by delivering the plans of West Point's defenses (these were captured with Major Andre), Arnold was awarded 6,315 pounds in compensation for his lost property. He and his entire family were granted pensions by the British Government. Arnold was made a Brigadier General in the British Army and given command of a "Tory legion" which he had offered to help raise. In January, 1781 he led a 1600-man force in a raid against Hampton Roads, Virginia. Continuing up the James River, Arnold's troops attacked Rebel artillery positions near Jamestown and briefly looted and occupied Richmond.

Despised and ultimately rejected by the British, in the long run Arnold paid a heavy price for his ill-gotten "fortune." Ever optimistic and entrepreneurial, for a decade (1782 to 1792) he moved his second family back and forth between Canada and England, seeking social acceptance and commercial opportunities. Arnold's many post-war business ventures achieved limited success, however, and when he died in 1801 he was deeply in debt. Both Arnold and his wife were permanently estranged from their relatives in the newly-independent United States. The three sons from Arnold's first marriage remained in America. Four of his sons by Peggy Shippen (she died in 1804) served in the British Army, one of them becoming a Lieutenant General.

Dr. Edward Bancroft[19]

Among the many spies the British recruited and placed inside the American Commission in Paris under Benjamin Franklin, was one who had access to every secret move, conversation and agreement negotiated between the American delegation and the intermediaries representing the French government. French support and aid was critical to the American revolutionary cause, without it the dream of American independence would have expired. Yet, despite the British intelligence success, the government of Lord North was ineffective in stopping American-French activities. The spy, Dr. Edward Bancroft, was never discovered until seventy years after his death when the British government provided access to its diplomatic archives.

Bancroft was born on 9 January 1744 in Westfield, Massachusetts. When he was two years old his father died of an epileptic seizure leaving his mother to care for the family. Five years later, his mother, Mary, remarried and the family moved with her new husband, David Bull, to Hartford, Connecticut. Bull owned "The Bunch of Grapes" tavern which, on 23 May 1781, hosted a meeting between George Washington and General Jean-Baptiste de Vimeur, Comte de Rochambeau, to plan their siege against British General Lord Charles Cornwallis at Yorktown.

While growing up in Hartford, Bancroft studied under Silas Deane, after the latter's graduation from Yale. Two years later, at age 16, Bancroft was apprenticed to a physician in Killingsworth, Connecticut. Then, on 14 July 1763, Bancroft left the colonies for Surinam where he found employment as a medical chief on one of the plantations. Bancroft expanded his medical practice to several additional plantations and also found time to write a study of Surinam's environment. Bancroft soon grew weary of Surinam and in 1766 began one year of travel between North and South America before sailing for England.

After his arrival in London, Bancroft became a physician's student at St. Bartholomew's Hospital. He also published, in 1769, a book titled, "Natural History of Guiana," which brought him to the attention of Paul Wentworth, the colonial agent for New Hampshire in London. Wentworth hired Bancroft to survey his plantation in Surinam with the hope that Bancroft could uncover ways for Wentworth to increase his profits from the land. Bancroft returned to Surinam for several months and then returned to London.

Also in London at the time was Benjamin Franklin, who was the colonial agent for several colonies. Franklin met Bancroft and they became friends. Franklin used Bancroft as a spy to support several of

Franklin's colonial activities.[20] When Franklin returned to America, it is unknown if Bancroft continued his spying for Franklin but evidence exists that this may have been the case. For example, when the Committee for Secret Correspondence sent Silas Deane to Paris to examine the political climate of France, Franklin provided Deane instructions to contact Bancroft. Deane was told that to arrange the meeting:

> *"...by writing a letter to him, under cover to Mr. Griffiths, at Turnham Green, near London, and desiring him to come over to you in France or Holland, on the score of old acquaintance. From him you may obtain a good deal of information of what is now going forward in England, and settle a mode of continuing correspondence. It may be well to remit a small bill to defray his expenses in coming to see you, and avoid all political matters in your letter to him."*[21]

If Bancroft was not an agent, why is it suggested that the letter be sent to a cover address rather than to Bancroft directly. Deane had been Bancroft's teacher, so it would be natural for a teacher to try to contact a former successful student. Also, Deane's instructions to devise a contact plan to meet with Bancroft adds further proof of some clandestine relationship.

A day after Deane arrived in France, 7 June 1776, he mailed a letter requesting Bancroft come to Paris to discuss some assistance to Deane in procuring goods for Indian trade and enclosing 30 pounds to defray travel expenses. Bancroft agreed and on 8 July both men met in Paris. Deane and Bancroft quickly established a close rapport, so much so that Deane informed Bancroft of his true mission in Paris.

He told Bancroft that he was attempting to devise a clandestine relationship with the French to obtain military aid for the colonies. Bancroft declined an invitation to attend the negotiations between Deane and the French but agreed to serve as Deane's assistant and interpreter during meetings with French agents, Pierre Augustin Caron de Beaumarchais and Monsieur Donatien le Rey de Chaumont. It was at these meetings the details of transferring to the Americans some forty thousand strands of arms, including two hundred cannon with French markings removed, as well as four million lives credit for miscellaneous military supplies.[22]

Deane informed Bancroft that the American objective was to motivate a Bourbon-Prussian coalition against England on the continent to force the British to redirect their power to a continental conflict and leave the colonies alone. The Americans expected the French to agree to the alliance. In fact, French Foreign Minister, Charles Gravier, the Comte de Vergennes was leaning towards war with England when he learned that General Sir William Howe evacuated Boston but wanted to enlist Spain's assistance and agreement to go to war with Portugal, England's ally. The situation changed when the French learned that Britain defeated Washington's forces on Long Island on 27 August 1776.[23]

Bancroft, saying business matters obliged him to return to London, left France on 26 July 1776. Before departing, he agreed to provide Deane with intelligence gleaned from his contacts in England. Despite his agreement to cooperate, Bancroft was troubled by his new role. He had always supported the British Empire's interest but also adhered to the belief that the colonies and the crown had to reconcile their positions through some compromise. He now realized that this was impossible and that French entry into the conflict would destroy the British empire. Bancroft considered informing the British government about Deane's efforts because he was convinced "that the government of France would endeavor to promote an absolute

Pierre Augustin Caron de Beaumarchais

separation of the then United Colonies from Great Britain; unless a speedy termination of the revolt by reconciliation, or conquest, should frustrate this project."[24]

Before Bancroft had an opportunity to contact the British, he was met by Paul Wentworth. Wentworth was recently recruited by William Eden, chief of the British Secret Service,[25] who assigned Wentworth the task of meeting with his old friend to obtain full details of Bancroft's visit to Paris. Wentworth informed Bancroft that the British knew he met and spent several days with Deane. Wentworth asked Bancroft to meet with Eden. Bancroft agreed and shortly thereafter a meeting was held between Bancroft, Eden, and Lords Suffolk and Weymouth to discuss the colonial rebellion. At this meeting, Bancroft was recruited as a double agent for the British. He later wrote of his decision:

> "I had then resided near ten years, and expected to reside the rest of my life in England; and all my views, interests and inclinations were adverse to the independency of the colonies, though I had advocated some of their claims, from a persuasion of their being founded in justice. I therefore wished, that the government of this country, might be informed, of the danger of French interference, though I could not resolve to become the informant. But Mr. Paul Wentworth, having gained some general knowledge of my journey to France, and of my intercourse with Mr. Deane, and having induced me to believe that the British Ministry were likewise informed on this subject, I at length consented to meet the then Secretaries of State, Lords Weymouth and Suffolk, and give them all the information in my power, which I did with the most disinterested views."[26]

When Benjamin Franklin arrived in Paris to take over the negotiations with the French, Lord Suffolk told Bancroft to move to Paris and inject himself in Franklin's circle. In return for his service, Bancroft was offered a life pension of 200 pounds per year, increasing to 500 pounds per year. Bancroft left England on 26 March 1977. After his arrival in Paris, it was not difficult for him to find a position with Franklin, his former friend and mentor. Bancroft was made secretary to the American commission. Also arriving in Paris was Paul Wentworth, who was sent to be Bancroft's handler.

To communicate with the British, Bancroft was instructed in the use of a timed deaddrop. He was told to compose a series of cover letters about gallantry which he was to address to a "Mr. Richards," and sign each with "Edward Edward." Between the lines of his letters, he was to write in secret ink the information he acquired on the French-American partnership. When the letter was complete, he was to place it in a bottle with a piece of string around the bottle's neck. Each Tuesday evening after 9:30, Bancroft was instructed to proceed to the south terrace of the Jardin de Tuilleries where he was to place the bottle in a hole in the roots of a certain box tree. The bottle was retrieved by Thomas Jeans, secretary to British diplomat Lord Stormont, who removed the contents and usually replaced it with taskings for Bancroft. Bancroft later that same evening returned to the drop site to recover the bottle. It is reported that Bancroft provided copies of hundreds of documents to his handlers. For example, it is said that the French-American treaty was in King George's hand 48 hours after its signing, courtesy of Bancroft.

Compliments of Franklin and Deane, who sent Bancroft on frequent secret intelligence missions to London, Bancroft had the luxury of sitting down in a relaxed atmosphere to be debriefed by Lord Suffolk and others. There is some suggestion by historians that Franklin was aware of Bancroft's betrayal, citing Franklin's comment in response to a friend's warning about British spies:

> "I have long observ'd one Rule which prevents any Inconvenience from such Practices. It is simply this, to be concern'd in no Affairs that I should blush to have made publick, and to do nothing but what Spies may see & welcome. When a Man's actions are just and honourable, the more they are known, the more his Reputation is increas'd and establish'd. If I was sure, therefore that my Valet de Place was a Spy, as probably he is, I think I should not discharge him for that, if in other Respects I lik'd him."[27]

Whether Franklin knew and used Bancroft to pass false information to the British or never knew Brancroft's true status is subject to interpretations of the facts because Franklin did not write about it and Bancroft's personal papers were later destroyed by a family member. No matter what the truth is, the fact remains that the British had placed an excellent double agent within the American Commission in Paris who provided a wealth of information on the French-American alliance. Even with Bancroft and the other British agents inside the Commission, the British were unable to take more effective action to destroy or diminish the negotiations and support which lead to the American-French Alliance and the final defeat of the British at Yorktown.

Secret Writing

While serving in Paris as an agent of the Committee of Secret Correspondence, Silas Deane is known to have used a heat-developing invisible ink, compounded of cobalt chloride, glycerin and water, for some of his intelligence reports back to America. Even more useful to him later was a "sympathetic stain" created for secret communications by James Jay, a physician and the brother of John Jay. Dr. Jay, who had been knighted by George III, used the "stain" for reporting military information from London to America. Later he supplied quantities of the stain to George Washington at home and to Silas Deane in Paris.

The stain required one chemical for writing the message and a second to develop it, affording greater security than the ink used by Deane earlier. Once, in a letter of John Jay, Robert Morris spoke of an innocuous letter from "Timothy Jones" (Deane) and the "concealed beauties therein," noting "the cursory examinations of a sea captain would never discover them, but transferred from his hand to the penetrating eye of a Jay, the diamonds stand confessed at once."

Washington instructed his agents in the use of the "sympathetic stain," noting in connection with "Culper Junior" that the ink "will not only render his communications less exposed to detection, but relieve the fears of such persons as may be entrusted in its conveyance . . ." Washington suggested that reports could be written in the invisible ink "on the blank leaves of a pamphlet . . .a common pocket book, or on the blank leaves at each end of registers, almanacs, or any publication or book of small value." Washington especially recommended that agents conceal their reports by using the ink in correspondence: "A much better way is to write a letter in the Tory stile with some mixture of family matters and between the lines and on the remaining part of the sheet communicate with the stain the intended intelligence."

Other Spies

**To Joseph Reed or
Colonel Cornelius Cox**

*Head Quarters, Morris Town,
April 7, 1777.*

Dear Sir:

I am informed, there is a certain Mr. Smith, who has been lately taken up by Genl. Lincoln as a Spy and sent to Philadelphia under that Character; I believe, for several reasons that he is the man who was employed by you to act for us, in that capacity, and that the apprehending him is a mistake, which may be attended with ill consequences. Lest he should be precipitately tried and punished, I must beg you will interpose in the affair without delay, and if you find him to be the person I suspect he is, take measures to have him released. I should be glad indeed, that some management might be used in the matter, in order to turn the Circumstance of his being apprehended to a good account. It would be well to make him a handsome present in money to secure his fidelity to us; and contrive his releasement, in such a manner, as to give it the appearance of an accidental escape from confinement. After concerting a plan with him, by which he will be enabled to be serviceable to us, in communicating intelligence from time to time, let him make the best of his way to the Enemy. Great care must be taken, so to conduct the scheme, as to make the escape appear natural and real; there must be neither too much facility, nor too much refinement, for doing too little, or over acting the part, would alike beget a suspicion of the true state of the case. I am etc.

To Governor William Livingston

Head Quarters, Valley Forge,

January 20, 1778

Sir:

I last night received a Letter from Colo. Dayton, informing me, that John and Baker Hendricks, and John Meeker had been apprehended upon a supposition of carrying on an illegal Correspondence with the Enemy, as they had been several times upon Staten Island and that they were to be tried for their lives in consequence.

In justice to these Men I am bound to take this earliest opportunity of informing you that they were employed by Colo. Dayton last Summer to procure intelligence of the movements of the Enemy while upon Staten Island, for which purpose I granted them passports, allowing them to carry small quantities of Provision, and to bring back a few Goods the better to cover their real designs. Colo Dayton acquaints me that they executed their trust faithfully; this I very well remember, that what intelligence he communicated to me and which he says, came principally thro' them, was generally confirmed by the Event. Upon these Considerations I hope you will put a stop to the prosecution, unless other matters appear against them. You must be well convinced, that is indispensibly necessary to make use of these men to procure intelligence. The persons employed must bear the suspicion of being thought inimical, and it is not in their powers to asset their innocence, because that would get abroad and destroy the confidence which the Enemy puts in them. I have the honour, etc.

To Governor William Livingston

Head Quarters, Valley Forge,
March 25, 1778.

Dear Sir:

I have strong reasons to suspect a Mr. Banskon,[28] late a Captain of Marines in our service, of being in the employ of the enemy as a Spy. His family lives at Princeton. We have nothing against him that amounts to proof, and to seize him at present would answer no end; but to put it out of our power to detect and punish him. It were to be wished, your Excellency, without discovering our suspicions could fall upon some method to have him well watched, and, if possible, find out something to ascertain the fact. He is lately from Philadelphia and has offered me his services in that way, as he proposes to return in a few days, taking this Camp in his way. If in the mean time any circumstances should arise within your knowledge you will be pleased to transmit it to me. I am etc.

To Colonel Stephen Moylan

Head Quarters,
April 3, 1778.

Sir:

By command of his Excellency, I am to desire, you will send a corporal and six Dragoons, with a Trumpeter to Head Quarters, without loss of time. They are wanted to escort the Commissioners on our part who are to meet on the subject of a General Cartel. You need not be told they must be picked Men and horses, must make the best possible appearance, must be very trusty and very intelligent. They should also be of the same regiment.

The General reminds you again of the necessity of keeping your Officers close to their quarters and duty; and of letting no attention be wanting to put the cavalry under your command, on the best footing you can, both with respect to condition and discipline.

There is a certain Mr. Bankson late of the Continental marines, who has a family at Princeton. We suspect him to be a spy to Mr. Howe, though he offers himself as one to us. We wish to find out his true history. He left this camp the 24th of March, on pretense of making a visit to his family, and is now returned with renewed offers of service. It is doubted whether he has not, in the mean time, been at Philadelphia. The General wrote some days since to Governor Livingston, requesting he would take measures to explore Mr. Bankson's conduct and views. He directs you immediately to see the Governor and learn from him, if he has been able to make any discovery, and to take cautious methods to ascertain whether Bankson has been at home, since he left camp, how long, and when he left home, in short any thing that may throw light upon his designs. Let him hear from you as soon as possible about the he subject. Manage the business with caution and address. Yours Affectionately.

To Governor William Livingston

Head Quarters, Valley Forge,
June 1, 1778.

Dear Sir:

I am honoured with yours of the 23rd and 29th Ultimo. The person who delivered me your letter of the 17th was one of our hired Expresses. He now out upon duty, but when he returns I will inquire how he came by the letter. The Christian name of Bankson, who I begged the favor of you to keep an eye upon, is Jacob[28], but as I am now satisfied concerning him, you need not trouble yourself further in the matter....

To Brigadier General William Swallowed

Head Quarters, Valley Forge,
June 1, 1778.

Dear Sir:

I received yours of the 30th May: A person, who I sent down to Chester to observe the movements of the Fleet, left that place on Sunday at dusk, he informs me that upwards of one hundred Sail had come down from Philadelphia and that they had not stopped near Wilmington, but proceeded towards the Capes. If this is so, it is a plain proof that they have no design to land any body of Men to molest our Stores. Captn. McLane who commands a scouting Party upon the Enemy's lines has been this Morning as near Philadelphia as Kensington, from whence he has a full view of the Harbour, he says very few ships remained and those chief armed Vessels. If therefore, upon sending an Office to Chester and another to Wilmington, you find that the Vessels have gone down and are below New Castle, you are immediately to join me, with your whole continental force. I am &ca.

P.S. Bring up your Tents with you and your lightest Baggage, as you will probably march immediately Northward.

To The Board Of General Officers

Head Quarters, Valley Forge,
June 2, 1778.

Gentlemen:

The Adjutant General has directions to send you one Shanks[29] formerly an Officer in the 10th Pennsylvania Regiment, charged with being a spy for the Enemy. There is a British deserter a serjeant of Grenadiers, who will attend as a Witness against him. His own confession is pretty ample. But to make the evidence as full as possible, I have directed Col. Morgan to send up the persons, who took the criminal, in order to ascertain the circumstances of his apprehension. To avoid the formality of a regular trial, which I think in such a case ought to be dispensed with, I am to request you will examine him and report the result; and if his guilt is clear, his punishment will be very summary.[30] If the Witnesses expected from Colonel Morgan, should not arrive speedily, so that it would detain the Board too much to wait for them; they may proceed to the examination, without them, but if it shod appear that their presence may materially affect the merits of the inquiry, I would wish it not to be brought to a conclusion. If it should be thought unessential, I should be glad the examination may be definitive. I am, etc.

P.S. I wish your report to be as full as possible, clear as to the criminality of the person, expressive of your opinion whether he is a proper subject for an example, and what kind of punishment may be most proper.

General Orders

Head Quarters, W. Plains,
Monday, September 14, 1778.

Parole St. Augustine. Countersigns Salem, Sandown.

After Orders

At a General Court Martial held in the Highlands January the 13th, 1778, by order of Major Genl. Putnam whereof Colo. Henry Sherburne, was

President, Matthias Colbhart of Rye, in the State of New-York, was tried for holding a Correspondence with the Enemy of the United States, living as a Spy among the Continental Troops and enlisting and persuading them to desert to the British Army, found guilty of the whole Charge alledg'd against him and in particular of a breach of the 19th Article of the 13th Section of the Articles of War and therefore sentenced to be punished with Death, by hanging him by the Neck until he is dead.[30] Which Sentence was approved of by Major General Putnam. His Excellency the Commander in Chief orders him to be executed tomorrow morning nine o'Clock on Gallows Hill.

To Major General Alexander McDougall

*Head Quarters, Middle Brook,
March 25, 1779.*

Dear Sir:

I duly received your favour of the 20th instant. Mr. H.———[31] has just delivered me that of the 22nd. (The Letter and inclosures referred to in it are not yet come to hand.) I have had a good deal of conversation with Mr. H———. He appears to be a sensible man capable of rendering important service, if he is sincerely disposed to do it. From what you say, I am led to hope he is; but nevertheless, if he is really in the confidence of the enemy, as he himself believes to be the case, it will be prudent to trust him with caution and to watch his conduct with a jealous eye.

I always think it necessary to be very circumspect with double spies. Their situation in a manner obliges them to trim a good deal in order to keep well with both sides; and the less they have it in their power to do us mischief, the better; especially if we consider that the enemy can purchase their fidelity at a higher price than we can. It is best to keep them in a way of knowing as little of our true circumstances as possible; and in order that they may really deceive the enemy in their reports, to endeavor in the first place to deceive them. I would recommend, that the same rule should be observed in making use of Mr. H———, who notwithstanding the most plausible appearances may possibly be more in earnest with the enemy than with us. By doing this we run the less risk and may derive essential benefit. He is gone on to Philadelphia.

Which so far as it affected the troops under your command you will be pleased to assist me in executing as speedily as possible. I am, etc.

To Major General Alexander McDougall

*Head Quarters, Middle Brook,
March 28, 1779.*

Dear Sir:

I yesterday Evening was favd. with yours of the 21st instant with the several inclosures to which it refers.

———[32] is gone to Philada. and will call upon me in his way back. In my last I took the liberty to drop you a hint upon the subject of the danger of our putting too much confidence in persons undertaking the office of double Spies. The person alluded to in the present instance appears very sensible, and we should, on that account, be more than commonly guarded until he has given full proofs of his attachment. The letter directed to Genl. Haldimand[33] was evidently intended to fall into our Hands. The manner of contriving that, and some other circumstances, makes me suspicious that he is as much in the interest of the enemy as in ours. I am etc.

Joseph Hyson[34]

Joseph Hyson was a Marylander, living in London where he was an unemployed seaman. While carousing among the bars, he met William Carmichael, a fellow Marylander and personal secretary to Silas Deane in Paris, who was visiting England and also liked to frequent the shadier sites of London. The two men became very close friends. When Carmichael was sent to England to recruit seamen to command privateers and munitions ships clandestinely fitted in France, he approached Hyson, who readily agreed because he was broke and wanted, he said, to see America again.

After Hyson was recruited by Carmichael, he was approached by Reverend John Vardill, a British agent of William Eden, an under-secretary of state, who directed British intelligence during the early years of the American Revolution. The meeting took place on 12 February 1777 and Hyson agreed to work for British intelligence. A plan, briefed to the British Admiralty which gave its approval, was devised whereby Hyson would slip out of England for France. After Hyson's arrival in France, he was to collect coastal and other maritime information on the country while waiting to take possession of one of the ships. Once he commanded a ship, he was to use elaborate signals, worked out with the British navy to make it appear that the ship was captured rather than Hyson having sailed it into British hands.

Hyson safely arrived in France and, while his ship was being fitted, he spent a great deal of time with Carmichael and the American Commissioners, Benjamin Franklin and Silas Deane. Hyson also began to collect data on French ports and shipping which he passed to Lt. Col. Edward Smith, a British intelligence officer. Carmichael detected Hyson's spy activities for Smith but did not reveal them to any of the American Commissioners. In fact, Carmichael offered to help Hyson obtain American dispatches, an offer Smith believed could help the British recruit Carmichael.[35] The British did try to recruit Carmichael but he rejected there overtures.

Benjamin Franklin and Silas Deane decided to send the Commissioners' important dispatches to the Continental Congress earlier than expected and selected a Captain Folger to take them aboard his ship. To get the dispatches to Captain Folger, Captain Hyson was selected as the courier. Hyson traveled to Havre, France where he turned over the dispatch pouch to Folger. Folger, after his arrival in America, gave the pouch to the Committee of Correspondence of the Continental Congress. When the Committee opened the pouch, they discovered a wad of blank paper. While the substituted pouch was on its way to America, Hyson delivered the real pouch to Lt. Col. Smith in London, who immediately turned it over to William Eden. Eden, in turn, displayed the entire pouch contents to King George III, who was often a harsh critic of the spies, alluding to his mistrust of them.

Hyson was paid for his services. Lord North gave him 200 pounds and a promise of 200 pounds a year. "He was an honest rascal, and no fool though apparently stupid."[36] An apt remark considering that Hyson returned to France to renew his contact with the American Commissioners. He could not understand why the Commissioners rejected any contact with him. The only one who came to visit him was Carmichael. He failed to realized that Carmichael was directed to make contact with him in order to get Lt. Col. Smith to come to Paris to meet with the Commissioners.

The Commissioners wanted to use Smith as a broker to determine if the British government was agreeable to negotiating a peace. When word was received on 30 November 1777 that General John Burgoyne surrendered, this plan was shelved. Hyson's value to the Commissioners was ended although he was offered the job of taking some dispatches to America. He refused. The French told him to leave their country or be arrested as a spy.

Hyson requested funds from Smith, who sent the request to Eden. Eden responded that he would support giving Hyson 40 pounds if Hyson would set sail and try to overtake either Silas Deane or Carmichael who had departed France in separate ships carrying dispatches. Hyson left for England, where he signed on a man-of-war, the Centaur, in which he was a key player in betraying an American munitions ship to the British. This is the last anyone heard of Hyson.

Lydia Darragh

Though it has been disputed as to accuracy and, indeed, truth, the story of Lydia Darragh deserves mention. Darragh, listening through a paper-thin wall of her home where British officers met, learned of British plans for the 4 December march on Philadelphia. Smuggling her notes in a "dirty, old needlebook" she was able to report the British would march out on 4 December and surprise General Washington at Whitemarsh with their superior forces against Washington's unprepared Continentals.

She reported that there would be 5,000 men under General William Howe, 13 pieces of cannon, baggage wagons and 11 boats on wheels, or pontoon equipment. The British did pull out of Philadelphia with more than 5,000 men on the night of 4 December, rolled through the city going in the wrong direction toward the Schuylkill River. Washington's intelligence and estimates were correct. He had strengthened the front, not the rear, and the British surprise failed.

After a day of confrontation, Howe withdrew to Philadelphia "like a parcel of damned fools." It was to his report of the Whitemarsh fiasco that General Charles Cornwallis first appended his view that the conquest of America was impossible. On other occasions, Lydia concealed reports in shorthand only her older brother, Lt. Charles Darragh could read, and covered them as buttons which her 14 year-old son wore on his clothing when traveling on regular visits to her brother. Charles would then decode the shorthand and deliver the report to Washington.

James Armistead

James Armistead was a slave who, with his master's permission, joined Marquis de Lafayette's service when the young French General arrived in Williamsburg in March 1781. Armistead had repeated success in penetrating the British lines and bringing out intelligence on Cornwallis' forces. Lafayette later commended the agent's "essential services," noting "His intelligences from the enemy camp were industriously collected and more faithfully reported."

As a courier between Lafayette and American agents in the Norfolk area, Armistead won this accolade from Lafayette: "He properly acquitted some important communications I gave him." But, the most valued role of this agent involved deception. Posing as a refugee, he crossed Cornwallis's lines, where he was recruited as a British spy and dispatched back against Lafayette.

Lafayette prepared a false order from himself to General Daniel Morgan, in which Morgan was instructed to move non-existent troop replacements into certain positions. With the properly crumpled and abused letter in hand, Armistead returned to the British, reporting that he had found no changes in the American position, but displaying the torn paper that he claimed to have found along the roadside, but could not read.

Cornwallis accepted the bait and did not learn he had been tricked until Lafayette completed the military operation. Cornwallis, during a courtesy visit to Lafayette after the British defeat at Yorktown, recognized Armistead on Lafayette's staff, and realized for the first time that his trusted agent, had, in actuality, been an American agent.

Following the war, the Virginia Assembly voted James Armistead his freedom and in later years approved both a bonus and a lifetime pension for his intelligence work, conducted "at the peril of his life." James reciprocated the honor, adopting the new surname, Lafayette.

John Honeyman

John Honeyman was denounced by George Washington as a traitor as part of a plan to get the American spy a warm welcome when he fled to the British lines. The "traitor" label worked so well that once Honeyman, who used the cover of butcher and horse trader, had his house raided by patriots. In order to expedite Honeyman's return, Washington issued order that Honeyman, upon returning to American lines, was to be "captured alive" and taken to Washington directly so that Washington could interrogate the "dangerous rascal" personally.

Honeyman, would of course, subsequently manage to escape back to British lines and provide deception information, as he did in telling the Hessians that Washington was not prepared to attack Trenton on Christmas.

Daniel Bissell

On 8 June 1783, Sargeant Daniel Bissell of the 2nd Connecticut Regiment was awarded the Honorary Badge of Military Merit, one of three men in the American Revolution to be cited with the award now known as the Military Order of the Purple Heart. Bissell was bestowed the award for his work as a military spy.

In August 1781, Lt. Col. Robert Harrison, Washington's aide-de-camp, dispatched Bissell into New York to gather intelligence. Finding he could not exfiltrate the city, he masqueraded as a Loyalist and joined Benedict Arnold's provincial regiment. For over a year, Bissell gathered intelligence, committing it to memory.

In September 1782, he was able to escape through British lines and report to Washington. Not only was

Bissell able to report first-hand on British fortifications, and intelligence gathered from others, he was able to present a twelve-month analysis of the British method of operation, which Washington commended him on.

Bissell's ideological motivation became clear when he refused both an honorable discharge and a pension for his work as an intelligence agent for Washington; he felt the nation could ill-afford the loss of his services, and he believed the nation should not be tasked with the pension payments.

David Gray

David Gray, a captain in the 1st Massachusetts, was highly effective in obtaining intelligence about the Loyalists and their plotting, which earned him the attention of Washington, who employed him as a spy. Gray made a number of trips to Conneticut and Long Island, New York and finally managed an introduction to Col. Beverly Robinson at British intelligence headquarters. He was recruited by Robinson as a courier to carry letters to Tories in New York, Conneticut, Vermont, and New Hampshire, which he did; after first delivering them to Washington for examination. After about a year with the British, he was sent to Canada with dispatches from Sir Henry Clinton.

The XYZ Affair

In 1798 a political scheme by three emissaries from French Foreign Minister, Charles Maurice de Talleyrand, outraged the American public, when it surfaced in the United States. The three emissaries, known by the initials, X, Y, and Z, attempted to bribe three American commissioners, who were seeking a treaty of commerce and amity with France. The uproar cause by the attempted bribe led to a complete break in relations with France and an undeclared naval war for two years.

The French, upset by the Jay Treaty of 1794 between the United States and Great Britain, giving Great Britain favored-nation status, felt the Americans were becoming too pro-British. The French were at war with Great Britain and began to seize American ships on the high seas looking for contraband believed headed for British ports. Suffering staggering financial losses, American ship owners demanded reprisals against the French.

In December 1796, the American minister to France, Charles C. Pinckney, tried unsuccessfully to present his credentials to the French Directory. This diplomatic slap in the face resulted in a heated outcry in America against the French. John Adams, the newly elected President, desired better relations with France and to avoid war. On 31 May 1797 he named a three-member commission, Pinckney, John Marshall and Elbridge Gerry, to negotiate with the French government. However, when they arrived in Paris in October 1797 to begin negotiations on a new commercial and friendship treaty, the French Directory refused to meet them. Instead, Talleyrand sent three emissaries to meet with them.

The emissaries advised the American commissioners that a "gift" of $25,000 to the Foreign Minister and a loan of $10 million to France was a prerequisite to any negotiations. Two other conditions demanded by the emissaries was an apology by the President for his past critical remarks about France and a reaffirmation by the United States of the old Franco-American Alliance of 1778. Although diplomatic bribes were customary, Pinckney, furious from twiddling his thumbs waiting for an appointment with Talleyrand, said, "Not a sixpence." His diplomatic note to President Adam was more articulate, "Millions for defense but not one cent for tribute."

The American commissioners decided to appeal to Talleyrand directly in a diplomatic note. Talleyrand did not respond for two months and when he did, his reply was terse. He blamed the Americans for the problems, said the President should have sent only Republicans (Pinckney and Marshall were Federalists) to negotiate and stated he would deal only with Gerry. Talleyrand also said that if Gerry left France, war between the two countries was likely. Although the commissioners made no concessions to the French, Pinckney and Marshall returned to the United States, leaving Gerry in France. Gerry's presence in France did not sit well with the Americans and President Adams recalled him.

President Adams informed Congress about the failed mission and provided Congress with the XYZ correspondence. The Federalists were overjoyed by the news. Alexander Hamilton suggested raising an army of 10,000 men. George Washington said he would come out of retirement to lead the new army, but in title only. Washington wanted Hamilton as his second-in-command. President Adams, fearful of promoting Hamilton over several Revolutionary War officers, who then might lead a coup against him, decided to authorize the building of 40 frigates and lesser warships. An undeclared naval war ensued for two years (1798-1800) in which American naval forces captured 84 armed French ship while only losing one. The Convention of 1800 ended the fighting. The diplomatic dispute ended six months later when Napoleon Bonaparte officially received the American commissioners to France.

The Burr Conspiracy

When Vice President Aaron Burr killed Alexander Hamilton in a duel in 1804, he also killed his chance to be president. Wanted for murder in New York, he fled the state and went to Philadelphia. Realizing that he had no future on the east coast, Burr, in a frantic effort to salvage his destroyed political power and heavily in debt, conceived a plan to seek political fortunes beyond the Alleghenies. He first contacted the British Minister, Anthony Merry, living in Philadelphia. He offered Merry his services in any efforts by Great Britain to take control over the western part of the United States. Merry, who hated the United States, wrote his Foreign Ministry that while Burr was notoriously profligate, nevertheless, his ambition and spirit of revenge would be useful to the British government. Merry became a strong supporter of Burr's schemes.

One of Burr's schemes was to organize a revolution in the West, take the Ohio and Mississippi Valleys and form them into a separate republic. His other scheme was to establish a republic bordering the United States by seizing Spanish possessions. To gain further support for his plans, Burr approached an old friend, General James Wilkinson; both had served as aides to then Colonel Benedict Arnold during the Quebec expedition. Wilkerson played a crucial role in the conspiracy for he not only conspired with Burr but conspired against him.

Wilkinson, after being commissioned a captain in the Continental Army in 1776, rose rapidly in rank and position. Assigned as aide-de-camp to General Horatio Gates, Wilkinson became involved in a plot, called the Conway Cabal, to replace George Washington as commander-in-chief with Gates. Wilkinson, himself, leaked aspects of the plot, probably believing in doing so he could gain some advantage for himself, but his scheme and the original plot failed. Wilkinson lost his job and military honors but kept his rank.

Despite this reversal, Wilkinson proceeded with several conspiracies. Replacing George Rogers Clark as leader in Kentucky, Wilkinson embarked on an attempt to separate Kentucky from Virginia. At the same time, he reasoned that an opportunity existed to make money from national resentment toward Spain. He traveled to New Orleans, where he convinced the Spanish authorities he was secretly working for the partition of the United States. He offered his services to the Spaniards, who identified him as "agent 13" in Spanish messages. Washington and Hamilton both thought that Wilkinson was a spy for the Spanish but felt that his loyalty could be purchased with a promotion.

Not satisfied with his intrigues involving Kentucky statehood and working an agent for the Spanish, Wilkinson accepted in 1792 a commission as brigadier general of a volunteer army fighting Indians north of the Ohio River. He then contrived to replace his commander, General "Mad Anthony" Wayne. Wilkinson succeeded only because Wayne died in 1796. He then seized Detroit from the British and became its military governor. His administration was short-lived as the citizens protested his greed and he returned to the South.

After arriving in the South, Wilkinson wheeled and dealed in land speculation and lucrative Army contracts and contrived to become governor or surveyor-general of the Mississippi Territory. President George Washington became uneasy about Wilkinson's activities and ordered his surveillance. Wilkinson discovered the surveillance and was able to have the surveillant withdrawn. Presidents John Adams and Thomas Jefferson did not share Washington's distrust of Wilkinson. In fact, in 1803 Jefferson fully trusted Wilkinson that he commissioned him to be one of two individuals to take formal possession of the Louisiana Purchase from the French.

In New Orleans, Wilkinson returned to his old ways and acted on Spanish fears concerning Florida, which was Spanish territory until 1819. For his ruse he received a $12,000 bribe. He purchased a boatload of sugar, took it to New York to sell and while there began secret negotiations with Burr, Jefferson's vice-president.

Burr, aware that war between the United States and Spain over boundary disputes was a possibility because of various Spanish conspiracies to achieve control of the lower Mississippi Valley, made covert plans with Wilkinson to invade and colonize Spanish territory in the West. They also schemed to establish an independent "Empire of the West" on a Napoleonic model. The conspirators even considered invading and annexing Mexico to add to their empire with New Orleans as capital.

Burr was dropped from the presidential ticket by Jefferson and in April 1805 commenced to put his plans into motion. He again approached the British via Minister Merry. He informed Merry that Louisiana was ready to break with the United States and once it did all the western country would follow suit. To be successful, Burr requested that Britain assure his protection, provide him with a half of million dollar loan, and dispatch a British naval squadron to the mouth of the Mississippi River. The British might have entertained Burr's requests but Prime Minister Pitt died and was succeeded by Charles James Fox, a life-long friend of the United States. Fox considered the Merry-Burr discussions indiscreet, dangerous and damnable and recalled Merry to England on June 1, 1806. Having failed to secure British aid in an attempt to separate western states from the United States, Burr then headed west across Pennsylvania. In Pittsburgh, he procured a riverboat and embarked down the Ohio River. He stopped to visit Harman Blennerhassett, a wealthy, gentleman-scholar and Irish emigrant, who lived with his wife Margaret on an island in the middle of the river. Burr explained his plan to Blennerhassett, who enthusiastically expressed his support by giving Burr money. Burr used the funds to later purchase the Batrop lands on the Ouachita River, in present-day northern Louisiana, to serve as his base of operations into the Southwest.

Burr continued down the river to New Orleans, recruiting frontiersmen, filibusters, adventurers, and others along the way. When he arrived in New Orleans in 1806, he was fervently welcomed because his game plan to colonize or conquer the Spanish possessions touched an appealing cord in many of the people. As rumors of his plan reached Washington, the political establishment suspected that Burr was talking treason. Wilkinson, who was stationed on the Sabine River on the Spanish border with the United States, learned of Washington's reaction and decided to inform on Burr to avoid being charged with treason himself. On November 25, 1806 a courier arrived in Washington carrying a dispatch for President Jefferson. In the dispatch, Wilkinson warned President Jefferson about Burr's threatening plan. Jefferson ordered Burr arrested and he was apprehended in late 1806 near Nachez, Mississippi, while attempting to flee into Spanish territory.

In May 1807, Burr was tried for treason in front of U.S. Chief Justice John Marshall in the circuit court at Richmond, Virginia. Jefferson prepared an account of Burr's criminal activity for Congress and wanted to present it to the court but Marshall requested President Jefferson appearance instead. The President refused, consequently establishing a precedent for future presidents. Marshall, who was not on amicable terms with Jefferson found Burr not guilty, explaining that Burr committed no overt act of treason. Although innocent of the charges against him, Burr was never able to overcome the accusations. He died in New York City in 1836.

In 1805, Jefferson appointed Wilkinson governor of the Louisiana Territory. To distance himself from Burr, Wilkinson made an effort to cozy up to Jefferson. His effort was successful as he averted indictment by the Richmond, Virginia grand jury investigating Burr. These efforts, however, caused him to neglect his duty as governor. The situation became so serious that troops were deployed to calm an angry populace, upset by his mismanagement.

After his wife died in 1807, Wilkinson appeared to lose the shrewdness that saved him in the past. He was reappointed by Jefferson to govern Louisiana but his administration was so openly corrupt that President Monroe ordered a court-martial in 1811. The court found him not guilty. Even his military acumen failed him. During the war of 1812, he made a complete mess of the campaign against Montreal that he lost his commission in the Army.

Wilkinson refused to give up and in 1812, at the age of 64, he once more attempted to defraud the Spanish. Using the cover as agent for the American Bible Society, he traveled to Mexico City to seek a Texas land grant. He secured the grant, but died in 1825 before fulfilling all of its provisions.

The Alien and Sedition Acts 1798

Following publication of the XYZ correspondence, Congress passed the Alien and Sedition Acts. Prompted by a spirit of nationalism by the Federalists, the real targets of the acts were the anti-Federalist editors and pamphleteers of English and French extraction. The Alien Acts were never enforced but did cause a number of French refugees to flee the country or go into hiding. The Sedition Act extended the jurisdiction of the federal courts but there was serious questions as to its constitutionality. The law was never challenged in court. In 1812 the Supreme Court ruled that the federal courts do not have common law jurisdiction in criminal cases. Of the twenty-five persons arrested under the Sedition Act only ten were convicted.

The Naturalization Act–June 18, 1798

An Act supplementary to and to amend the act, entitled "An act to establish an uniform rule of naturalization," and to repeal the act heretofore passed on that subject.

Section 1. *Be it enacted...,* That no alien shall be admitted to become a citizen of the United States, or of any state, unless ...he shall have declared his intention to become a citizen of the United States, five years, at least, before his admission, and shall, at the time of his application to be admitted, declare and prove, to the satisfaction of the court having jurisdiction in the case, that he has resided within the United States fourteen years, at least, and within the state or territory where, or for which such court is at the time held, five years, at least, besides conforming to the other declarations, renunciations and proofs, by the said act required, any thing therein to the contrary hereof notwithstanding: Provided that any Alien, who was residing within the limits, and under the jurisdiction of the United States, before...(January 29, 1795,)...may, within one year after the passing of this act-and any alien who shall have made the declaration of his intention to become a citizen of the United States, in conformity to the provisions of the act (of Jan. 29, 1795), may, within four years after having made the declaration aforesaid, be admitted to become a citizen, in the manner prescribed by the said act, ... *And provided also,* that no alien, who shall be a native, citizen, denizen or subject of any nation or state with whom the United States shall be at war, at the time of his application, shall be then admitted to become a citizen of the United States....

Section 4. *And be it further enacted,* That all white persons, aliens,...who, after the passing of this act, shall continue to reside in any port or place within the territory of the United States, shall be reported,...to the clerk of the district court of the district, if living within ten miles of the port or place, in which their residence or arrival shall be, and otherwise, to the collector of such port or place, or some officer or other person there, or nearest thereto, who shall be authorized by the President of the United States, to register aliens: and report, as aforesaid, shall be made in all cases of residence, within forty-eight hours after the first arrival or coming into the territory of the United States, and shall ascertain the sex, place of birth, age, nation, place of allegiance or citizenship, condition or occupation, and place of actual or intended residence within the United States, of the alien or aliens reported, and by whom the report is made....

Section 5. *And be it further enacted,* That every alien who shall continue to reside, or who shall arrive, as aforesaid, of whom a report is required as aforesaid, who shall refuse or neglect to make such a report, and to receive a certificate thereof, shall forfeit and pay the sum of two dollars; and any justice of the peace, or other civil magistrate, who has authority to require surety of the peace, shall and may, on complaint to him made thereof, cause such alien to be brought before him, and there to give surety of the peace and good behavior during his residence within the United States, or for such term as the justice or other magistrate shall deem reasonable, and until a report and registry of such alien shall be made, and a certificate of such surety, such alien shall and may be committed to the common goal, and shall be three held, until the order which the justice or magistrate shall and may reasonable make, in the premises, shall be performed....

2. The Alien Act–*June 25, 1798*
An Act concerning Aliens

Section 1. Be it enacted..., That it shall be lawful for the President of the United States at any time during the continuance of this act, to *order* all such aliens as he shall judge dangerous to the peace and safety of the United States, or shall have reasonable grounds to suspect are concerned in any treasonable or secret machinations against the government thereof, to depart out of the territory of the United States, within such time as shall be expressed in such order, which order shall be served on such alien by delivering him a copy thereof, or leaving the same at his usual abode, and returned to the Office of the Secretary of State by the marshal or other person to whom the same shall be directed. And in the case any alien, so ordered to depart, shall be found at large within the United States after the time limited in such order for his departure, and not having obtained a *license* from the President to reside therein, or having obtained such a *license* shall not have conformed thereto, every such alien shall, on conviction thereof, be imprisoned for a term not exceeding three years, and shall never after be admitted to become a citizen of the United States. *Provided always, and be it further enacted,* that if any alien so ordered to depart shall prove to the satisfaction of the President, by evidence to be taken before such person or persons as the President shall direct, who are for that purpose hereby authorized to administer oaths, that no injury or danger to the United States will arise from suffering such alien to reside therein, the President may grant a *license* to such alien to remain within the United States for such time as he shall judge proper, and at such place as he may designate. And the President may also require of such alien to enter into a bond to the United States, in such penal sum as he may direct, with one or more sufficient sureties to the satisfaction of the person authorized by the President to take the same, conditioned for the good behavior of such alien during his residence in the United States, and not violating his license, which license the President may revoke, whenever he shall think proper.

Section 2. And be it further enacted, That it shall be lawful for the President of the United States, whenever he may deem it necessary for the public safety, to order to be removed out of the territory thereof, any alien who may or shall be in prison in pursuance of this act; and to cause to be arrested and sent out of the United States such of those aliens as shall have been ordered to depart therefrom and shall not have obtained a license as aforesaid, in all cases where, in the opinion of the President, the public safety requires a speedy removal. And if any alien so removed or sent out of the United States by the President shall voluntarily return thereto, unless by permission of the President of the United States, such alien on conviction thereof, shall be imprisoned so long as, in the opinion of the President, the public safety may require....

Section 6. And be it further enacted, That this act shall continue and be in force for and during the term of two years from the passing thereof.

The Alien Enemies Act–July 6, 1798
An Act respecting Alien Enemies

Section 1. Be it enacted..., That whenever there shall be a declared war between the United States and any foreign nation or government, or any invasion or predatory incursion shall be perpetrated, attempted, or threatened against the territory of the United States, by any foreign nation or government,... all natives, citizens, denizens, or subjects of the hostile nation or government, being males of the age of fourteen years and upward, who shall be within the United States, and not actually naturalized, shall be liable to be apprehended, restrained, secured and removed, as alien enemies. And the President of the United States shall be, and he is hereby authorized,... to direct the conduct to be observed, on the part of the United States, towards the aliens who shall become liable, as aforesaid; the manner and degree of the restraint to which they shall be subject, and in what cases, and upon what security their residence shall be permitted, and to provide for the removal of those, who, not being permitted to reside within the United States, shall refuse or neglect to depart therefrom; and to establish any other regulations which shall be found necesary in the premises and for the publlic safety....

The Sedition Act–July 14, 1798

An Act in addition to the act, entitled "An act for the punishment of cerain crimes against the United States."

Section 1. Be it enacted..., That if any persons shall unlawfully combine or conspire together, with intent to oppose any measure or measures of the government of the United States, which are or shall be directed by proper authority, or to impede the operation of any law of the United States, or to intimidate or prevent any person holding a place of office in or under the government of the United States, from undertaking, performing or executing his trust or duty; and if any person or persons, with intent as aforesaid, shall counsel, advise or attempt to procure any insurrection, riot, unlawful assembly, or combination, whether such conspiracy, threatening, counsel, advice or attempt shall have the proposed effect or not, he or they shall be deemed guilty of a high misdemeanor, and on conviction, before any court of the United States having jurisdiction thereof, shall be punished by a fine not exceeding five thousands dollars, and by imprisonment during a term not less than six months nor exceeding five years; and further, at the discretion of the court may be holden to find sureties for his good behavior in such sum, and for such time, as the said court may direct.

Section 2. That if any person shall write, print, utter, or publish, or shall cause or procure to be written, printed, uttered or published, or shall knowingly and willingly assist or aid in writing, printing, uttering or publishing any false, scandalous and mallows writing or writings against the government of the United States, or either house of the Congress of the United States, or the President of the United States, with intent to defame the said government, or either house of the said Congress, or the said President, or to bring them, or either of them, into contempt or disrepute; or to excite against them, or either of any of them, the hatred of the good people of the United States, or to stir up sedition within the United States, or to excite any unlawful combination therein, for opposing or resisting any law of the United States, or any act of the President of the United States, done inpursuance of any such law, or of the powers in him vested by the constitution of the United States, or to resist, oppose, or defeat any such law or act, or to aid, encourage or abet any hostile designs of any foreign nations against the United States, their people or government, then such person therof convicted before any court of the United States having jurisdiction thereof, shall be punished by a fine not exceeding two thousand dollars, and by imprisonment not exceeding two years.

Section 3. That if any person shall be prosecuted under this act, for the writing or pusblishing any libel aforesaid, it shall be lawful for the defendant, upon the trial of the cause, to give in evidence in his defense, the truth of the matter contained in the publication charged as libel. And the jury who shall try the cause, shall have a right to determine the law and the fact, under the direction of the court, as in other cases.

Section 4. That this act shall continue to be in force until March 3, 1801, and no longer....

Revolutionary Soldier

American Revolution Bibliography

Arnold, Benedict. Daybook of Financial Transactions, 1777-1779. Journal of his Expeditions to Canada: March to Quebec. Revolutionary Government Papers. Archives & Man., Pennsylvania Historical & Museum, Harrisburg, PA.

Augur, Helen. The Secret War of Independence, New York: Duell, Sloan & Pearce; Boston: Little, Brown, 1955. 341 pp.

Bakeless, John. Turncoats, Traitors, and Heroes, Lippincott, Philadelphia, 1959.

Barnum, H.L. The Spy Unmasked; or, Memoirs of Enoch Crosby, Alias Harvey Birch. New York: J. & J. Harper, 1828. Reprinted with additional material, Harrison, NY: Harbor Hill Books, 1975.

Beirne, Francis F. Shout Treason: The Trial of Aaron Burr. New York: Hastings House, 1959.

Boatner, Mark Mayo, Encyclopedia of the American Revolution. New York, David McKay Company, Inc., 1966.

Brown, Charles H. Agents of Manifest Destiny. Chapel Hill: University of North Carolina, 1980.

Bryan, George S. The Spy in America. Philadelphia: J. B. Lippincott, 1943.

Campbell, Kenneth J. & Edmund R. Thompson. General Gage's Spies. 1990.

Campbell, Kenneth J. Benedict Arnold, America's First Defector. 1990.

Central Intelligence Agency. Intelligence In The War Of Independence. Washington, D.C.: CIA, 1976.

Cooper, James Fenimore, The Spy. 1821. Numerous 20th Century editions. (Novel based on the exploits of double agent Enoch Crosby.)

Cummings, Richard. Paul Revere & the Mechanics, Copy. 1989.

Currey, Cecil B. Code Number 72: Ben Franklin: Patriot or Spy. Englewood Cliffs, N.J.: Prentice-Hall, 1972.

Dann, John C. The Revolution Remembered: Eyewitness Accounts of the War on Independence. University of Chicago Press, 1980.

Einstein, Lewis D. Divided Loyalties, Americans in the British Service, Spies, Secret Agents and Adventurers. Boston, MA: Houghton Mifflin, 1933 Reprint 1969.

Engle, Paul. Women in the American Revolution. New York, 1976.

Flexner, James Thomas, George Washington. Boston, MA Little, Brown and Co., 1968.

Flexner, James Thomas, The Traitor and the Spy, Benedict Arnold and John Andre. New York: Harcourt Brace, 1953. Little, Brown and Co., Reprint, 1975.

Ford, Corey, A Peculiar Service. (Nathan Hale, Benjamin Tallmadge, Culper Net.) Boston, MA: Little, Brown & Co, 1965.

French, Allen, General Gage's Informers, Ann Arbor, MI: University of Michigan Press, 1932; Reprint, New York: Greenwood Press, 1968.

Groh, Lynn. The Culper Spy Ring. Philadelphia: Westminster Press, 1969.

Hatch, Robert McConnell. Major John Andre: A Gallant in Spy's Clothing. Boston: Houghton Mifflin Company, 1977.

Hoehling, Adolph A., Women Who Spied. New York: Dodd, Mead & Company, 1967.

Hoffman, Daniel N. Governmental Secrecy and the Founding Fathers: A Study in Constitutional Controls. Westport, CT: Greenwood, 1981.

Jacobs, James R. Tarnished Warrior: Maj. Gen. James Wilkinson. New York: Macmillan, 1938.

Jellison, Charles A. Ethan Allen: Frontier Rebel. Syracuse, New York, 1983.

Johnson, David R. Benedict Arnold: The Traitor as a Hero in American Literature. Unpublished doctoral dissertation, Pennsylvania State University, 1975.

Morpurgo, J.E., Treason at West Point: The Arnold-Andre' Conspiracy. New York: Vantage Press, 1977.

Nathan, Adele Gutman. Major John Andre: Gentleman Spy. New York: Franklin Watts, 1969.

O'Conner, David B. General Washington's Spymaster. Copyright 1990.

Palsgrave Wyllys: A Digressive History. New Haven, CT; Privately Printed, 1941.

Partridge, William, Nathan Hale: The Ideal Patriot. New York: Funk and Wagnalls Company, 1902.

Peckham, H.H. British secret Writing in the Revolutionary War. Michigan Alumnus Review, 44, pages 126-31, 1938.

Pennypacker, Morton, General Washington's Spies on Long Island and in New York. Vol. 1 Brooklyn, NY Long Island Historical Society, 1939; Vol. 2 East Hampton, NY.

Pennypacker, Morton. The Two Spies: Nathan Hale and Robert Townsend. Boston: Houghton Mifflin, 1930.

Randall, Willard Sterne. Benedict Arnold Patriot and Traitor. William Morrow and Company, Inc. New York. 1990.

Reno, J. David Sergeant Bissell's Purple Heart. Copy. 1989.

Seymour, George Dudley, Captain Nathan Hale, Major John.

Smith, Joseph B. The Plot to Steal Florida: James Madison's Phony War. New York: Arbor House, 1983.

Taplin, Winn L. The King's Green Mountain Spymaster. Copyright 1989.

Thompson, Edmund R. Secret Places: A Spies Guide to Revolutionary New England. Copyright 1990.

Thompson, Edmund R. Nathan Hale's Necessary Service. Copyright 1989.

Thompson, Edmund R. ed. Secret New England: Spies of American Revolution. Published by The David Atlee Phillips New England Chapter, Association of Former Intelligence Officers, Kennebunk, Maine. 1991.

Van Doren, Carl, Secret History of the American Revolution, Viking, New York, 1941.

Wallace, Willard M. Traitorous Hero: The Life and Fortunes of Benedict Arnold. New York: Harper and Brothers, 1954.

Wise, William. The Spy and General Washington. New York: Dutton, 1965.

IMPORTANT DATES AND COUNTERINTELLIGENCE EVENTS
THE AMERICAN REVOLUTION AND POST ERA, 1770-1859

1770	5 March	Five colonists killed by British troops during a demonstration. Becomes known as the Boston Massacre.
1774	13 May	General Gage, the commander of British forces in the colonies, is named Royal Governor of Massachusetts.
	5 September	First Continental Congress opens in Philadelphia, Pennsylvania.
1775	19 April	British troops clash with colonials at Lexington and Concord.
	15 June	George Washington named chief of the continental forces.
	17 June	Battle of Bunker Hill.
	30 September	Benjamin Church is arrested and later convicted of being a British spy.
	10 October	General Howe succeeds General Gage as British commander.
	20 November	Continental Congress establishes a Committee to review intercepted mail to determine who is authorized to conduct such operations.
	29 November	Second Continental Congress creates Committee of Secret Correspondence. Members are Benjamin Franklin, John Dickinson, Benjamin Harrison, John Jay, and Thomas Johnson.
1776	2 May	France decides to aid America and sets up a cover company to supply munitions to the colonies.
	June	Committee (later Commission) for Detecting and Defeating Conspiracies established in New York.
	12 June	Continental Congress adopts first secrecy agreement for government employees.
	28 June	Sgt. Thomas Hickey, a member of Washington's guards, is hanged for his role in a plot to kill the General. First American soldier executed by military court.
	4 July	Declaration of American Independence signed in Philadelphia.

IMPORTANT DATES AND COUNTERINTELLIGENCE EVENTS
THE AMERICAN REVOLUTION AND POST ERA, 1770-1859

1776	16 July	The Provincial Congress passes a motion by John Jay prescribing the death penalty for treason.
	August	Enoch Crosby contacts Committee for Detecting and Defeating Conspiracies and agrees to become a double agent.
	21 August	The first Espionage Act adopted by the Continental Congress.
	23 December	Enoch Crosby dispatched on his second double agent mission by the Committee.
	26 December	George Washington crosses the Delaware River and attacks and captures the Hessians.
	21 September	The New York Convention reestablished the committee to detect, and defeat all conspiracies which may be formed in the State against the liberties of America.
	22 September	Nathan Hale is captured and hanged as a spy by the British.
1777	4 January	Daniel Strang, British spy, tried at Peekskill, New York and sentenced to hang.
	12 February	Joseph Hyson recruited as a British spy to penetrate the American Commission in Paris, France.
	17 April	Committee of Secret Correspondence reconstituted as the Committee for Foreign Affairs.
	14 June	Washington notes execution of Abraham Patten as a spy and says that Patten conducted himself with great fidelity to the American cause.
	24 June	Treason defined by resolution of the Continental Congress.
	17 October	Americans defeat General Burgoyne at Saratoga which is considered the turning point in the war.
	17 December	France recognized the independence of the United States.

IMPORTANT DATES AND COUNTERINTELLIGENCE EVENTS
THE AMERICAN REVOLUTION AND POST ERA, 1770-1859

1778	13 January	Matthias Colbhart is tried as a British spy, found guilty and subsequently hanged.
	8 May	General Clinton succeeded General Howe as British commander in the colonies.
1779	12 January	Thomas Paine fired from his post with Foreign Affairs Committee for violation of government secrecy agreement.
1780	20 September	Major John Andre, head of British intelligence in the colonies, is captured by American miltiamen after meeting with General Benedict Arnold. Arnold escapes to the British lines.
	2 October	British spy John Andre is hanged in Tappan, New York.
1781	March	James Armistead volunteers to be an American spy against the British at Yorktown, Virgina.
	August	Daniel Bissell is dispatched as an American spy against the British in New York.
	19 October	Washington accepts formal surrender of Cronwallis' army at Yorktown.
1782	4 April	Sir Guy Carleton succeeds General Clinton as British commander.
1783	19 April	Continental Army receives official announcement of "cessation of hostilities" with Great Britain.
	8 June	Daniel Bissell is awarded the Purple Heart for his work as an American spy.
	3 September	Peace Treaty signed between England and the United States.
	4 December	Last of the British troops leave the United States.
1787	May	Consitutional Convention established the President as the manager of intelligence.
1789	27 July	Department of Foreign Affairs established; officially redesignated Department of State on 15 September 1789.

IMPORTANT DATES AND COUNTERINTELLIGENCE EVENTS
THE AMERICAN REVOLUTION AND POST ERA, 1770-1859

1789	7 August	Department of War created.
	2 September	Department of Treasury established.
1790	1 July	Congress authorizes Contingent Fund of Foreign Intercourse, the so-called secret fund.
1798	18 October	XYZ Affair; representatives of French Minister Talleyrand suggests US pay a bribe to France to recognize the American Commission.
	3 May	Department of Navy established.
	18 June	The Naturalization Act passed, establishing a uniform rule of naturalization in the US. This act was never enforced.
	25 June	Alien Act passed which gave the President the power to expel any alien from the country. The act was never enforced.
	6 July	The Alien Enemies Act passed. This act made any aliens subject to arrest during a time of war. The act was never enforced.
	14 July	The Sedition Act passed (expired/repealed in 1800-1802).
1803	18 January	President Jefferson requests covert funding from Congress for the Lewis and Clark expedition, an intelligence gathering operation.
1805	9 August	Zebulon Pike leads expedition as part of an intelligence operation targeting the Spanish lands in the west. His arrest as a spy created a controversy with Spain.
1807	19 February	Aaron Burr arrested and indicted for treason. Found not guilty.
1811	15 January	President Madison obtained secret Congressional approval for covert action to acquire the Florida's.
1812	20 February	Madison purchased letters from British spy, John Henry, proving British operations in the US.
1818	7 April	Andrew Jackson invaded Florida.

IMPORTANT DATES AND COUNTERINTELLIGENCE EVENTS
THE AMERICAN REVOLUTION AND POST ERA, 1770-1859

1818	22 March	Congress declassifies the first SECRET journals, except for those the President determines to require continued protection.
1819	22 February	Spain ceded East Florida to the US.
1831	October	Senator John Forsyth gives first public description of the Contingent Fund of Foreign Intercourse.
1841	13 June	President Tyler defends sources and methods in responses to Congressional inquiry in Duff Green matter.
1846	11 June	After leaving office, Tyler defends his decision authorizing Daniel Webster expenditures of Contingent Funds in domestic propaganda operations.
1849	18 June	President Taylor publicly defends secret American Observers (spies) abroad.

CHAPTER 2

CHAPTER 2

The Civil War: Lack of a Centralized Direction

Introduction

Six weeks after the election of Abraham Lincoln as President, South Carolina seceded from the Union. In February 1861, six other states (Louisiana, Texas, Georgia, Alabama, Florida and Mississippi) followed. They formed the Confederate States of America. When President Lincoln called for 75,000 volunteers after Fort Sumter was fired upon in April, 1861, Virginia, Arkansas, North Carolina and Tennessee joined the Confederacy. The Civil War had begun.

When hostilities began, neither the North nor the South had any significant intelligence or counterintelligence capability. Generals operated their own espionage rings and personally recruited and directed their spies. In Washington, President Lincoln was concerned. He only had to look outside his window to realize that the capital was penetrated and surrounded by southern sympathizers. Although Maryland stayed loyal to the Union, many of its citizens favored the southern cause.

To protect the federal government, Secretary of State William H. Seward took the initiative. Under his directon, southern spies, sympathizers and others were arrested and detained as threats to the government. When General George McClellan was appointed commander of the Union Army, Allan Pinkerton and his detectives replaced Seward in his role as counterintelligence chief. Pinkerton was very effective in stopping the flow of intelligence out of the capital to the Confederacy.

In November 1862, Lincoln removed McClellan and replaced him with General Ambrose Burnside. With McClellan's dismissal, Pinkerton left Washington and his counterintelligence role to protect the city was given to Lafayette Baker. At the time, Baker was working for the War Department, targeting contraband channels. Like Pinkerton, Baker was successful in neutralizing southern agents and sympathizers.

The Confederacy did not formerly establish a Secret Service Bureau until 30 November 1864; the war would be over on 9 April 1865. The full extent of the Confederacy's counterintelligence operations and activities remain a mystery because Judah Benjamin, the Secretary of State for the confederacy, burned all espionage records as the Union Army entered Richmond.

William H. Seward[1]

When the Lincoln Administration suddenly found itself faced with open hostilities and accompanying espionage and spy intrigues in 1861, one of the first officials to react to the situation was Secretary of State Seward. His organization combined both the police function—pursing individuals with a view to their incarceration and prosecution—and the intelligence function—gathering information regarding the loyalty and political views of citizens without any particular regard for possible violations of the law. In combining the two tasks, of course, their distinction often became lost. One commentator notes:

The Government's first efforts to control the civilian population were conducted by the Secretary of State for reasons both personal and official. William H. Seward, the "Premier" of the Cabinet, had an unquenchable zeal for dabbling in everyone else's business. In addition, since the establishment of the Federal Government the office of the Secretary of State had been somewhat of a catchall for duties no other executive agency was designed to handle. With the war, and the new problem of subversion on the home front, Seward soon began to busy himself about arrests of political prisoners, their incarceration, and then the next step of setting up secret agents to ferret them out.[2]

There are no informative records as to how or why the initial arrests of political prisoners and the creation

William H. Seward

of a secret service fell to Secretary Seward. It is entirely likely that he requested these duties. The more important consideration, however, concerns the extent to which he responsibly carried out these obligations. According to one of the Secretary's biographers:

Arrests were made for any one of many reasons: where men were suspected of having given, or intending to give, aid or comfort to the enemy in any substantial way,—as by helping in the organization of troops, by supplying arms or provisions, or selling the bonds of the states in secession; by public or private communications that opposed United States enlistment or encouraged those of the Confederacy; by expressing sympathy with the South or attacking the administration; by belonging to organizations designed to obstruct the progress of the war—in fact for almost any act that indicated a desire to see the government fail in its effort to conquer disunion.[3]

But the question was not simply one of fact. The manner and nature of the arrest and detention of political offenders raised a number of due process considerations.

The person suspected of disloyalty was often seized at night, searched, borne off to the nearest fort, deprived of his valuables, and locked up in a casemate, or in a battery generally crowded with men that had had similar experiences. It was not rare for arrests regarded as political to be made by order of the Secretary of War or of some military officer; but, with only a few exceptions, these prisoners came under the control of the Secretary of State just as if he had taken the original action.

For a few days the newcomer usually voiced varied reflection and loud denunciation of the administration. But the discomforts of his confinement soon led him to seek his freedom. When he resolved to send for friends and an attorney, he was informed that the rules forbade visitors, except in rate instances, that attorneys were entirely excluded and the prisoner who sought their aid would greatly prejudice his case. Only unsealed letters would be forwarded, and if they contained objectionable statements they were returned to the writer or filed in the Department of State with other papers relating to the case.

There still remained a possibility, it was generally assumed, of speedy relief by appeal to the Secretary in person. Then a long narrative, describing the experiences of a man whose innocence was equaled only by his misfortunes, was addressed to the nervous, wiry, all-powerful man keeping watch over international relations, political offenders, and affairs generally. The letter was read by the Chief Clerk or Assistant Secretary, and then merely filed. A second, third, and fourth petition for liberation and explanations was sent to the department—but with no result save that the materials for the study of history and human nature were thereby enlarged; the Secretary was calm in the belief that the man was a plotter and could do no harm while he remained in custody.[4]

To rectify this situation, two important steps were taken in February 1862. On St. Valentine's Day, an Executive order was issued providing for the wholesale release of most political prisoners, excepting only "persons detained as spies in the service of the insurgent, or others whose release at the present moment may be deemed incompatible with the public safety."[5] In addition, a special review panel, consisting of Judge Edwards Pierrepont and General John A. Dix, was established to expedite releases under this directive.[6]

With regard to intelligence activities, Seward apparently employed Allan Pinkerton for such operations during the summer of 1861, "but did not keep him long, perhaps because he felt that the detective was too close to the President, and Seward wanted his own man, whose loyalty would be direct to him."[7] A listening post was sought in Canada for purposes of checking on the activities of Confederate agents and to monitor the trend of sentiment in British North America during the secession crisis.[8] Former Massachusetts Congressman George Ashmun was appointed special agent to Canada for three months in early 1861 at a salary of $10 a day plus expenses. Seward advanced $500 cash on account. Another operative, Charles S. Ogden, took residence in Quebec and additional stations were subsequently established at Halifax and St. John's, among other seaports.[9]

A domestic network also came into being while the Canadian group struggled to recruit confidential agents.

Seward's "Secret Service Letter Book" for 1861 was full of inquiries dispatched to friends and trusted official associates throughout the country asking them to discover persons who could be put on important investigating tasks. He wanted "a discreet and active" man for the Northern frontier, to arrest spies seeking entrance from Canada, and offered to pay such a man $100 a month. A little later he appointed a special agent at Niagara Falls, to examine the persons coming over the Suspension Bridge, and seize and hold any whom seemed suspicious. He sought, without immediate results, a good man for Chicago and another for Detroit. He authorized the United States Marshall at Boston to employ two detectives for two-month's time, each at $150 a month. This was particularly urgent; therefore let the Marshall consult the governor of the State, "and take effective measures to break up the business of making and sending shoes for the Rebel Army."[10]

Almost unnoticed, Seward's intelligence organization began to grow; though its agents often proved to be ineffective amateurs. Shortly, however, professionalism, discipline, and a careful sense of mission came to the Secretary's spy corps in the person of Lafayette Charles Baker.

Allan Pinkerton[11]

Allan Pinkerton (1819-1884), a Scottish immigrant, is best known as the founder of the Pinkerton detective agency, one of the most famous organizations of its kind. Pinkerton emigrated to Chicago in 1842 and moved to Dundee, Kane County, Illinois in 1843. After apprehending a gang of counterfeiters, he was appointed deputy sheriff of Kane County in 1846 and immediately afterward of Cook County, headquartered in Chicago. There he organized a force of detectives to counter theft of railroad property, and in 1850 he established the North Western Police Detective agency, later renamed Pinkerton's National Detective Agency.

A group of Union Spies.

Members of the Bureau of Military Information, Army of the Potomac.

Pinkerton also was an important player in intelligence gathering during the Civil War years of 1861 and 1862 when he organized a system of obtaining military information in the Southern states. Pinkerton recorded his exploits as a Union operative, under the *nom-de-plume* of Major E. J. Allen, in the book, *The Spy of the Rebellion: Being a True History of the Spy System of the United States Army During the Late Rebellion*, published in 1883. Unfortunately for the historian, the book was published after Pinkerton lost his records during the Chicago fire of 1871. The majority of his narrative relied upon his few remaining notes, official reports, and his memory of events that had occurred 20 years before. The book also served the purpose of refuting claims that Pinkerton's spies had provided inflated numbers of Confederate troops, a claim that has become an accepted part of Civil War history.

Pinkerton felt the need to defend his spy system's record during the first years of the war and his close association with Major General George B. McClellan. Pinkerton had been well acquainted with McClellan before the Civil War, during his years as railroad detective when McClellan was president of the Ohio and Mississippi Railroad.

Pinkerton began his intelligence activity before President-elect Lincoln's arrival in Washington, D.C. for his inauguration in 1861. Pinkerton had received a letter from Samuel H. Felton, the president of the Philadelphia, Wilmington and Baltimore Railroad, warning of a plan to disrupt Lincoln's trip by destroying rail transportation between Washington, D.C. and cities in the west and north. In response, Pinkerton dispatched surveillance agents along the roads, selecting places where intelligence indicated there were secessionist supporters. He also employed two agents to infiltrate secessionist groups, one of whom learned of plans to assassinate Lincoln as he passed through Baltimore, Maryland.

These agents established their credibility through ethnic ties, collegiate studies, foreign travel, knowledge of foreign languages, familiarity with local customs and prominent individuals, vocal support for secessionist causes, and participation in secret secessionist societies. They discovered that the conspirators, in league with members of the Baltimore police force, planned to assassinate Lincoln as he rode in an open carriage for a half-mile between the Northern Central Railroad Station to the Washington depot.

Pinkerton Letter

Chicago, April 21st 1861
To His Excellency
A Lincoln, Pres. of the U-S

Dear Sir

When I saw you last I said that if the time should ever come that I could be of service to you I was ready-If that time has come I am on hand.

I have in my Force from Sixteen to Eighteen persons on whose courage, Skill & Devotion to their Country I can rely. If they with myself at the head can be of service in the way of obtaining information of the movements of the Traitors, or Safely conveying your letters or dispatches, or that class of Secret Service which is the most dangerous, I am at your command-

In the present disturbed state of Affairs I dare not trust this to the mail-so send by one of My Force who was with me at Baltimore-You may safely trust him with any message for me-Written or Verbal-I fully guarantee his fidelity-He will act as you direct-and return here with your answer.

Secrecy is the great lever, I propose to operate with-Hence the necessity of this movement (If you contemplate it) being kept Strictly Private-and that should you desire another interview with the Bearer that you should so arrange it-as that he will not be noticed.

The Bearer will hand you A Copy of A Telegraph Cipher which you may use if you desire to Telegraph me-

My Force comprises both Sexes-All of Good Character-And well Skilled in their Business.

Respectfully yours,

Allan Pinkerton

In a tale with as many twists and turns as any good spy novel, Lincoln is secretly whisked from a public appearance in Harrisburg, Pennsylvania, by a special train to Philadelphia, then through the "lines of treason" in Baltimore and safely on to Washington, D.C. Key to the success of this plan was Pinkerton's arrangement to have the telegraph lines out of Harrisburg cut so that news of Lincoln's abrupt departure was contained. He also detained two journalists by force of arms from immediately reporting the plan and assumed responsibility for the security of the railroad tracks, on which the special train traveled.

The identity of Pinkerton's infiltrated agents was closely held and led to an incident that added to the credibility of his chief operative, Timothy Webster. Webster had become well entrenched among secessionist groups in the Baltimore area, frequently socializing with them and carrying letters through Union lines for them. He played his role so well that another secret service agent, who was not aware of his identity and activities, arrested him in Baltimore. Webster had to contact Pinkerton to obtain his release.

His escape, arranged by Pinkerton, increased Webster's standing among the Southern sympathizers and allowed him to continue his successful spy operations. He became a trusted emissary of the Confederate government, delivering letters and other communications to relatives in the North.

These documents were first inspected by Pinkerton's service before being delivered and in this way served two purposes. Webster not only won the trust of the Confederate authorities, but he also provided the federal government with valuable information. In one case, the intercepted documents revealed the presence of a Confederate spy ring in the Provost Marshal's office in Washington, D.C.

When General George B. McClellan was given command of the Army of the Potomac in November 1861, Pinkerton came to Washington with him. It was at this time that Pinkerton was given the responsibility for security and counterintelligence within the nation's capital. How Pinkerton was going to handle this new assignment was spelled out in a letter to McClellan. In it, Pinkerton wrote:

> *In operating with my detective force, I shall endeavor to test all suspected persons in various ways. I shall seek access to their houses, clubs, and places of resort, managing that among the members of my force shall be ostensible representatives of every grade of society, from the highest to the most*

John C. Babcock (center standing) pictured while a member of Pinkerton's organization. Standing with him are (left) Augustus K. Littlefield and (right) George H. Bangs. Seated (left) William Moore, Secretary to War Secretary Stanton and Allen Pinkerton.

menial. Some shall have the entree *to the gilded salon of the suspected aristocratic traitors, and be their honored guests, while others will act in the capacity of valets, or domestics of various kinds, and try the efficacy of such relations with the household to gain evidence. Other suspected ones will be tracked by the "Shadow" detective, who will follow their every foot step, and note their every action.*

I also propose to employ a division of my force for the discovery of any secret traitorous organization which may be in existence; and if any such society is discovered, I will have my operatives become members of the same, with a view to ascertaining the means employed in transmitting messages through the lines, and also for the purpose of learning, if possible, the plans of the rebels. All strangers arriving in the city, whose associations or acts may lay them open to suspicion, will be subjected to a strict surveillance.[12]

Another counterintelligence technique used by Pinkerton was the double agent. As Pinkerton wrote:

In war, as in a game of chess, if you know the moves of your adversary in advance, it is then an easy matter to shape your own plans, and make your moves accordingly, and, of course always to your own decided advantage. So in this case, I concluded that if the information intended for the rebels could first be had by us, after that, they were welcome to all the benefit they might derive from them.[13]

Another of Pinkerton's agents infiltrated the Southern bureau of intelligence in Richmond, managed partly by the Confederate government and partly by wealthy merchants in Richmond and Baltimore. This bureau was said to employ about 50 persons to carry information across Union lines. Pinkerton's agent, George Curtis, gained access to the "subterranean headquarters" of this bureau, which actually were located above ground in a Richmond hotel, by claiming to be a dealer in contraband material. According to Pinkerton, Curtis was such an excellent spy that the "subterranean headquarters, with its corps of operatives, never did the Union cause any practical harm, but a great deal of good, in furnishing intelligence of the movements and intentions of the rebel forces."

Pinkerton's memoirs also recount how his service used women and slaves as spies. Mrs. E. H. Baker, a former resident of Richmond who had moved north at the war's start, was one notable woman agent. Returning to Richmond in Pinkerton's service, she renewed an acquaintance with a Confederate officer and his wife, and learned of a planned test of a submarine battery. She pursued this lead and asked to be invited to the test of a small working model of the Merrimac. She immediately carried news of the test back to Pinkerton who alerted General McClellan and the Secretary of the Navy. Pinkerton saw this incident as changing the destiny of the Union in the face of this "infernal machine."

Pinkerton stopped working with the Union Army after General McClellan was removed as commander, although he continued to investigate government fraud cases. In 1865 he severed his connection with the Secret Service and returned to Chicago to pursue his detective profession. What he provides in his memoir is his case that his wartime agents operated heroically in the service of their country.

Layfayette Baker[14]

Born in New York in 1826 and reared in the Michigan wilderness, Layfayette Baker engaged in mechanical and mercantile pursuits in the state of his birth and in Philadelphia in 1848 before departing, in 1853, for California. Three years later he was an active member of the Vigilance Committee. This experience and his admiration of Francios Vidocq (1775-1857),

Layfayette Baker

an infamous Paris detective whom Baker came to imitate, whetted his appetite for intrigue and the life of the sleuth. When hostilities broke out between the North and the South, Baker happened to be heading for New York City on business. When he became aware of the mischief and misdeeds of Confederate spies and saboteurs in and around Washington, he set out for the capital determined to offer his services as a Union agent.[15]

Arriving in the District of Columbia, Baker obtained an interview with General Winfield Scott, commander of the Army and himself not unfamiliar with spy services. In need of information about the rebel forces at Manassas, Scott, having already lost five previous agents on the mission, solicited Baker's assistance. After an adventure of daring and dash, the intrepid Baker returned three weeks later with the details sought by General Scott. The success of the mission earned Baker a permanent position with the War Department.[16]

The next assignment given Baker involved ferreting out two Baltimore brothers who were running the Union blockade to supply munitions to the Confederates. This he did, breaking up the smuggling operation and earning himself a considerable amount of press publicity.[17]

These activities came to the attention of Secretary Seward who hired Baker at the rate of $100 a month plus expenses[18] and sent him off to prowl wherever espionage, sabotage, or rebel spy agents were thought to be lurking.[19] Assisted by three hundred Indian cavalrymen, Baker was later ordered to probe the Maryland countryside for the presence of rebel agents and Confederate sympathies.

His mission took him to Chapico, Leonardstown, Port Tobacco, Old Factory, and the farmland of St. George's, St. Charles and St. Mary's counties.[20] As his column advanced, they punished the disloyal. As a result, "he left behind a trail of burning buildings, frightened men, women and children, terrified informers, (and) bullet-pierced Secesh Tobacco planters.[21]

As a consequence of this campaign, Baker attempted to interest Postmaster General Montgomery Blair in a purge of disloyal Maryland postmasters, replacing them with Union stalwarts or closing the stations. Blair was well aware of disloyalty among some of the Maryland postmasters and earlier had ordered their displacement. In a report to the Secretary of State, Baker claimed he had obtained unlimited authority to conduct the postmaster purge and requested a military force of two hundred to three hundred men to police the localities in Maryland where these disloyal officials had been discovered. The proposal was ignored but Baker had a variety of other tasks to occupy him as Seward's intelligence chief.[22]

With enough endurance for a dozen men, he worked almost without rest to educate himself in the ever-spreading operations of the rebels and their sympathizers. He traveled to Canada to see for himself what the South was doing to build a fire in the rear of the Union: he made the acquaintance of police chiefs of the big northern cities: he personally took prisoners to the harbor forts to look over conditions; he uncovered and jotted down identities of suppliers of war goods to the South; he acquired a firsthand knowledge of Secesh-supporting newspapers, in sedition-ridden New York, New Jersey, and the seething West. Only on rare occasions, when official duty took him there, did he see his wife Jennie, who had gone to the security of her parent's home in Philadelphia.[23]

As a consequence of Lincoln's St. Valentine's Day directive regarding the release of political prisoners and limiting "extraordinary arrests" to "the direction of the military authorities alone," Baker was recommended to the War Department and its new Secretary, Edwin M. Stanton. In accepting Baker's services, Stanton warned him of the grave and desperate situation facing the government, advised him that he would never be permitted to disclose the authority for his actions, and gave notice that he would be expected to pursue all enemies of the Union, regardless of their station, power, loyalty, partisanship, or profession. Baker's detective service was to be the terror of the North as well as the South, secretly funded, and accountable exclusively and directly to the Secretary of War.[24]

The enemies of the state took many forms. An enemy could be a pretty girl with swaying hips covered by an acre of crinoline, carrier of rebellion-sustaining contraband goods. Or an enemy could be a contractor selling the Union shoddy clothing. Or an enemy could be a Copperhead sapping the strength of the Union by discouraging enlistments. An enemy could also be a Union general with larceny in his soul, gambling away the pay of his soldiers. He could be a guerrilla with a torch firing a government corral within sight of the White House.[25]

For three years, Baker gathered intelligence on the enemies of the Union, reporting his findings to Stanton and Lincoln. In addition, at their direction and sometimes on his own authority, he functioned as an instrument for directly punishing the enemy or for arresting and incarcerating them. Utilizing his intelligence sources, Baker identified and prejudged the despoilers of the Union; relying upon extraordinary military authority and martial law, he seized his foe in his capacity as a Federal policeman; and as the custodian of the Old Capitol Prison and its nefarious annex, the Carroll Prison, he served as jailer of those he captured.

Of Baker's Commander-in-Chief, one authority has commented: "No one can ever know just what Lincoln conceived to be limits of his powers."[26]

In his own words, the Sixteenth President wrote:

"... my oath to preserve the Constitution to the best of my ability, imposed upon me the duty of preserving, by every indispensable means, that government—that nation—of which that Constitution was the organic law. Was it possible to lose the nation, and yet preserve the constitution? By general law life and limb must be protected; yet often a limb must be amputated to safe a life, but a life is never wisely given to save a limb. I felt that measures, otherwise unconstitutional, might become lawful, by becoming indispensable to the preservation of the constitution through the preservation of the nation. Right or wrong, I assumed this ground, and now avow it. I could not feel that, to the best of my ability, I had ever tried to preserve the constitution, if, to save slavery, or any minor matter, I should permit the wreck of the government, county, and Constitution all together."[27]

And in the more contemporary view of Clinton Rossiter:

"Mr. Lincoln subscribed to a theory that in the absence of Congress and in the presence of an emergency the President has the right and duty to adopt measures which would ordinarily be illegal, subject to the necessity of subsequent congressional approval. He did more than this; he seemed to assert that the war powers for the Constitution could upon occasion devolve completely upon the President, if their exercise was based upon public opinion and an inexorable necessity. They were then sufficient to embrace any action within the fields of executive or legislative or even judicial power essential to the preservation of the Union. (He) ... implied that this government, like all others, possessed an absolute power of self defense, a power to be exerted by the President of the United States. And this power extended to the breaking of the fundamental laws of the nation, if such a step were unavoidable.[28]

Mary E. Walker, Winner of the Medal of Honor, who worked for Layfayette Baker.

The presence of this operating viewpoint at the highest level of the Executive Branch, coupled with his own personal ambitions for power and prestige, contributed significantly to Baker's zealous, authoritarian, and often illegal manner of carrying out his War Department mission. Nevertheless, Baker must be recognized as a professional thoroughly familiar with the methods and tactics of his profession. Reflecting a classically Machiavellian perspective, he once wrote:

> *"It may be said that the deception and misstatements resorted to, and inseparable from the detective service, are demoralizing and prove unsoundness of character in its officers. But is must be borne in mind that, in war, no commander fails to deceive the enemy when possible, to secure the best advantage. Spies, scouts, intercepted correspondence, feints in army movements, misrepresentations of military strength and position, are regarded as honorable means of securing victory over the foe. The work of the detectives is simply deception reduced to a science or profession; and whatever objection, on ethical grounds, may lie against the secret service, lies with equal force against the strategy and tactics of Washington, Scott, Grant, and the host of their illustrious associates in the wars of the world. War is a last and terrible resort in the defense of even a righteous cause, and sets at defiance all of the ordinary laws and customs of society, overriding the rights of property and the sanctity of the Sabbath. And not until the nation learns war no more, will the work of deception and waste of morals, men and treasures cease."* [29]

Establishing offices at 217 Pennsylvania Avenue, in close proximity to both the White House and the War Department, Baker began gathering recruits and organizing his unit. Operating without official status, the group was generally referred to as the Secret Service Bureau. Its personnel, known only to Baker in terms of number and complete identity, bore no credentials other than a small silver badge.[30] Secretly commissioned as a colonel; Baker initially represented himself, when absolutely necessary, as an agent of the War Department. Later, he publicly cited his military rank and held the title of Provost Marshal.

He initiated the nation's first police dossier system although the rebels, the Copperheads, and the misguided among the Loyalists in the North charged him with poking his private eyes into the homes of the innocent. He gathered systematically the first criminal photo file, enabling a more efficient pursuit of the enemies of the nation. He instituted a policy of seizing suspects in the dead of the night when their resistance to interrogation and their ability to seek help would be at the lowest ebb. He made a science of the interrogation of prisoners, using teams of detectives to work over a suspect until he was satisfied he either had the full story or he could drag no more information from his victim.

He established a secret fund for building and feeding a vast army of informers and unlisted agents. No one except he knew the full range of his organization. Even his most trusted aides were not allowed to know the identity of all of his operatives.[31]

For reasons of both security and strategy, Baker's agents were divided into daylight and nighttime units—the men in one group did not know the identity of those in the other—and another section counted operatives who infiltrated and trafficked in the capital's high society.[32] He cultivated contacts with the police in the nation's society. He cultivated contacts with the police in the nation's major cities[33] and kept a close watch on Confederate activities in Canada.[34] By the summer of 1863, a branch office had been set up in New York City[35] and he succeeded in placing his personnel in the Post Office for purposes of inspecting the mails.[36]

On two occasions Baker's spy service gathered intelligence which probably contributed to the downfall of General McClellan: Baker's personal penetration of the Confederate forces at Manassas resulted in the discovery that the fortifications and artillery which were supposedly keeping McClellan's army at bay were actually earthen and wooden fakes and later Lincoln utilized the services of one of Baker's agents to secretly observe McClellan's conduct on the battlefield.[37] With the decline of McClellan, Allan Pinkerton, whom Baker regarded as "sagacious," departed from the scene, leaving some agents and the spy field to Baker.[38] The only other threat to Baker's supreme command of the secret service operations was the reputed organizer of the old Mexican Spy Company, Ethan Allen Hitchcock, but he was founded to be an old man seized with mysticism and pursuits of alchemy with no desires for any responsibility in the hostilities.[39]

In June of 1863, Baker gained an open commission in the army with the rank of colonel, the opportunity to wear the Union uniform, and command of a military police force he had sought for some time.[40] The exact size of the unit is not known, or its losses, or its complete record of action. After much pressuring from Baker, Stanton agreed to establish the troop utilizing authority entitling the District Columbia to a battalion of infantry and cavalry for use within its confines.[41] Placed under a direct authority of the Secretary of War, the first Regiment Cavalry, known as "Baker's Rangers," consisted, ironically, of recruits from Robert E. Lee's former command, the Second Dragoons, renamed the Second Regular United States Cavalry at the outbreak of the war.[42]

Hundreds of men sought places in the new regiment; some offered bribes. Whether the attraction was the promise that no soldier in the Baker command would ever be sent outside the immediate vicinity of the District of Columbia or whether Baker's fame inspired all types of adventurers to flock to his banner was the subject of much conjecture at that time.[43]

In an appeal to the Governor of New York, Baker wrote:

> "...the duties to be performed by this regiment demand on the part of both men and officers qualities of a high order, both mental and physical. Among these, I may enumerate intelligence, sobriety, self dependence, bodily vigor, the power of endurance, and though last not least, that knowledge of the horse which results from early practical experience and management of that noble animal.[44]

The personal qualifications of Baker's recruits, of course, cannot be assessed. By their actions, however, they demonstrated great military ability, intense loyalty to their commander, and a complete insensitivity to the property, liberties and lives of those they encountered as enemies. For reasons of high morality and public image, the Rangers were unleashed upon the gambling parlors and vice dens of Washington.[45] Soon, however, they began engaging in forays of destruction against enemies of the Union beyond the confines of the capital.[46]

The Rangers were an auxiliary to Baker's intelligence activities; they were his agents of espionage, enforcement, and protection. Secret operatives gathered information in both the cities and the countryside of the Potomac region. Baker devoured their reports, conferred with Stanton and/or Lincoln, and then set out with enforcements against the subversives.

In addition to ferreting out spies, blockade runners, and locals giving aid and comfort to the rebels, Baker engaged in three major intelligence enterprises: unmasking crimes in the Treasury Department, smashing the Northwest conspiracy, and capturing the President's assassin.[47] The opportunity to probe the Treasury Department regarding allegations that it had become a bawdy house and command post for certain predatory interests arose around Christmas, 1863, when Treasury Secretary Salmon P. Chase invited Baker to investigate the situation.

There was growing talk of scandals in the Treasury Department. Newspapers were saying that the hundreds of girls busy scissoring the new greenbacks were hussies in the night. There were oyster feasts in the bonnet room. Clerks were making off with sheets of uncut currency.

Counterfeiters were discovering it was easier to steal a plate and run off bales of money rather than go to the trouble of making an imitation engraving in some hideaway. The Treasury's own police seemed helpless to stem the tide of corruption and debauchery. The Blair family, avowed enemies of Chase, was giving support to the rumors. (Postmaster General) Montgomery Blair's brother, Frank, cried out for congressional inquiry.[48]

The probe was charged and politically explosive. Seward, eyes upon the 1864 election and the White House beyond, might well have wanted Lincoln's top detective mired in the scandals, defused and defamed along with most of the Administration. In Hanson A. Risley, special Treasury agent, Seward had his own source of intelligence. So close were the two men that Risley gave over one of his daughters to Seward to adoption and, after Mrs. Seward's death, the old man sought her for his second wife.

In detailing Baker to Treasury, Stanton probably thought he would be the best man to vindicate the President as untainted, honest and ignorant of the conditions there. Himself a frequent critic of Lincoln, the Secretary of War nevertheless realized that public confidence in the President must be maintained in the midst of the country's perils and he might well have been aware that Lincoln had no direct involvement in the treasury calamities.

Factions within Congress were ready to intervene to attack Lincoln, Chase, and Baker. Ultimately, a committee of investigation was formed, probed the situation, and beclouded the facts and the guilt of those involved.

Baker plunged into the Treasury probe with ferocity and determination. He temporarily relinquished command of the Rangers and established an office in the dark basement of the Treasury building. His techniques were direct and dauntless; he stalked the printing facilities and subjected clerks and lesser officials to ruthless and merciless interrogation. At one juncture he halted a funeral cortege in the midst of the city, seized the corpse of a Treasury girl and had an examination made to determine if her death had resulted from an abortion.[49]

And what did Baker find? At the outset he discovered that young James Cornwell, who had the function of burning mutilated bonds and notes, had pocketed $2,000 worth of notes. Cornwell was convicted and sent to jail for this offense, the only individual to be prosecuted for crimes against the Treasury in this probe.

Next, Baker alleged that two printers who had sold the Treasury new presses, paper, and a technique for printing currency were conspiring to sell the government worthless machinery and processes. Their presses were weakening the upper floors of the Treasury building and their security procedures were virtually non-existent, allowing ready access to both plates and process. In the midst of the inquiry, the new presses began malfunctioning and greater demands were placed on the building for "improved" printing devices.

Baker discovered that the head of the department of printing and engraving, Spencer Clark, was involved with a number of young women who were cutting and preparing new currency. An associate of Clark's was also implicated and Baker named both men for dismissal. Eventually it came to pass that it was Secretary Chase who was to resign and the great Treasury scandal passed into history.[50]

In mid-November of 1863, a full month before the Treasury investigation got underway, rumors of a dangerous conspiracy along the Canadian border began circulating. Baker's agents pursued the facts of the matter and by late spring of the following year a fairly clear image of the attack planned by the Confederates was evident. In Richmond, Judal P. Benjamin, Secretary of State for the rebel government, a holder of three cabinet posts in the Confederacy, and a man of imagination, conceived a desperate plan of havoc utilizing secret societies reminiscent of the later Klu Klux Klan guerrillas. Warriors behind Union lines would burn down New York City, free rebel troops imprisoned in the North to loot and pillage throughout the industrial Northeast, and seize Chicago, Buffalo, and Indianapolis. The plan failed to recognize the drift of northern morale; those disenchanted with the war still supported Lincoln, sought the Union as was and the Constitution as is, and otherwise had no interest in or sympathy for a separate Confederate nation.

In the aftermath of the destructive campaigns of Generals Sheridan in the Shenandoah Valley and Sherman in Georgia, the rebels were ready for unconventional warfare of their own making.

The Copperhead firebrand Clement Vallandigham was recruited to obtain support for a new nation composed of states adjacent to the Canadian border. Army officers in civilian dress were dispatched north to act as terrorists. The first target for revenge was Chicago. Assembled in Toronto, the band of insurgents made their plans—all of which were carefully recorded by a Baker informer.

Commanders of military prisons were informed of these developments and advised to be prepared for uprisings within or attacks from outside of their institutions. Baker advanced a squadron of agents to Toronto to maintain surveillance of the conspirators who were followed and observed as they straggled into Chicago in the midst of the Democratic National Convention. More than 2,000 civilian-clad Confederate soldiers were scattered around the city.

At the height of the convention proceedings, the area would be put to the torch. While police and firemen fought the flames, an attack would be made on Camp Douglas and its prisoners freed. The banks would be looted, City Hall seized, and the police headquarters occupied. Thus, the second largest city in the land fell to rebel control.

Politics among the conspirators caused a postponement of their assault until Election Day. After reassembling in Toronto, burnings and attacks on local authorities were scheduled for simultaneous occurrence in Chicago, New York, Cincinnati, and Boston. Surveillance of these preparations continued and information from the informer flowed to Baker.

Offensive actions were unleashed against the terrorists. Without warning, General Benjamin F. Butler, seasoned in maintaining the security and serenity of New Orleans, marched into New York with 10,000 Union troops as the clock moved toward Election Day. Confederate arsonists abandoned their grandiose plan of havoc, set a few fires in some hotels (which were quickly distinguished), and fled to Canada. Across the border, they soon learned that they had been fortunate in their escape. A Baker spy in Chicago brought about the ruination of terrorist activities in that city and a Union operative in Indiana gathered enough information to implicate almost the entire band of Confederate conspirators in that state.

While these elements were being rounded up and jailed, Union authorities took an imprisoned Confederate officer into their intelligence corps, swore him to loyalty to the Union cause, and released him to make contact with some of the remaining members of the Northwest Conspiracy. Followed by Baker's agents, the man soon met with a group seeking to liberate 3,000 rebel officers incarcerated on Johnson's Island in Lake Michigan. The intervention of this spy cost the conspirators a cache of arms and the loss of a few men in Chicago and indirectly contributed to the scuttling of the Johnson's Island mission.

By late fall, 1864, the Northwest Conspiracy had collapsed and its principal leaders and organizers had been jailed.[51] The excitement and stimulation of the chase ended. Baker founded himself in an unfamiliar situation. He was given no public credit for his part in smashing the great conspiracy. On the contrary, his enemies increased their efforts to build up the ugly image of the Bastille master, and he continued to be identified in the public mind with unjust arrests and imprisonment, invasions of the rights of private persons and rumored profiteering. Baker still knew that, as a secret agent, the details of his activities must remain secret.

If, however he had hoped that this sensational case would change the attitude toward him in Congress and Administration circles, or would convince the Copperheads that he put the Union before personal gain, he must have been sadly disappointed. His success in securing and transmitting information which led to the dramatic collapse of the great conspiracy and the punishment of its leaders in the North still brought him no evidence that his services were to be fairly judged by the results he achieved for the Union cause.[52]

Baker had just completed a successful investigation of fraud and deception surrounding the draft, bounty-hunting, defrauding sailors out of prize money, and efforts at morally corrupting Union troops in the New York City area when he received the news of Lincoln's assassination. Undoubtedly he felt guilt for not having had more advance information about the conspiracy against the President and for not having had agents near the Chief Executive when the murderer struck. Upon receiving word that Lincoln had been shot and was dead, Baker threw himself into the pursuit and capture of those responsible for the crime. After producing a handbill, the first to be circulated for a nationally wanted criminal, describing John Wilkes Booth in detail, Baker set about interrogating everyone and anyone who knew anything about the conspirators involved in the assassination.[53]

Stanton went along with the detective's thinking and supported his tigerish moves to stalk his prey. One by one, Booth's accomplices were rounded up. Baker's rival police agencies did most of the work. But he took charge of the prisoners, dragged incriminating admissions from them, put black hoods on their heads, and stuffed them in the hold of a monitor in the river.[54]

Finally, Baker found Booth's track, pursued him with a command of cavalry, and came at least to the

Garrett farm where the assassin had taken refuge in a barn. His prey cornered, Baker confronted the killer, demanded his surrender or the alternative of firing the barn. In the midst of negotiations and flames, Booth was shot by either himself or by Sergeant Boston Corbett. Baker took charge of the body and later sought a portion of the rewards for capturing Booth. The amount subsequently awarded Baker was reduced to $3,750 from a potential of $17,500: the secret service chief continued to be unpopular with the Congress.[55]

With the death of Lincoln, Baker became the protector of the new President, Andrew Johnson, and set up the first White House secret service details in the history of the Republic.[56] With the peace of Appomattox, however, the career of the spy chief began to rapidly decline. The rebel foe of wartime now walked the streets of the capital. Many of the prostitutes and gamblers Baker had jailed under military law were again free. These, together with political enemies, taunted and reproached the once powerful secret service, a vestige of war, which seemed to have no future mission.

Nevertheless, Baker attempted to carry on in the old style. His task was to protect the President: his immediate foe, he surmised, were various female pardon brokers, lately sympathetic to the South, who prevailed upon the President to grant clemency and forgiveness to all manner of rebels. In attempting to halt this traffic in and out of the White House, Baker incurred the wrath of President Johnson and a lawsuit that successfully damaged his status and role. In the midst of the trial, he was routinely mustered out of the army and effectively left without a friend or defender.[57] He departed Washington in disgrace, returned to his wife in Philadelphia, wrote his memoirs in lieu of finding other work, contracted spinal meningitis and died on the evening of July 3, 1868.

Lafayette Baker was a zealot who, imbued with a strong sense of righteousness and a taste of vigilantism, in the name of a cause became oblivious to the ends-means relationship underlying his function. In his defense of the Union and democratic government, he resorted to extreme actions obnoxious to popular rule and, in some instances, in violation of constitutional guarantees. He actively sought to exceed his intelligence role and became policeman, judge, and jailer. His desires in this regard, and his capacity for achievement of same, were fostered and fed by the exigencies of the moment and the liberties Lincoln took in administering (or not administering) the law.

When Lincoln died and the war ended, Baker became a political pariah with a vestigial function. His activities had annoyed many, frightened some, and made bitter enemies of an important and powerful few. With the onset of peace in the Nation, he was virtually stripped of his organization and official status and left vulnerable to legal, political, and financial reprisals. These forces converged, coalesced, and crushed. Due to the secret nature of Baker's operations and his tendency to embellish fact, the full account of the activities of this spy chief may never be known. In all likelihood, his record of service will always be controversial, and of debatable value.

Henry Beebee Carrington[58]

Henry Beebee Carrington conducted intelligence operations against political enemies—the Copperheads and rebel conspirators attempting to undermine the Union cause. Born in Connecticut in 1824, Carrington became an ardent abolitionist in his youth, graduated from Yale in 1845, and taught for a while in the Irving Institute at Tarrytown, New York. Under the influence of the school's founder, Washington Irving, he subsequently wrote *Battles of the American Revolution*, which appeared in 1876. He was also to write seven other major titles. Leaving New York, he taught at the New Haven Collegiate Institute while pursing a law degree at his old alma mater.

In 1848 he moved to Ohio and entered upon a law practice. Over the next dozen years Carrington represented a variety of commercial, manufacturing, banking, and railroad interests and became a pioneer in Republican politics. A close friend and supporter of Governor Salmon P. Chase, he was subsequently appointed to a position to reorganize the state militia (1857). He subsequently became an adjutant general for Ohio, mustering nine regiments of militia at the outbreak of the Civil War. He then was commissioned a colonel of the 18th United States Infantry and took command of an army camp near Columbus.

In neighboring Indiana, Governor Olive P. Morton had need of Carrington's services. For reasons not altogether clear—perhaps it was his partisan political past and /or his ardent abolitionism—Carrington was ordered, upon the request of Morton, to organize the state's levies for service.

When Carrington arrived in Indiana, political warfare between the adherents of the administration and its opponents was beginning in earnest. The favorite weapon of the Republicans was that ephemeral and elusive order, the Knights of the Golden Circle. Carrington joined in wholeheartedly. On December 22, 1862, he blamed the appalling rate of desertion on the treasonable secret societies, whose penetration of the army was shown by knowledge among soldiers of a "battle sign" which would save them from rebel bullets.

In a long report dated March 19, 1863, he described the situation as so alarming that it bordered on open revolt. He claimed that the Knights had ninety-two thousand members between sixteen and seventy who were drilling constantly. They were plotting to seize the arsenals, the railroads, and the telegraph in order to revolutionize Indiana and "assert independent authority as a state." They communicated with Confederates, in particular with General Morgan, whose picture hung in many homes and who name was "daily praised." Thousands of them believed the bold raider would shortly appear to "raise the standard of revolt in Indiana." If he did, Carrington was sure Morgan could raise "an army of 20,000 traitors."[59]

What prompted these comments by Carrington and where he get his information? The answer to these questions appears to derive from the activities of Governor Morton. Taking advantage of the crisis conditions that the war created, Morton had established himself as virtual dictator of the state. He dealt harshly with rebel sympathizers, Copperheads, Democrats, and anyone opposed to his rule. By the end of 1861, a spy system had been inaugurated to keep watch of these enemies.[60] Carrington was given charge of this intelligence organization and thus became familiar with the "foes of the Union" which it kept under surveillance. There is strong evidence that Carrington had no desire for combat service and twice Morton intervened to prevent his transferal to the front lines. Thus, it was important that Carrington cast himself in the role of an intelligence chief devoted to maintaining the security of the state, even though disaster appeared to be just around the corner.

In March 1863, Carrington was promoted to brigadier-general and made commander of the District of Indiana of the Department of the Ohio, later renamed the Northern Department. By this time, however, he had intelligence activities organized and operating under his direction. His secret service:

> *"... was composed of spies, informers, betrayers, and outside secret agents. Inside officials who were jealous of more important leaders were worked on; the itch for money played a part; in quite a few instances, unsuspecting loyal men who had joined the casts were amazed at the lengths to which love of constitutional rights or Southern sympathies could carry the assertion of dissent. From many sources, and for almost as many motives, disclosures flowed in to Carrington's headquarters."*[61]

Claiming to have between two and three thousand men reporting to him, Carrington enlisted the services of almost anyone who would provide information about an "enemy." Unsolicited reports were gratefully accepted as well. The amateur sleuths and informers were supplemented with a few choice agents and detectives. Spies apparently were paid from state

Henry Beebee Carrington

funds at the rate of $100 per month, over six times the amount received by a Federal soldier.[62]

Early in 1863 Carrington claimed to have emissaries at the meetings of the secret societies. In April 1864, he asked Adjutant General Lorenzo Thomas for money to organize a twelve-man detective force. One of his agents said he had eighteen men at such work early in 1864.

General Alvin P. Hovey, who succeeded Carrington August 25, 1864, continued his espionage organization. Colonel Conrad Baker, the state provost marshal, also employed informers who reported directly to him. At least one of the district provost marshals, Colonel Thompson, had an agent who worked for him among Democrats of the Seventh District. He signed his reports only as "H.," and his identity was not even known to Colonel Baker, Thompson's supervisor.

Carrington claimed he participated personally in his work, once attending "in disguise" a meeting of the Sons of Liberty in Indianapolis. Be that as it may, the general was probably not exaggerating when he claimed to know every morning what had happened in the lodges the night before. Not only did he have his own spies, but also he kept in close touch with other officials who conducted espionage.[63]

While Carrington's operatives were effective in breaking up the Sons of Liberty, the Knights of the Golden Circle, and elements of the Northwest Conspiracy, they also contributed to arbitrary arrests, infringements upon the freedom of speech and freedom of association, and otherwise maintained a corrupt and despotic regime. The manner in which the intelligence organization was recruited—utilizing betrayers, jealous and disgruntled officials, informers, and invalidated hearsay from unsolicited sources—caused it to traffic in unreliable information of generally more political than military value. And the suspicion prevails that the whole arrangement served to maintain Governor Morton's administration and coincidentally counteracted Confederate operatives who happened to count among his foes.

General Alvin P. Hovey replaced Carrington in August 1864. With less than a year of warfare ahead of him, Hovey assumed control of the espionage organization as the new commander of the Indian District. It is not immediately evident if he made any changes in the intelligence operation other than to gain access to the funds seized from bounty jumpers to pay his agents.[64] If the spy system did not collapse at the end of the war, it must certainly have been discarded in 1867, when Governor Morton resigned to enter the United States Senate.

Carrington was first mustered out of service as a brigadier-general of volunteers, rejoined his old regiment in the Army of the Cumberland, completed war duty and saw Indian campaigns in the West. He built and commanded Fort Phil Kearny but lost the respect of his fellow officers due to his reputation as a "political warrior" and his demonstrated lack of aggressiveness in several Indian skirmishes. Before a decision to remove him from command could be implemented, Carrington became further embroiled in controversy.

In December 1866, a force of fifteen hundred to three thousand Indians massacred a force of eighty officers and men under Captain William J. Fetterman. The disaster was attributed to Fetterman's disobeyance of Carrington's order to proceed on a certain route of march: instead, he had directly engaged the war party from their rear while they were attacking a group of woodcutters.

Stanton's Letter

The Secretary of War
Washington City, D.C.
May 2, 1863—11 a.m.

Major-General Hooker,

We cannot control intelligence in relationship to your movements while your generals write letters giving details. A letter from General VanAllen to a person not connected with the War Department describes your position as entrenched near Chancellorsville.

Can't you give his sword something to do, so that he will have less time for a pen?

/s/ Edwin M. Stanton

The Indians turned on Fetterman's force and annihilated them. Because no one had heard Carrington's orders to Fetterman, coupled with existing distrust of the colonel's leadership, rumors persisted that the men had been ordered into tragedy. General Grant moved to court-martial Carrington but, at the suggestion of General William T. Sherman, submitted the matter to a court of inquiry, which subsequently exonerated Carrington. Nevertheless, Carrington was relieved of command and, with his military career ruined; he resigned and spent the rest of his life attempting to convince the public of his innocence in the incident. He also wrote a number of books and taught military science at Wabash College in Indiana before his death in 1912.

Spies

Belle Boyd

Belle Boyd is probably the Civil War's most famous spy; but, in the view of a present-day student of her career, she is also the War's most overrated spy.

A Shenandoah Valley girl, Belle Boyd was only 17 years old in 1861. However, she was persevering in her efforts to aid the South by procuring useful information on Northern activities, much of it for the use of General "Stonewall" Jackson. To support her claims to success in secret service, Miss Boyd held an honorary Confederate Army rank, as well as the firm opinion as to her abilities of the entire North (especially that of its counterintelligence officers). The extent to which her efforts actually aided Southern arms is, however, uncertain and will probably remain so. One can admit that she was a woman of great spirit and charm.

On several occasions, the Union forces captured Belle Boyd, and each time she was released from imprisonment. However, Miss Boyd's activities became increasingly a matter of public knowledge, thus reducing her effectiveness.

Early in 1864, her health somewhat undermined, Miss Boyd decided to go to England. Jefferson Davis concurred in this decision, as she could be used as a courier to carry dispatches on her trip. On the day after her ship sailed from Wilmington, North Carolina, it was captured by a Northern warship and escorted to Boston.

Ensign Harding was placed in charge of the prize, and, on the trip north, he became completely mesmerized by Belle Boyd, finally proposing marriage, an offer that she accepted. Arriving in Boston, Miss Boyd was shortly exiled to Canada, from whence she went to England.

Through carelessness, Ensign Harding permitted the captain of the blockade-runner to escape in Boston, and Harding was cashiered from the Navy. He too made his way to England, where he and Belle Boyd were married. While in England in 1865, Belle Boyd published her memoirs, which is considered to be essentially sound with the usual embellishments of color and detail.

Spencer Kellogg Brown

After brief service in the Union Army, Spencer Brown enlisted as a sailor on a Federal gunboat on the Mississippi River. With the permission of his commander, he "deserted" in January 1862, to begin an espionage mission within the Confederate lines. Brown succeeded in making his way back to General Ulysses S. Grant's headquarters during the battle of Shiloh with useful information on the Confederate order of battle.

Belle Boyd

In August 1862, Brown was captured while on a naval mission to blow up a Confederate vessel. He was charged with being a Union spy and a deserter from the Confederate Army. The charge of desertion was based on his alleged "service" with Confederate troops while accompanying them on his espionage mission before the battle of Shiloh earlier in 1862. He was executed in the fall of 1863.

While Spencer Brown is only a minor figure as a spy, he is remembered in part because the Confederacy executed him as a spy in defiance of a rule of military law adhered to by the Union forces. This rule was that when a person, who was formerly a spy, was subsequently taken prisoner while not engaged in espionage, he would not be tried as a spy.

Rose O'Neil Greenhow

Rose O'Neil Greenhow was the widow of the celebrated Dr. Robert Greenhow, who was librarian and chief translator of the Department of State from 1831-1850. Because of her husband's status, she was one of the chief figures in Washington society during that period. A native of Port Tobacco, Maryland, in 1861, she identified herself with the cause of the South in the Civil War and became the first of the Confederate secret agents in the nation's capital.

She was arrested on 21 August 1861 by Allan Pinkerton, chief of the Secret Service on the staff of General McClellen, at the instigation of President Abraham Lincoln. She was first imprisoned in her own home at 16th and H Streets, NW (where the Hay-Adams Hotel now stands) and then for five months in the Capital Prison, which stood where the Supreme Court building now sits. Her little daughter and namesake, Rose, then age eight, shared her imprisonment with her.

Historians and writers have overestimated the value of Greenhow's spying for the South. Except for confirming that General Irvin McDowell's was moving his troops to Manassas, which gave General P. G. Beauregard the time he needed to prepare for battle, Greenhow's espionage activities were of little value to the Southern cause. Much of her information was obtained by having people walk around Washington, D.C. and report to her what they saw. She did have one "knowledgeable" source, Senator Henry Wilson, who chaired the Senate's Military Affairs Committee. He was reportedly her lover but it is doubtful that he provided any important military or political information to her.

She, like many spies, also failed to destroy incriminating evidence she kept in her house. After her arrest, a search of her home by Pinkerton's men, discovered copies of her intelligence reports. Although Greenhow used a code to write portions of her reports, she also left a copy of one of the plain-text messages, which allowed Pinkerton to decipher her messages.

After her arrest she continued to send messages to her Confederate handler, Thomas Jordan, who was General Beauregard's adjutant.

Historians cite this fact to prove Greenhow's resourcefulness but any counterintelligence analysis shows just the opposite. Pinkerton was no fool. He kept an airtight watch on Greenhow, allowing only a few visitors to see her, and punishing any of the guards who failed to inspect anything leaving the house. In fact, the Confederates no longer trusted any information she sent to them.

She was released on 1 June 1862 and taken through the Union lines to Richmond, Virginia, where she resided for a short time. While in Richmond, she wrote a book, *My Imprisonment and the First Year of Abolition Rule in Washington*. In autumn 1862 she boarded a ship, which ran the Union blockade at Wilmington, North Carolina and landed in England

Rose O'Neil Greenhow

via Nassau. In London she had her book published. She also represented the Confederacy in diplomatic negotiations with England and France.

She decided to return to the United States and, in the fall of 1864, she boarded a ship that attempted to run the blockade at Wilmington. The ship ran aground in high seas at Cape Fear River. Greenhow was determined to go ashore and persuaded the captain to lower a small boat. The small boat capsized and all abroad was saved but Greenhow who drown.

C. Lorain Ruggles

C. Lorain Ruggles was a member of the 20th Ohio Volunteer Infantry, serving in the Mississippi-Tennessee Theater as a scout, spy and detective. He claimed to be the brother of a Confederate general, in whose command he sometimes operated. Ruggles expressed his philosophy as follows: "People often ask me, 'What is the essential qualification of a good spy?' My answer is, 'It requires an accomplished liar.' I mean by that a man that can successfully practice deception. I do not mean that a man must be a habitual liar. There is nothing that I despise more than a man whose word cannot be relied upon. Whether deception, as I have practiced it in the discharge of my duty as a spy, is a moral wrong, I shall not attempt here to argue. Of this much I am sure: it has many times saved my life, and perhaps the lives of thousands of others, besides saving immense sums of money to the Government."

One of Ruggles' superiors, Brigadier General Wiles, stated that "I never knew him to give false information," and Ruggles' book contains several official comments on his success. Ruggles' book is titled, *Four Years a Scout and Spy*. It was ghost written for him by one of his officers, Major Edward C. Downs, who enlisted Ruggles in 1861. The book went through several editions, and in a later edition, Ruggles listed himself as the author and eliminated Major Downs' introduction. The title was also changed to *Perils of Scout-Life*.

Henry Bascom Smith

Lieutenant Henry Smith (whose self-assumed post-war rank was that of major) was occupied for much of the Civil War in basic counterintelligence work, including detection of blockade-runners and supervision of Confederate prisoners. Smith operated in Baltimore, Maryland, a center of secret service activity for both the Union and the Confederacy.

He joined the Union army as a second lieutenant in a New York heavy artillery regiment in January 1862. The following May his unit was ordered to Baltimore. After several adventures as a prisoner escort, Smith was appointed Assistant Provost Marshal at Fort McHenry, where he had his first experience in counterintelligence activities. He wrote: "Confederate mail carrying, spy promoting, blockade promoting, recruiting for Confederate service, were being engineered right from among these prisoners. I under-grounded it all. Through this channel, I enlisted for the Confederate service ... to discover their actions ...."

Smith did not "under-ground" by any means all such activity at Baltimore, but even so his claim is more modest, and more convincingly presented, than those others who overemphasized or glorified their intelligence and counterintelligence worth. His secret service rationale also was less overstated than most others.

Felix Grundy Stidger

Felix Stidger, after serving part of the war in a Kentucky (Federal) regiment, took his discharge and went to work as a detective. Despite his Union background, he was accepted as a member of the Copperhead secret societies in Kentucky, Indiana and Ohio. He was so successful in his penetration that he rose to a high office in the society His penetration was very instrumental in the arrest and prosecution of the chief conspirators.

Although he had testified in public, Stidger waited nearly 40 years to publish his story. While his story is not entirely verifiable, it is among the most trustworthy of the Civil War secret service memoirs. In producing such an account, Stidger unwittingly lent credence to his belief that the Copperheads trusted him because his manner had a certain straightforwardness about it. He wrote: "I know of no other reason why I should have been able to look them so steadily in their eyes except an innate consciousness of my being in the performance of a just and honorable duty to my government."

Benjamin Franklin Stringfellow

Following the First Battle of Bull Run, Frank Stringfellow was trained as a scout under the command of Colonel J.E.B. Stuart. He became one of Stuart's better scouts and spies, and is one of the few Confederate intelligence operatives whose service can be even slightly documented. He is said to have spent weeks in occupied Alexandria collecting information; was in the environs of most of the great battles fought by the Army of Northern Virginia; was captured once and exchanged.

Of Captain Stringfellow's service, Colonel Stuart wrote, "In determining the enemy's real design, I rely upon you, as well as the quick transmission of the information. . . . Your service is too important and many be worth all the Yankee trains." Lauded by Confederate President Jefferson Davis, *Stringfellow* summed up: "My business was to get information."

Elizabeth Van Lew

Her parents were Northerners who had moved to Richmond, Virginia, where they became prominent citizens and where Elizabeth was born. Her father John Van Lew died when she was a young girl, leaving her and her mother to carry on. They stayed in Richmond but did not hold with southern thinking. They freed their family slaves and used their money to purchase relatives of their slaves in order to set them free also. Elizabeth was considered an eccentric by Richmond society.

Benjamin Franklin Stringfellow

When the Civil War came, Elizabeth became the center of a northern spy network, called the Richmond Ring. She established five safehouses from which messages could be relayed to Union lines. The information came from a variety of sources. She succeeded in planting one of her former slaves within the Confederate White House of Jefferson Davis. She coordinated the underground activities of her brother, John Newton Van Lew and a black marketeer, Frederick Lohmann.

She secured the services of Samuel Ruth, the superintendent of the vital Richmond, Fredericksburg & Potomac Railroad. Ruth was effective in making the railroad inefficient, causing delays in moving valuable Confederate troops and supplies, without raising suspicion.

The Confederates arrested Ruth for aiding southerners, who no longer wanted to live in the Confederacy, to defect to the north. She was tried but the charges were dismissed for lack of evidence.

Elizabeth came under Confederate counter-intelligence scrutiny because she and her mother visited and provided food and clothing to Union Army officers held in Richmond's notorious Libby prison. Union operatives tasked Elizabeth to obtain from the prisoners the latest information on battle information and estimates of Confederate army strength. Even when prison authorities refused to allow her to speak with the prisoners, she was able through other means to secure the information. Confederate counter-intelligence made every effort to catch her. They kept her house under constant surveillance and conducted unannounced and random searches of her home. In the end, they failed to find any incriminating evidence against her.

When the Confederate Government abandoned Richmond, Elizabeth raised the American flag and welcomed General Ulysses Grant into her home upon his arrival in the city. After the war, she put in a claim to be reimbursed for her expenses. She was supported in her effort by then President Grant, but Congress rejected the claim. She might have died penniless but the Union officers she comforted in Libby prison raised enough funds to provide her with a steady income for the rest of her life.

Col. George H. Sharpe following the Battle of Gettysburg, 1863

Civil War Bibliography

Ayer, I. Winslow. *The Great Treason Plot in the North during the War*. Chicago: U.S. Publishing, 1895.

Anderson, Nancy Scott. *The Generals: Ulysses S. Grant and Robert E. Lee, 1861-1885*. New York, Knopf 1988.

Axelrod, Alan. *The War Between the Spies: A History of Espionage during the American Civil War*. Intelligence Services during the Civil War. New York, Atlantic Monthly Press 1992.

Bakeless, Katherine Little. *Confederate Spy Stories. Biographies of men and women who, for patriotic or mercenary reasons, engaged in espionage for the Confederacy*. Philadelphia, Lippincott. 1973.

Bakeless, John Edwin. *Spies of the Confederacy. Secret Service in the Civil War, 1861-1865*. Philadelphia: J.B. Lippincott, 1970.

Baker, La Fayette Charles. *History of the U.S. Secret Service during the Civil War*. New York, AMS Press, 1973.

Baker, La Fayette Charles. *Spies, Espionage, Traitors, Secret Service and Conspirators of the late Civil War. 1861-65*. Philadelphia, J. Potter and Co. 1894.

Bates, David Homer. *Lincoln in the Telegraph Office: Recollections of the U.S. Military Telegraph Corps during the Civil War*. New York: Appleton-Century, 1939.

Beymer, William Gilmore. *On Hazardous Service: Scouts and Spies of the North and South*. New York: Harper & Brothers, 1912.

Benson, Blackwood Ketcham. *Who goes there? The Story of a Spy in the Civil War*. New York: MacMillan, 1900.

Botkin, Benjamin Albert. *A Civil War treasury of anecdotes, tales, legends, and folklore*. New York, Random House 1960.

Bovey, Wilfrid. "Confederate Agents in Canada During the American Civil War." Canadian Historical Review 2 (Mar. 1921): 46-57.

Brandt, Nat. *The Man Who Tried to Burn New York*. New York: Berkley, 1990. (Robert Cobb Kennedy, Confederate spy and saboteur.)

Brockett, Linus Pierpont. *Intelligence Service in the Civil War: Scouts, Spies, and detectives of the Great Civil War. Including Thrilling adventures, daring deeds, and heroic exploits*. Washington, D.C., The National Tribune, 1899.

Brown, R. Shepard. *Stringfellow of the Fourth: The Amazing Career of the Most Successful Confederate Scout*. New York: Crown, 1960. (Frank Stringfellow.)

Brown, Spencer Kellogg. *Spencer Kellogg Brown, His Life in Kansas and His Death as a Spy, 1842-1863, as Disclosed in His Diary*. Ed. by George Gardner Smith. New York: D. Appleton, 1903.

Brownlee, Richard S. *Gray Ghost of the Confederacy: Guerrilla Warfare in the West, 1861-1865*. Baton Rouge, Louisiana State University Press. 1958.

Bulloch, James Dunwody. *The Secret Service of the Confederate States in Europe*. New York: Putnam's, 1884. Reprinted. New York: Thomas Yoseloff, 1959.

Case, Lynn M. and Warren F. Spencer. *The United States and France: Civil War Diplomacy*. Philadelphia: U. Penn. Press, 1970.

Conrad, Thomas Nelson. *A Confederate Spy: A Story of the Civil War*. Confederate States of America. New York: J.S. Ogilie Publishing Company, 1892.

Crouch, Tom D. *The Eagle Aloft: Two Centuries of the Balloon in America*. Washington: Smithsonian Institution Press, 1983.

Current, Richard N. *Lincoln's Loyalists: Union Soldiers from the Confederacy.* Boston: Northeastern Univ. Press, 1992.

Dannett, Sylvia G. L. *Noble Women of the North: Women of the Civil War, Personal Narratives.* New York T. Yoseloff, 1959.

Downs, Edward C. *The Great American Scout and Spy, "General Bunker"... A Truthful and thrilling narrative of the experiences of C. Lorain. Ruggles, of the Twentieth Ohio Volunteer infantry. Exploits, Perils, Adventures of a government scout and spy.* New York, Olmsted, 1870.

Drake, James Madison. *Historical sketches, maps, anecdotes etc. used for the Revolutionary and Civil War for infiltration purposes.* New York: Printed for the author by the Webster Press, 1908.

Edmonds, Sarah Emma Evelyn, 1841-1898. *The Female Spy of the Union Army: the thrilling adventures, experiences and escapes of a women as nurse, spy a female soldier, and scout.* Boston, DeWolfe, Fiske. 1864.

Estabrooks, Henry L. *Adrift in Dixie; or, a Yankee Officer among the Rebels.* New York, Carleton, 1866.

Fishel, Edwin C. *The Secret War for the Union: The Untold Story of Military Intelligence in the Civil War.* Houghton Mifflin Company, Boston New York 1996.

Fishel, Edwin C. *"Myths That Never Die" International Journal of Intelligence and Counterintelligence* 2. No. 1 (Spring 1988).

Foote, Morris C. *A Narrative of an escape from a Rebel Prison Camp, Evasion and Escape during the civil war.* Camp Sorghum. Columbia, South Carolina.

Forman, Allan. *A Bit of Secret Service History: Intelligence Services during the Civil War.* 1861-1865.

Foster, G. Allen. *The eyes and ears of the Civil War: Communications, Intelligence Services, and Espionage.* New York: Criterion Books, 1963.

Gaddy, David W. "William Norris and the Confederate Signal and Secret Service Bureau." *Maryland Historical Magazine* 70, No 2 (Summer 1975).

Glazier, Willard Worcester. 1841-1905. *The Capture, the prison pen, and the escape of a courier.* Giving a complete history of prison life in the South during the Civil War. New York: R.H. Ferguson, 1870.

Gray, Wood. *The Hidden Civil War: The Story of the Copperheads.* New York: Viking, 1942.

Grimes, Absalom Carlisle, 1834-1911. *Absalom Carlisle Grimes and Milo Milton Quaife 1880-1959. Confederate mail runners.* New Haven, Yale University Press; 1926.

Hagerman. Edward. *The American Civil War and the origins of modern warfare: ideas, organizations, and field commands and intelligence history.* Bloomington: Indiana University Press, 1988.

Hall, James O. "The Spy Harrison," *Civil War Times Illustrated,* Feb. 1986.

Hardinge, Sam Wilde. *Spies of the Confederate States of America. Belle Boyd in camp and prison.* South Brunswick, New Jersey. 1968.

Headley, John William. *Confederate Covert Operations in Canada and New York.* New York and Washington: Neale Pub. Co. 1906.

Horan, James David., and Howard Swiggett. *The Pinkerton Story.* New York: Putnam's, 1951.

Horan, James David., *A Confederate agent in the Civil War. A discovery in history.* New York: Crown Publishers. 1954.

Johns, George Sibley, 1857-1941. *Philip Henson, the Southern Union Spy. The hitherto unwritten record of a hero of the War of the Rebellion, History of the Secret Service.* St. Louis, Nixon-Jones Print. Co, 1887.

Johnston, Joseph E. *Narrative of Military Operations*. New York: D. Appleton, 1874.

Jones, Virgil Carrington. *Gray Ghost and Rebel Raiders. Underground Movements during the Civil War*. New York, Holt. 1956.

Kane, Harnett. *Spies For The Blue and the Gray: Secret Service during the Civil War.*. New York: Doubleday, Ace Books, 1954.

Kerby, Joseph Orton. *The Boy Spyin Dixie: A Substantially true record of the Secret Service during the Civil War, the only practical history of espionage during the war of the rebellion. Service under the shadow of the Scaffold*. Chicago: Donohue and Co., Henneberry, 1892.

Kinchen, Oscar Arvle. *Confederate Covert Operations in Canada and the North; A little known phase of the American Underground and Secret Service during the Civil War*. North Quincy, Mass, Christopher Publishing House, 1970.

Klement, Frank L. Dark Lanterns: *Secret Political Societies, Conspiracies, and Treason Trials in the Civil War*. Baton Rouge, La: Louisiana State University Press, 1984.

Landis, Arthur H. *The Abraham Lincoln Brigade, Participation in the American Civil War*. New York, Citadel Press, 1967.

Maslowski, Peter. *"Military Intelligence Services in the American Civil War: A Case Study."* The Intelligence Revolution: A Historical Perspective. 13th Military History Symposium, U.S. Air Force Academy, 1988.

McIntosh, Elizabeth P. Association of Former Intelligence Officers: *The role of Women spies and intelligence officers in intelligence History, beginning with the American Revolution and the Civil War*. McLean, Virginia. 1989.

Military Signals Intelligence Communications. Ed. Paul J. Scheips, 2 Vols. New York: Arno Press, 1980.

Mogelever, Jacob. *Death to Traitors: The Story of General LaFayette C. Baker, Lincoln's Forgotten Secret Service Chief*. Garden City, NY: Doubleday, 1960.

Newcomer, Louis A. *Lincoln's Boy Spy. Personal narratives from the Civil War*. New York, G. P. Putnam's sons, 1929.

Pinkerton, Allan. *The Spy of the Rebellion. A True history of the Spy system of the United States Army during the late rebellion of the Civil War.*, Chicago: A.G. Netteton, 1883. Rep. Lincoln: Univ. of Nebraska Press, 1989.

Plum, William Rattle. *The Military telegraph during the Civil War in the United States, with an exposition of ancient and modern means of communication*. Chicago, Jansen, McClurg & Co. 1882.

Popchock, Barry. "His Lordship, the adventures of Union spy Pryce Lewis (1828-1911), Espionage during the Civil War," *Civil War Times Illustrated*, September 1988.

Raskin, Edith & Joseph. *Spies and Traitors; Tales of the Revolutionary and Civil wars*. New York: Lothrop, Lee and Shepard Co. 1976.

Richardson, Albert Deane. *The Secret Service, the Field, the Dungeon, and the Escape, Experiences of a correspondent of the New York Tribune within the Confederate lines in 1861, and later with the Union Army*. Hartford, Conn. American Publishing Co. 1865.

Ross, Ishbel. *Rebel Rose: Life of Rose O'Neal Greenhow*. New York: Harper & Brothers, 1954.

Rowan, Richard W. *The Story of the Secret Service*. New York: Literary Guild of America, 1937.

Sarmiento, Ferdinand L. *Life of Pauline Cushman Fryer (1833-1893): the celebrated Union Spy and scout of the Civil War*. Chicago: W.H. Harrison, 1865.

Schmidt, C.T. "G-2 Army of the Potomac." *Military Review* 28:4, (July 1948) 45-56.

Sigaud, Louis A. *Belle Boyd: Confederate Spy.* Richmond: Dietz Press, 1944.

Siepel, Kevin H. *Rebel, the life and times of John Singleton Mosby (1833-1916): Guerrillas of the Civil War.* New York: St. Martin's Press, 1983.

Smith, Henry B. *Between the Lines: Secret Service Stories Told Fifty Years After.* New York: Booz Brothers, 1911.

Sparks, David S. "General Patrick's Progress: Intelligence and Security in the Army of the Potomac," *Civil War History* 10:4 (1964): 371-384.

Stern, Philip Van Doren. *Secret Missions of the Civil War; first hand accounts of covert activity conducted during the Civil War.* New York, Bonanza Books, 1975.

Taylor, Charles E. *The Signal and Secret Service of the Confederate States.* Hamlet, NC: North Carolina Bookley, 1903.

Tidwell, William A. April '65: *Confederate Covert Action in the American Civil War.* Kent State University Press, 1995.

Tidwell, William A. *Confederate intelligence expenditures for the Secret Service.* Biographical references, Kent State U. Press, 1995.

Time Life Books. *Spies, Scouts, and Raiders: irregular operations and intelligence services during the Civil War.* Alexandria, Virginia. Time Life Books, 1985.

Trumbull, Henry Clay. *The captured scout of the Army of the James. A sketch of the life of Sergeant Henry H. Manning, of the Twenty-fourth Massachusetts regiment.* Boston, Nichols and Noyes, 1869.

Van Lew, Elizabeth L. and Ryan, David D. *A Yankee spy in Richmond: the Civil War diary of a Union spy "Crazy Bet" Elizabeth Van Lew.* Mechanicsburg, PA. Stackpole Books, 1996.

Wagner, Arthur L. *The Service of Security and Information.* 11th Edition Kansas City: Hudson-Kimberly, 1903.

IMPORTANT DATES AND COUNTERINTELLIGENCE EVENTS
THE CIVIL WAR, 1859-1865

1859	25 October	John Brown indicted and convicted of treason for leading a raid on Harpers Ferry.
	2 December	John Brown is hanged for treason.
1860	20 December	South Carolina seceded from the Union.
1861	22 February	President-elect Abraham Lincoln warned by Allan Pinkerton of an assassination plot against him.
	2 April	Allan Pinkerton offered the services of his detective agency to President Lincoln, who does not respond.
	12 April	Fort Sumter is attacked and surrenders two days later.
	1 November	George McClellan becomes general-in-chief of the Union forces.
	1 November	Allan Pinkerton given responsibility for security and counterintelligence within the nation's capital.
	20 December	Radical Republicans in Congress set-up a Joint Committee on the Conduct of the War to investigate Lincoln's assumption of vast powers.
1862	15 January	Edwin Stanton becomes Secretary of War.
	14 February	Executive Order No. 1 issued by President Lincoln which provided for wholesale release of most political prisoners.
	23 May	Rebel Spy, Belle Boyd, arrested for spying.
	August	Spencer Kellogg Brown, a Union spy, arrested and in the fall of 1863 was executed.
	23 August	Rose Greenhow, a Confederate spy, arrested in Washington, D.C.
	22 September	Lincoln issued his Emancipation Proclamation.
	7 November	General Ambrose E. Burnside replaces McClellan.
1863	3 March	The Signal Corps is created.
	30 March	Col. George Sharpe appointed first professional intelligence officer and established the Bureau of Military Information for the Union Army of the Potomac.
1865	9 April	The Civil War ends.
	14 April	President Lincoln is assassinated.
	5 July	William P. Wood becomes the first chief of the U.S. Secret Service.

CHAPTER 3

CHAPTER 3

Post Civil War to World War I

Introduction

At the end of the Civil War, counterintelligence fell by the wayside as the Federal Government focused on the reconstruction of the South. The only practitioners of the discipline were the private detective agencies which, before the American entry into World War I, did a booming business from an increase in demand for strikebreakers and labor spies. By 1917 there were nearly three hundred detective agencies across the country investigating labor activity.

The Pinkerton Detective Agency's unsavory history in industrial labor quarrels led Congress in 1893 to proscribe the hiring of private detectives by any Federal agency. In World War I, however, the demand for professional operatives was so great and the private detective companies so available that Military Intelligence deliberately violated the law.

For many years, after it was organized in July 1865, the Secret Service was the only detective force in the Federal Government, other than a Division of Special Agents of the Office of the Secretary of the Treasury, the investigations of which were concerned primarily with customs matters. When the short-lived Spanish-American War came along, it was the Secret Service and not the newly established War Department's Military Intelligence (MI) or Navy's Office of Naval Intelligence (ONI) which received money from Congress for increased counterintelligence activities. The Service investigated spy leads from MI, ONI, and also from the Post Office, the Justice Department and from U.S. Senators. They also conducted an operation to break up a spy system operated by the Spanish Government in Canada.

Until 1908, when the practice was prohibited by law, Secret Service agents were engaged in special investigations for other departments. They were not permitted to resume this practice until World War I, when the President was authorized to direct the use of the Service wherever necessary. Agents then conducted investigations for alleged pro-German sympathizers and spies in 1918-19 and suspected infractions by firms and individuals of laws, regulations, and orders governing exports during the war.

The Mexican revolution and counterrevolutions of 1914 posed exceptional problems for American counterintelligence. The buying and transporting of weapons from the border states into Mexico, Mexican intelligence operating in the states, and German schemes to use Mexico against the United States during

World War I, were some of the threats facing the meager counterintelligence resources of the U.S. Government.

The most famous activity to occur in the border region was Poncho Villa's raid on the small New Mexico town of Columbus, where several soldiers and civilians were killed. Furious over this brazen violation of American sovereignty, President Wilson ordered General John Pershing to pursue Villa. Pershing's efforts became known as the Punitive Expedition.

During this expedition, human intelligence (HUMINT) and signals intelligence (SIGINT) took on new proportions. Although an embryo intelligence staff had been organized in 1903 as part of the General Staff of the Army, it was up to Pershing to organize his own field intelligence network. He started an "Information Department" which employed a network of agents who reportedly penetrated Villa's camp. He also intercepted and deciphered Mexican communications. "By tapping the various telegraph and telephone wires and picking up wireless messages," according to Pershing, "we were able to get practically all the information passing between various leaders in Mexico."

When World War I began, no single federal agency had any substantial investigative capability, and the modern concept of a counterintelligence community did not exist. The counterintelligence efforts of the Secret Service, the Bureau of Investigation (later Federal Bureau of Investigation), and War Department's Military Intelligence and Navy's Office of Naval Intelligence were insignificant and not coordinated. In fact, these agencies were totally unprepared to deal with the disingenuous espionage and sabotage ring organized in the United States by German Ambassador Johann von Bernstorff.

During the war these agencies expanded and new federal offices emerged, many with intelligence departments. In this atmosphere, interagency competition became particularly acrimonious, first between the Department of Justice and the Secret Service, and later between Justice and Military Intelligence. This situation was noted by the Secretary of State who offered his department as the "clearinghouse" of information obtained from each of these agencies. However, an agreement concluded in 1918 shared the counterintelligence mission between Justice, State, Army and Navy.

The Office Of Naval Intelligence: A Proud Tradition Of Service[1]

During the period immediately following our Civil War, the United States Navy found itself in a state of disarray and woefully incapable of protecting the nation. Along with ships and men, the ravages of conflict destroyed naval strength and readiness, leaving few seaworthy ships when peace finally arrived.

Yet fueled by the indomitable American spirit and spurred with challenge, there arose a class of naval officer who recognized the need for rebuilding a United States Navy that had come to be ignored in the postwar period by government and citizen alike.

The change that came was wholly owed to a recognition amongst the officer class that emerging technological and educational advances had to be adopted if the service was ever to fulfill its duty to the nation. It was precisely during this time and for those reasons that our nation's first organized agency devoted entirely to intelligence collection and associated activities was founded.

Years before, the U.S. Navy had come to recognize the importance of capitalizing on intelligence to counter enemy plans and movements during both the Revolutionary War and the War of 1812; however, those efforts were best characterized as disorganized and fragmented to such a degree as to be ineffectual.

On 23 March 1892, the Office of Naval Intelligence (ONI) was created with the signing of General Order 292 by William H. Hunt, Secretary of the Navy, and became the first U.S. Government agency devoted solely to the systematic collection of information regarding foreign military affairs.

Originally subordinate to the Bureau of Navigation, ONI would routinely acquire information from military attaches posted abroad or naval officers making cruises to foreign ports, where numerous collection opportunities were presented to command staff personnel. Whether it was charting foreign passages, rivers or other bodies of water, touring overseas fortifications and building yards or conducting other naval related activities as necessary, naval personnel busied themselves collecting information for ONI regarding the strengths and weaknesses of any alien power that could someday pose a threat to U.S. national security interests.[2]

ONI quickly gained an enviable reputation and for three decades was considered by U.S. government officials to be the most authoritative and reliable source of information regarding foreign military affairs. Even so, a great deal of information collected by this organization, especially that dealing with European shipbuilding advances and associated industrial improvements, would never be put to substantive use.

In fact, volumes of valuable data frequently lay totally wasted and squirreled away in various navy bureaus because ONI lacked the capability in its infancy to render. In-depth analysis that would have insured the material was more thoroughly understood and better used. ONI's shortcomings were recognized as especially critical when it was finally realized that the United States, with a fleet of wooden sailing ships,

---

General Order No. 292

Navy Department
Washington, March 23, 1882

An "Office of Intelligence" is hereby established in the Bureau of Navigation for the purpose of collecting and recording such information as may be useful to the Department in time of war, as well as peace.

To facilitate this work, the Department of Library will be combined with the "Office of Intelligence" and placed under the direction of the Chief of the Bureau of Navigation.

Commanding and all other Officers are directed to avail themselves of all opportunities which may arise to collect and forward to the "Office of Intelligence" professional matters likely to serve the object in view.

William H. Hunt
Secretary of the Navy

---

was quickly shrinking to inferiority in the face of European navies producing iron hulled men-of-war with rifled guns and metal turrets.[3]

During its early days, ONI was officially tasked by the Department of the Navy to collect specifically categorized information deemed essential to the U.S. defense. To fulfill this duty, the Secretary of the Navy mandated that naval officers who could objectively and skillfully collect and report matters of interest to the Navy be chosen for service with ONI in Washington, D.C., posted to any one of several naval attaché positions at U.S. foreign legations, or appointed as special aides to senior military personnel posted abroad. Generally all would restrict their collection to information that was publicly available and could be acquired through overt means like open source publications, from foreign officers with whom the naval attaché or aide might associate and through contacts with knowledgeable political or industrial figures.

Initially, the military and naval attaché system formally established by passage of Congressional Law on 22 September 1888, allowed for the posting that following year of five officers to Berlin, Paris, London, Vienna and St. Petersburg.

Within five years this rudimentary intelligence network expanded modestly and attaché personnel came to be posted in Rome, Brussels, Madrid, Tokyo and Mexico City. For years, the number of naval officers assigned such duties remained limited and at a fixed level or, in some cases, attaches would only be posted to a foreign nation in times of international tension or strife.

It became the primary responsibility of naval attaches to visit naval bases, shipyards, industrial sites and any other commercial or government facilities associated with building, supporting or directing foreign commercial and military maritime efforts. Though officially instructed to perform their duty in an open manner, our former attaches sometimes found it necessary to employ covert measures and the use of "secret agents" to gather information that would be unavailable by any other means.

Even as it was successful in certain regards, the attaché system was probably no more than moderately effective due to a continual lack of funding and because the posts were difficult to fill with line officers, who generally did not regard such duty as prestigious or career enhancing.[4]

Initially, ONI was more concerned with collecting information regarding the characteristics and weaponry of foreign vessels than with tactics, movements, dispositions or the intentions of those navies. However, by 1915, when it became one of nine subdivisions organized into the Office of the Chief of Naval Operations, ONI would assume responsibility given it by the Navy "General plan" to develop and gather all manner of information on the Navy's possible adversaries.

The plan allowed for certain collection to be done by covert means and by 1916 the first undercover operation, termed Branch Office, had commenced activity in New York City under the control of ONI. Staffed by naval reservists on active duty or civilian volunteers working without pay, the Branch Office garnered some impressive successes in the field of counterespionage while protecting U.S. persons and properties from subversion and sabotage in the wake of growing world conflict.

Simultaneous to these endeavors, a separate organization called the Aides for Information was developing and employing personnel who were locally assigned to the staffs of fifteen Naval District Commandants.

Individuals affiliated with this effort routinely searched passengers on incoming vessels, provided security at docks, warehouses and factories, investigated subversive activity and executed other necessary duties during this extraordinary period to protect the Navy and country from possible foreign inspired subversion. With Branch Offices centrally controlled from Washington, while aides were supervised by their respective districts it was inevitable that confusion, conflict and duplication arose to such an extent that all investigative activities came to be consolidated under the District Aides.

The War Years
The preeminent concern of ONI when our nation finally declared war on Germany and its allies was the ferreting out of individuals deemed a threat to the

U.S. Navy or national security. Often working on tips provided by a variety of government agencies or patriotic organizations or on information acquired from private citizens swept up by the furor of the time, ONI pursued and worked tirelessly against all those suspected of subversive activity.

ONI operations became quite skilled at a variety of investigative techniques like surveillance and wiretapping and at one point it was actively involved in some 15,000 subversive investigations each week. The identification and neutralization of subversive elements became especially important to ONI after being assigned responsibility for protecting those war plants executing U.S. Navy contracts. ONI field agents routinely checked those plants for physical security, indications of labor unrest that would affect production, loyalty of factory workers and managers and the identification and elimination of anyone who could pose a threat to that company's vital work for the U.S. Navy.

There is no question that ONI did materially contribute to our nation's security and war-making capacity during this trying time although there was a certain amount of attendant frustration. In its enthusiasm to seek out individuals posing a possible threat to national security, ONI could be blame for periodically engaging in "witch hunts" or using questionable methods that would later be judged an affront to justice. Intolerance for different tactics or the needs of other government agencies led ONI into repeated conflicts with Army Intelligence and the U.S. Justice Department. Eventually, Rear Admiral Leigh V. Palmer, Chief of the Bureau of Navigation was forced to comment in August 1918, "...ONI might be pursuing suspects a bit too enthusiastically."

The Director of ONI at that time was further warned, apparently in the interest of fairness, "...to permit people accused of misdeeds to explain their actions before Naval Intelligence recommended dismissal, arrest or internment."[5]

During the First World War, ONI assigned four times the personnel and resources to domestic security work, as it did on foreign collection, after deciding that protecting the home front was its most important mission.

Yet in all fairness, it should be recalled that ONI traditionally considered its primary responsibility to be the collection, evaluation and dissemination of foreign intelligence that was of interest to the U.S. Navy. With our nation's declaration of war and involvement in armed hostilities, ONI was quickly forced to adopt many new responsibilities, like domestic security, without the luxury of extensive planning or very much forethought. Considering the seriousness of the time and overall circumstances, it is not entirely surprising that ONI would be chastised for being a bit too over zealous as it attempted to executive its duties in what was thought to be the most effective manner.

As had traditionally been the case, the bulk of all foreign intelligence collection continued to be performed by those naval attaches posted to U.S. diplomatic establishments in foreign countries. During the war years, naval attaches were forced to rely on the use of agent networks to insure the development of necessary and ever-increasing amounts of information. Emphasis was placed on the development of covert capabilities and the establishment of a global spy network that enlisted a string of agents throughout Latin American and the Far East.

The Lean Years
Some of these networks proved to be quite effective and lent themselves to the development of valuable information while others suffered poor organization and management, producing little other than scant or erroneous information that had disastrous effects at times.

The end of World War I brought a general demobilization and the country's desire to rapidly return to normalcy. With the Armistice signed and our country at peace, few could give reason to the need for maintaining other than a modest military.

Though not completely expendable, ONI with a war machine to support, came to be ignored in large part by the Department of the Navy which cut funding for personnel or operations and pared the organization back in all aspects to its barest minimum. Several years would elapse until 1926 when a limited effort was undertaken to establish groups of volunteer reserve intelligence officers whose goal became the gathering of information on individuals and activities that could pose a threat to U.S. naval security.

The intent was to create a cadre of personnel who could be called upon to render service in time of national emergency and by the beginning of 1927, some such groups had been created and started to operate in a manner that would be refined during the ensuing several years. Yet the mood of our nation was slow to change and it remained the strongest wish of many citizens that we continue to isolate ourselves from problems and entangling involvement with other nations.

Naturally, few could see the need to collect foreign intelligence and during these years such assignments continued to be regarded as especially undesirable by the regular Army and Navy officers given such responsibilities.

Though ONI by 1934 remained a small and neglected organization with only twenty-four officers and a clerical staff of eighteen, attitudes were slowly beginning to change in certain quarters of government where it was considered necessary to begin collecting more earnestly, information relating to the naval strength, war making capabilities and national intentions of certain foreign powers.

The chief source of this information continued to be the naval attaché system which had generally proven itself to be competent and capable in the past.

Brigadier General Frederick Funston

Additionally, a certain amount of data was collected by persons assigned to intelligence staffs of each Naval District although their contribution was quite often weakened by routinely being assigned too many diverse or non-intelligence activities. When the national ambitions of the Axis Powers finally brought Europe and the Far East to war, President Roosevelt mandated in June 1939, that ONI be responsible for the investigation of sabotage, espionage and subversive activities that pose any kind of threat to the Navy.

By the fall of 1940, a selective call-up of intelligence reservists for investigative and counterintelligence duties began, and following our entry into World War II, the Navy's investigative arm was manned almost entirely by reserve officer personnel.

A Tardy Awakening

For some time before the spring of 1914, events along the southern border of the United States had plainly foreshadowed an unfavorable turn in American relations with Mexico. President William H. Taft, therefore, on 21 February 1913, directed the movement of an Army division to the Galveston-Texas City area in order to be prepared to meet any eventuality. Because the War Department General Staff had already gained considerable experience from the similar but poorly planned and executed venture of some two years earlier, this troop concentration was accomplished in a comparatively smooth manner. The anticipated crisis, though, came to an unexpected head on the Gulf Coast rater than along the border, with the Mexican authorities at Tampico seizing a United States navy launch and holding its crews and passengers as prisoners. While these personnel were soon released, apologies and amends in strict compliance with the demands of the commander of the Atlantic Squadron were not forthcoming, so the entire Atlantic Fleet was moved into a position of readiness off Vera Cruz. A small naval force was also put ashore within that city to prevent the landing of an arms shipment destined for Mexican Army use. Military skirmishes promptly occurred and there was consequent loss of life on both sides.

Thoroughly aroused by these provocative developments, Congress jointly resolved, effective 22 April 1914, that the President was fully justified in utilizing the armed forces of the United States to support the enforcement of his demands for redress against the Mexican Government.[6] Due principally to prior staff planning by the Joint (Army-Navy) Board, a reinforced brigade of Army troops under the command of Brig. General Frederick Funston was then successfully transported from several different American ports to disembark without major incident at Vera Cruz on 26 April 1914. This force proceeded to remain in Mexico until November of that same year.

Even though these significant military operations were taking place far to the south, the unsatisfactory military intelligence situation in Washington showed little real improvement. Only one bright spot had appeared on the horizon, with General Wood approving an order which stated that all units operating along the Mexican border would detail carefully selected officers to act, in addition to their other duties, as intelligence officers for collecting "such information as is possible from refugees and other sources, without leaving the limits of the United States."[7] The main obstacle continuing to stand in the way of any fruitful results from a program of this nature, however, was the fact that the War Department still lacked a staff agency capable of properly processing information derived therefrom. Besides, the officers involved could hardly be expected to put forth much of an effort as long as they were being called upon to perform their intelligence tasks in addition to their normal troop duties.

An event of enormous future portent from the military intelligence standpoint occurred on 18 July 1914, when Congress authorized the formation of an Aviation Section within the Army Signal Corps.[8] While airplanes had previously been utilized on an experimental basis for reconnaissance during maneuvers near New York City in 1912 and an aviation school was already functioning at College Park, Maryland, this legislative enactment served measurably to stimulate further air development throughout the United States Army.[9] It would thus not be long before the eyes of military commanders could be extended over undreamed of distances in seeking information about the enemy and terrain but this same improved capability would also generate a number of complex problems dealing with command, communications and logistics, so as to alter completely the entire existing military intelligence system.

Congress was at this time still appropriating separate funds each year for "Army War College Expenses" and "Contingencies, Military Information Section, General Staff Corps."[10] With the departmental military intelligence agency forming an integral part of the War College Division of the General Staff, this outmoded fiscal arrangement naturally provoked a large number of upsetting administrative difficulties. Wanting to respect Congressional wishes in the matter but also desiring to insure that the War College officials would have full control of both funds, it was decided to alter the departmental organization by splitting the War College Division up into a "Military Information Section" and an "Army War College Section." From this, it might be reasonable to assume that all the work performed by the Division, except that which was connected with operating the War College itself, would now bear directly upon military information activities. Such was not the case, however, because the so-called Military Information Section of the War College Division in May 1915 actually consisted of ten different standing committees, designated as follows:

> Military Preparation and Policy
> *War Plans*
> *Organization, Equipment and Training*
> *Regular Troops*
> *Militia*
> *Militia Education*
> *Military Information and Monographs*
> *History*
> *Library and Map Room*
> *Legislation*[11]

According to a statement made by the Chief of the War College Division when this two-section was first adopted, the primary function of the new Military Information Section would be "to do current General Staff work."[12] It thus becomes readily apparent that the departmental military intelligence agency had finally reached the end of its disastrous journey down the road toward total extinction. The remnants of the original agency were now effectively buried within the Military Information and Monographs Committee of a misnamed Military Information Section comprising a regular part of the War College Division. Moreover, the members of this standing committee were principally engaged in handling current staff action papers of many different kinds. There was no appropriate agency in being therefore, that could be counted on to supervise a suitable military intelligence collection program, process any information obtained from a collection program, or conduct counter-intelligence activities to satisfy the needs of the War Department and Army at large. This was the vital element so plainly missing in the general staff organization toward the close of 1915, even though the earth-shaking assassination at Sarajevo had already taken place more than a year before.[13]

When World War I suddenly broke out in Europe during the summer of 1914, the War Department found itself right in the midst of a determined campaign, launched earlier by General Wood himself, to reduce the number of Army officers serving on detached service.[14] This drive had been occasioned mainly by a severe shortage of officers that kept reappearing whenever important maneuvers were planned, since there was no adequate provision in the existing tables of organization to compensate for an ever-growing number of officer positions requiring duty away from troops. It carried very serious implications from the standpoint of military intelligence operations because all the military attaches and observers, as well as the officers attending foreign schools, came under this detached service classification. Even as late as February 1914, the Chief of the War College Division had forwarded to his superiors a most amazing official opinion to the effect that he considered American military attaches unnecessary in Spain, Italy, Austria and Belgium; Switzerland warranted a retired officer only; Russian remained doubtful; and the Balkan States and Turkey were merely of temporary importance.

This last item was apparently in reference to the Balkan Wars of 1912-13. An effort had been made in December 1912 to introduce a large group of American officers into the combat area, including a four-officer cavalry board headed by Brig. Gen. Edward J. McClernaud, to function as official military observers on the Balkan Allies side against the Turks. When the Bulgarian government refused to permit the presence of these observers, the cavalry board return to the United States. During a subsequent campaign, however, two of the other officers did manage to gain permission to visit "certain points of interest" in Serbia and were then able to secure a considerable amount of valuable military information.[15]

A Counterintelligence Officer of the American Expeditonary Force and Belgian Intelligence questions a suspected enemy agent.

Furthermore, in the event that the United States Army was called upon to perform any extensive field operations, five military attaches, four of them from Europe, plus all nine student officers stationed in France and Germany, could be quickly relieved and returned to the United States for troop duty.[16]

This threatening intelligence personnel situation commenced to clear up right after the start of the war in Europe because the departmental authorities promptly realized the tremendous importance of obtaining as much information as possible about the combat operations in order to keep the United States fully abreast of all the latest military developments. The matter actually came to an immediate head during the opening days of the hostilities, when the American Military Attaches in Paris and Vienna, both requested permission to take to the field with their respective host armies and function in the capacity of military observers. This memorandum wisely concluded that it would be much better for the American military attaches in Europe to remain at their regular posts and execute intelligence tasks within the capital cities, while other officers, especially selected due to their technical ability and physical stamina, were detailed to act as observers in the field.[17]

General Blackjack Pershing leading the Mexican Punitive Expedition to capture Poncho Villa in 1916.

By November 1914, therefore, in addition to the thirteen military attache posts already established, which now included Austria, France, Germany, Great Britain, Italy, Japan, and Russia, American military observer groups were found to be operating with the combatant forces of France, Germany, Austria and Japanese. Two American military observers were also accepted by the Rumania Army early in 1916.

With this expanded military observer program resulting in a sizeable expenditure of extremely scarce War Department funds, Congress was soon persuaded to increase by $15,000 the appropriation under "Contingencies, Military Information Section, General Staff" for that particular purpose during FY 1916.

Apparently all went well with these several American military observer groups except the one which was initially formed in France. In that country, despite repeated complaints on the part of the officers directly concerned, the French authorities consistently refused to permit non-Allied personnel to accompany their armies in the field and thereby accomplish any worthwhile military observations. When this frustrating restriction was continued, the entire American group in France signed a "round robin" letter dated 19 July 1916 and addressed to the Chief of the War College Division, asking that they be granted the status of a Military Mission. They would then not only be able to operate independently of the United States Military Attaché in Paris but also

Poncho Villa (second from left) with two of his Generals, Toribio Ortega and Juan Medina. On Villa's right is Rodolfo Fierro, AKA the "Butcher."

acquire additional prestige for dealing with the recalcitrant French authorities.[18] While this move was strongly opposed by Lt. Col. Spencer Cosby, the American Military Attaché, it duly received official approval and the necessary inter-government negotiations were completed in November 1916.[19] No real improvement seems to have come from the change, though, because as late as 29 December 1916, the Chief of the American Military Mission in France was still complaining that the privileges being offered to his personnel by the French Army for observing under field conditions were "practically the same as those extended to small unimportant countries, such as, for example, Ecuador and Siam."[20]

Mexican border incidents were now again on the rise. These disturbances reached a critical peak early in March 1916, when the Mexican bandit leader Pancho Villa crossed the international boundary and launched an attack against Columbus, New Mexico, killing both US soldiers and civilians. With the revolutionary Mexican Government under Provisional President Carranza having thus proved itself incapable of protecting American lives and property along the border, it was decided to organize a Punitive Expedition under Brig. Gen. John J. Pershing, for the specific purpose of entering Mexico and capturing Villa.[21] This turned out to be an exceedingly difficult military task, especially in view of the fact that General Pershing's orders not only called for him to proceed against Villa and his followers but also directed him to pay scrupulous regard at all times to Mexican sovereignty.[22] The latter proviso became increasingly embarrassing after military contacts were developed with Mexican Federal troops following a relatively large scale skirmish with Villistas on 29 March 1916, near Guerrero, some 250 miles south of the border. From then on, clashes between the two regular forces stemmed chiefly from a growing hostile attitude taken by the Carranza government toward the continued presence of American troops in Mexican territory. The Punitive Expedition was finally withdrawn, effective 5 February 1917, with Poncho Villa still remaining at large but his military capabilities having been effectively curtailed.

As an experienced cavalry officer, General Pershing was fully aware of the direct relationship that must always exist between adequate reconnaissance and the security of a military command. He further recognized that the ultimate success or failure of his isolated expedition into Mexico would hinge largely upon an ability to secure timely and dependable information about the forces opposing him, as well as the terrain over which he would have to operate. Since he had previously held military intelligence and general staff duty assignments, he also realized the necessity for keeping the War Department properly informed on his current military situation. He thus took prompt steps to appoint as his intelligence officer Maj. (later Brig. Gen.) James A. Ryan, 13th Cavalry, an officer he considered well-qualified for directing an efficient field intelligence organization and one who was already proficient in the Spanish language.[23] Similarly, carefully chosen military intelligence personnel from both the War Department and the Southern Department were ordered to serve at his expedition headquarters. The net result of all this intelligence appreciation was that frequent and copious information reports were sent back to the War Department, mostly in the forms of telegrams. Although an officer of the War College Division had been detailed to read these reports, this was apparently the only positive action taken in connection with them. As a matter of fact, it remains very doubtful that the bulk of them ever found their way into the War College files.[24]

General Pershing was given tactical control of the First Squadron, Aviation Section, Signal Corps,

The interior of an Intercept Station operated by the Signal Corps on the Mexican Border in 1918.

Post Civil War

stationed at San Antonio, Texas, to assist him in solving his difficult reconnaissance problems and to utilize as a supplementary means of communications.[25] Because of the low power of the eight available airplanes, however, in contrast to the high altitude and long distance required for flights over Mexican territory, this service did not prove to be of "material benefit" for either of these purposes.[26] On the other hand, his intelligence organization seems to have made full and excellent use of native agents hired to provide the command with needed information concerning both the Villistas and Carranzistas.[27] Approximately 20 Apache Scouts were also engaged in performing local reconnaissance and tracking missions.[28]

While these historic events were taking place in Europe and Mexico, the unsatisfactory situation with reference to the submerged status of the departmental military intelligence agency continued to remain essentially unchanged. On the other hand, military information was still flowing into Washington from a steadily increasing number of established collection sources throughout the field. Most of this material sooner or later did find its way to the Military Information Committee of the War College Division, but the problem of properly processing it had admittedly become more than its limited membership could manage. Since the Committee was also unable to give any due consideration to the matter of publishing military information for use by the Army at large, this important phase of the intelligence effort was likewise being noticeably neglected.[29]

Recognizing that this failure to disseminate available military information to the Army was a major deficiency, the departmental officials attempted early in 1916 to take one remedial step which had some rather embarrassing repercussions. Acting upon a suggestion from the Chief of the War College Division himself, arrangements were made with the Commandant of the Command and Staff School at Fort Leavenworth, Kansas, to have certain intelligence reports, forwarded to that institution for the purpose of preparing intelligence publications for appropriate Army distribution. The first publication issued under this new system, however, brought forth a strong note of protest from the British government because the information upon which it was based had been given to the American Military Attaché in London only after securing his solemn promise to maintain an utmost secrecy in the matter. Hence, this promising experimental program was abruptly cancelled.[30]

The dangerous state of affairs, relative to the manner in which the War Department was failing to fulfill its military intelligence responsibilities, during this period of ever-worsening international relations, was not permitted to go unchallenged by the few experienced intelligence officers remaining assigned to the War College Division.

As a matter of fact, they kept forwarding strenuous complaints on the subject to the Chief of Staff at regular intervals. One of the most comprehensive and forceful presentations along such lines was prepared by Maj. (later Maj. Gen.) Ralph H. Van Deman of the General Staff Corps, who had been an early member of the original Military Information Division, and had later played a key role in connection with Army intelligence operations in the Far East. As a true intelligence zealot he became gravely perturbed when, following his arrival in May 1915 for duty within the War College Division, he observed how the War Department was neglecting to execute its basic military intelligence mission. During March 1916, he drew up a detailed summary of historical facts bearing upon the problem and concluded therefrom that the reestablishment of a separate Military Information Section without further delay

Col. Ralph M. Van Deman became the first Chief of the War Department's Intelligence Organization when it was established in World War I.

was plainly indicated. This study was then not only promptly approved by Brig. Gen. H.H. Macomb, Chief of the War College Division, but also forwarded to the Chief of Staff with an added comment that he personally believed the time had now come to effect a sweeping reorganization of the entire General Staff structure on a totally new basis.[31]

Although no immediate improvement resulted from these particular War College Division recommendations, the Chief of Staff soon did authorize one important action, long advocated by the military intelligence officials, which was deliberately aimed at achieving a better coordination of effort for collection activities in the field. A general order was thus published, on 25 April 1916, directing as follows:

    1. Department commanders will establish and maintain an intelligence office at their headquarters to operate under the personal supervision of the Department chief of staff.

    2. This will also arrange for the detail of intelligence officers at such posts and field detachments of their subordinate commands as is deemed necessary by the circumstances.

    3. Each Department intelligence, insofar as its intelligence duties are concerned, will be considered a branch of the War College Division.

    4. The Department chief of staff is authorized direct communication in intelligence matters with the War College Division but all military information will first be brought to the attention of the Department commander before being forward thereto.

    5. The duties of the intelligence officers will consist generally of collecting and preparing military information for use by the headquarters to which they are attached but, in addition, they should keep the superior headquarters properly informed.

    6. Department intelligence officers will set up a complete file and index of all maps, reports, communications, and other intelligence data in accordance with subsequent instructions to be issued from the Office of the War Department Chief of Staff. Moreover, all intelligence items will be regarded as confidential until released by authority of the Chief of Staff.

This general order did initiate several progressive steps in the direction of improving intelligence collection practices for the United States Army but it also represented a distinct compromise with reference to the key question of what direct command authority, if any, the departmental military intelligence agency should exercise over intelligence personnel operating in the field. Even though it included a statement that the department intelligence offices would function as "branches" of the War College Division, the strict application of this particular provision of the original statement remained clear, however, with the intelligence officials in Washington recalling the completely dependent status of the previous Havana and Manila Branch Offices, and wanting to form an Army-wide military intelligence system along parallel lines.

During 1915, when the Nation was simultaneously faced with the threat of further trouble in Mexico and the growing possibility of becoming directly involved in the European War, the matter of military reform again came under active consideration.[32] Secretary of War Lindley M. Garrison had already instructed the War College Division of the General Staff to prepare a broad study covering the entire field of America military policy. This study, which was finished in 1915, then led to a thorough airing of that politically explosive subject in Congress.[33]

With these Congressional discussions still in progress, Garrison chose to resign in order to register a sharp protest over President Wilson's refusal to accept his proposal for the establishment of a Federal Reserve force which could favorably supplement an enlarged Regular Army and improved National Guard.[34] This personal sacrifice on the part of a notably courageous Secretary of War served to dramatize the issue of military reform and helped materially to insure Congressional passage of a new and comprehensive National Defense Act in June 1916. The Act not only called for the creation of an Army of the United States to consist of a Regular Army, Volunteer Army, Officer's Reserve Corps, Enlisted Reserve Corps, National Guard while in the service of the United States, and other land forces authorized by law, but also permitted an increase in the strength of the Regular Army up to a total of 175,000 by means of annual increments extending over the next five years.

Post Civil War

Meanwhile, on 9 March 1916, Newton D. Baker was appointed the new Secretary of War. Although possessed of a strong pacifist background and, like Secretary Elihu Root, without any previous experience in military matters, Baker was destined to be regarded as one of the truly great American Secretaries of War. This seems all the more noteworthy because, during a lengthy term of office, from 9 March 1916 to 4 March 1921, his extraordinary talents were constantly taxed to the utmost by the terrific demands of World War I and its complicated aftermath. When he first assumed office, for example, he was immediately faced with the tremendous task of revitalizing a newly-created Army of the United States under legislative authority granted to him by an untried National Defense Act that had been optimistically designed to mature over a lengthy period of five years. Actually, of course, it was to be less than one year before the war clouds descended upon the country in full force.

The National Defense Act of 1916 did represent a forward advance of major proportions for providing the War Department with badly needed legislative assistance in solving some of its more important national defense problems but it also included several unfavorable stipulations which were pointedly aimed at the Army General Staff. Unfortunately, these same stipulations could only serve to handicap the proper execution of the Act itself. One of them, for example, specified that not more than half of the officers detailed to the General Staff Corps "could be at any time station or assigned to or employed upon any duty in or near the District of Columbia." Although the Act also granted an increase of 18 officers for the General Staff Corps, this expansion was scheduled to come in annual increments extending over a five-year period. In June 1916, therefore, the total number of General Staff Corps officers was fixed at 41 officers, with only 19 of them on duty within the Washington area. Since highly technical and difficult staff problems had already become the order of the day throughout the War Department, these personnel restrictions gravely hindered the successful conduct of any effective planning for a prewar expansion program.

The serious shortage of General Staff personnel was promptly reflected, of course, in the War College Division, which soon found itself reduced to a total complement of just nine officers. At the same time, though, the flow of information into its so-called Military Information Section kept rapidly mounting. The problem of processing this huge amount of material thus soon became so overwhelming that toward the close of 1916, Brig. Gen. Joseph E. Kuhn, the Acting Division Chief, decided to cancel the remainder of the War College course and to utilize all available personnel in making an "extensive study of military intelligence reports from abroad, so the information compiled might be imparted to the troops." Before doing this, he had also requested authority from the Chief of Staff to reorganize his division into three new sections and to designate them respectively as the Military Information, Military Operations and Military Preparedness Sections.[35] While such a move would have plainly helped to restore the lost independence of the departmental military intelligence agency, no definite action could be taken along those lines until after the war actually started.

General Kuhn also took several other positive steps to remedy glaring deficiencies in the military intelligence effort. During March 1917, for instance, he opened a series of discussions with the Chief of the Militia Bureau concerning the practicability of having selected National Guard officers nominated to become intelligence officers and receive special training under War Department direction. The result was that the Chief of Staff shortly authorized the dispatch of a confidential letter addressed to the Adjutants General of all States, the Territory of Hawaii and the District of Columbia, instructing them to make such appointments. On the eve of America's entrance into World War I and prior to the start of a general mobilization, therefore, the War Department was assured of having at least the nucleus of an intelligence organization installed in most of the larger cities throughout the country. Likewise, a number of National Guard officers had already received a worthwhile amount of preliminary intelligence training, especially within the counterintelligence field.

Nevertheless, despite these few scattered signs of a tardy awakening, when the United States declared war against Germany on 6 April 1917, the period of imposed adversity for the departmental military intelligence agency was still essentially in force. The agency thus continued to remain s deeply submerged with the General Staff organization that it could not execute any of its fundamental intelligence responsibilities in a proper manner. At the same time, along with the rest of the War Department, it was also suffering markedly from a lack of trained general staff personnel stemming from the restrictive provisions of the National Defense Act of 1916. Under the far-sighted leadership of General Kuhn, Chief of War College Division, strenuous last minute efforts had been made to improve this distressing situation but events were now marching ahead so swiftly that the cumulative mistakes of more than ten years duration could not possibly be rectified prior to the entrance of the United States into World War I. As a result, most of the indicated intelligence reforms had to be undertaken at a greatly accelerated rate right in the midst of the widespread confusion and uncertainties that habitually accompany large-scale military expansions. The marvel is that any satisfactory progress could be achieved at all in the face of the seemingly insuperable obstacles which were actually encountered.

With the advent of World War I, the general period representing the preliminary development of the departmental military intelligence agency came to an abrupt conclusion. Although the Military Intelligence Division was not officially reestablished until 26 August 1918, to all intents and purposes it started to function on a comparatively independent basis just three weeks after the declaration of war against Germany. Strongly influenced by sound operational principles that were originally formulated by General Washington during the course of the American Revolution and then subjected to trail in the field over a lengthy succession of formative years, the agency had experienced a highly promising start in 1855 under the direct sponsorship of the Adjutant General. Following the creation of a General Staff Corps within the United States Army in 1903, however, it became a victim of a series of unfavorable decisions by higher authority which promptly led to a disastrous decade of imposed adversity. Notwithstanding, the full period did witness a large number of intelligence activities that not only remain of important historical significance but also furnish several enlightening lessons of major concern to the future.

Pursuant to the Freedom of Information Act, 5 U.S.C. §552B(4), the article: "The Underside of the Mexican Revolution: El Paso 1912", pp.83-89, has been redacted at the request of the author.

Post Civil War

This page intentionally left blank.

This page intentionally left blank.

Post Civil War

This page intentionally left blank.

This page intentionally left blank.

Post Civil War

This page intentionally left blank.

Imperial Germany's Sabotage Operations In The U.S.

As the industrial revolution swept across Western Europe, the nations there sought an outlet for their manufactured products in the less developed regions of the world. Great Britain grabbed the lion's share, but in the decade after 1870, the other European nations moved aggressively to obtain what was left. An imperialistic rivalry was born. France wanted to restore her national spirit after her defeat in 1870. Germany, with an astonishing industrial development and with the most powerful army in the world, demanded "a place in the sun." Russia desired an ice-free port on the Pacific Ocean and Japan searched for new markets to support her overflowing population. In this scramble for markets and territories, Africa was carved up into colonies and protectorates and there was every indication that the same fate awaited Asia.

The rivalries between these European nations were a continuous menace to peace. With Europe wallowing in an orgy of militarism, imperialism, nationalism and intelligence intrigues, it was unlikely that any balance of power could be maintained. It was finally upset in the Balkans where racial hatred and nationalist strivings were complicated by the conflicting ambitions of Austria and Russia.

In was June 28, 1914 in late morning as an inconspicuous Bosnian student waited by a cobble street in Sarajevo. He observed Archduke Franz Ferdinand and his wife drive by on their way to the town hall. The student was Gavrilo Princip, a member of the Young Bosnians, a group that was organized in 1910 to protest against the annexation in 1908 of Bosnia and Herzegovina. A few minutes earlier, another member of the Young Bosnians had tossed a bomb into the Archduke's car but it was deflected by Ferdinand and exploded beneath the security vehicle following the Archduke's car.

After his town meeting, the Archduke ordered his driver to take him to the hospital to visit the injured security guards. Although the driver wanted to take a different road, the Archduke insisted on using the same route where the attack took place. Princip saw them returning and as the Archduke's car passed slowly by, he stepped from the crowd into the street and fired several rounds at point-blank range into the archduke and his wife, killing both. World War I began less than two months later.

Following a century-old tradition, the United States declared a policy of neutrality. President Woodrow Wilson attempted to steer a neutral position among the belligerents but several major influences within the United States eventually caused this policy to be abandoned.

The least effectual of these influences was the heterogeneous character of the American population. When the war in Europe began, about one-third of the American population was foreign-born or of foreign-born parentage. It was this group that the European propagandists first focused their efforts. They had limited success but, in the last analyst, targeting this audience was of little importance in determining how the United States finally acted.

Count Johann von Bernstorff, German Ambassador to the United States.

The other three influences played a greater role in President Wilson's decision to declare war on Germany. The first of these was the economic affect the war had on the United States. It caused a tremendous upswing in the economy. The war was destroying the industrial and agricultural base in Europe and the United States became the major source for all types of commodities, particularly foodstuffs and munitions. All this meant a sudden and widespread prosperity. The profits came almost entirely from the Allied Powers. As Great Britain tightened the blockade around Germany and extended the contraband list, it became difficult to export to the Central Powers (Germany and its allies).

While economic interests were tying the United States more closely to the allied nations, organized propaganda was effectively used. Both the Allied and Central Powers exerted themselves to the utmost to influence public opinion, but in this effort, the allied Powers were far more successful. The success was due to Great Britain's control of the cables and strict censorship, which allowed only the news it wanted Americans to hear from the war front to reach the United States. Honest, unbiased news largely disappeared from American papers after August 1914. According to one journalist, the British censors eliminated three-quarters of the dispatches from American correspondents in Central Europe.[83] The British portrayed themselves as saviors of the world from the Teutonic hordes. The French reminded Americans of their contributions to American independence. Against the skillful Allied propaganda, the blundering efforts of Germany to subsidize the American press and influence American opinion made scant progress and were eventually utterly discredited by 1915.

As Franz Rintelen admitted,

> *Everybody in Germany was raging. Large packets of newspapers had been received from America, and there was not a word of truth in the reports that were being made about the military situation. We were particularly indignant at the numerous stories of atrocities, which had found their way into the American papers. With this kind of journalism it was inevitable that not only the mass of newspaper readers, but gradually also official circles in America, would assume an anti German attitude.*[84]

The last major influence was the violations of America's neutral rights by the Germans. To the Germans, the United States remained a problem and they had to develop a strategy to deal with it. The strategy they chose was to keep the United States neutral while at the same time closing off the flow of food and war material from the United States to the Allied Powers. The first part of the strategy depended on diplomacy and the second relied on sabotage.

To conduct this strategy in the United States, the German High Command selected Johann Heinrich Count von Bernstorff, the German Ambassador to the United States.

"Bernstorff, a seasoned diplomat, came to Washington as Imperial German Ambassador during a placid and superficially cordial period in German-American relations and played very well what was largely a ceremonial role before the summer of 1914. However, the outbreak of the World War, and particularly his government's decision in early 1915 to launch an unrestricted submarine campaign against merchant shipping, thrust Bernstorff into the center of a diplomatic firestorm that grew in intensity and culminated in an American declaration of war against the German Empire in 1917."[85]

In July 1914, nine days after the Archduke is assassinated in Sarajevo, Bernstorff left the United States for Germany. He believed his summons home was to consult with the German Foreign Ministry. Instead, he met with Section 3B, military intelligence, of the German General Staff. Bernstorff was told that German military intelligence had no experienced officers it can devote to the United States. They informed Bernstorff that all their best officers and espionage agents had been deployed against Germany's enemies in the war, Great Britain, France and Russia. Even if Section 3B could identify a sufficient number of trained agents and mobilize them against the United States, the odds of infiltrating them into America undetected was remote.

Section 3-B told Bernstorff that he was to be Germany's espionage and sabotage chief for the Western Hemisphere. To support his effort, he would be assisted by Captain Franz von Papen, currently military attaché in Mexico who was to be transferred to the United States, Captain Karl Boy-Ed, naval attaché, and Dr. Heinrich Albert, the commercial attaché who would be the finance officer for the sabotage operations. With this small group of men, Bernstorff had to carry out the German strategy against the United States.

With Bernstorff in Washington, the other three officials established their operational base in New York City. Albert opened an office at 45 Broadway and von Papen and Boy-Ed use an office in the Wall Street area. Their first task was to identify and recruit agents for their sabotage and subversion operations. The early efforts of the group were ragged and ineffectual.

One of the first enlistee in their plans was Horst von der Goltz, who devised a plan to dynamite the Welland Canal, which linked Lakes Ontario and Erie on the Canadian side of the border, just west of Buffalo. Shippers to transport raw material to American munitions and commodities companies used the Canal.

Using the pretext of blasting tree stumps on a farm, a Captain Hans Tauscher, the Krupp representative in New York obtained dynamite from the Dupont Powder Company. Tauscher gave the dynamite to von der Goltz who stored it at a German safehouse operated by Martha Held. Held's row house at 123

Captain Karl Boy-Ed

Post Civil War

West 50th Street in Manhattan was also the gathering place for German ship captains who docked in New York.

To help him in his plan, von der Goltz, using the alias Bridgeman H. Taylor, engaged the services of several men. Several days after obtaining the dynamite, the small group of saboteurs left New York for Buffalo by train. Following them was the Secret Service. After surveying the canal and seeing that it was heavily guarded, the men got cold feet and abandoned the plan.

Von Papen reported back to Berlin about the failure and von der Goltz was recalled to Germany. Instead of being reprimanded, German military intelligence ordered him to return to the United States. On his return, the ship stopped in England and von der Goltz walked in to Scotland Yard with an offer of information on German air raids on Britain. Scotland Yard arrested him and during his interrogation, he informed them that he prevented a sabotage plot against the Welland Canal. The British extradited him to the United States to stand trial.

Once he was in the hands of the American authorities, von der Goltz repeated his story about the sabotage plot. He also guided Department of Justice officers to the safehouse run by Martha Held. Held was interviewed about the dynamite by the Justice officers but claimed she was asked to hold a suitcase but did not know what it contained. Although Justice was aware of this safehouse, they never investigated nor conducted surveillance against it. Horst von der Goltz was tried convicted and sent to prison in 1916.

The next operational plan conducted by von Papen and Albert was to obtain U.S. passports for use by German army reservists residing in the United States to return to Germany to fight against its enemies. After the reservists reached Germany, military intelligence took the passports and used them to send spies into Britain, France and Russia. The problem was that the Department of State had tightened the loose passport regulations by requiring more extensive proof of American citizenship and a photograph of the applicant. To circumvent the new regulations, the Germans resorted to passport fraud.

To conduct the operation, von Papen and Albert recruited a German, Hans von Wedell. Von Wedell devised a plan to have American longshoremen, sailors and street bums in the New York environs apply for American passports. Once they had the passports, von Wedell purchased the passport from them for a small amount of money, usually from ten to twenty-five dollars. It was a great scheme and worked well until some of the street-smart individuals realized what was happening and attempted to blackmail von Wedell for more money. American authorities got wind of the scam and began to investigate but Von Wedell left for Cuba before they had a chance to identify him.

Instead of curtailing their operation after von Wedell left, the Germans recruited another individual, Carl Ruroede, to take von Wedell's place. Ruroede's career as a German agent was short-lived. The Department of Justice's investigation had zeroed in on the location of the office used by the Germans. An undercover agent, Albert Adams, was sent in to make contact

NOTICE!

TRAVELLERS intending to embark on the Atlantic voyage are reminded that a state of war exists between Germany and her allies and Great Britain and her allies; that the zone of war includes the waters adjacent to the British Isles; that, in accordance with formal notice given by the Imperial German Government, vessels flying the flag of Great Britain, or of any of her allies, are liable to destruction in those waters and that travellers sailing in the war zone on ships of Great Britain or her allies do so at their own risk.

IMPERIAL GERMAN EMBASSY
WASHINGTON, D. C., APRIL 22, 1915.

Notice in an American Newspaper advising travelers of the danger of sailing on British Ships.

with Ruroede. Posing as a Bowery bum with pro-German views, Adams was immediately enlisted to procure American passports.

With Department of State support, Adams was given four passports to give to Ruroede. Ruroede, an inexperienced agent, made the foolish mistake of showing Adams how the passports were doctored and saying that the passports were going to be used by four Germans to sail to Europe in a few days.

On 2 January 1915 the Department of Justice arrested Ruroede. The ship, *Bergensfjord*, carrying the four Germans using the false passports, was stopped in the harbor and boarded by Justice officials who promptly arrested the men. On board the ship was von Wedell but the officials missed him.

A few days prior to sailing aboard the Bergensfjord, von Wedell wrote the following letter, dated 26 December 1914, to von Bernstorff:

"His excellency The Imperial German Ambassador, Count von Bernstorff, Washington, D.C. Your Excellency: Allow me most obediently to put before you the following facts: It seems that an attempt has been made to produce the impression upon you that I prematurely abandoned my post, in New York. That is not true.

I. My work was done. At my departure I left the service, well organized and worked out to its minutest details, in the hands of my successor, Mr. Carl Ruroede, picked out by myself, and, despite many warnings, still tarried for several days in New York in order to give him the necessary final directions and in order to hold in check the blackmailers thrown on my hands by the German officers until after the passage of my travelers through Gibraltar; in which I succeeded. Mr. Ruroede will testify to you that without my suitable preliminary labors, in which I left no conceivable means untried and in which I took not the slightest consideration of my personal weal or woe, it would be impossible for him, as well as for Mr. Von Papen, to forward officers and 'aspirants' in any number whatever to Europe. This merit I lay claim to and the occurrences of the last days have unfortunately compelled me, out of sheer self-respect, to emphasize this to your Excellency.

II. The motives which induced me to leave New York and which, to my astonishment, were not communicated to you, are the following:

1. I knew that the State Department had, for three weeks, withheld a passport application forged by me. Why?

2. Ten days before my departure, I learnt from a telegram sent me by Mr. Von Papen, which stirred me up very much, and further through the omission of a cable, that Dr. Stark had fallen into the hands of the English. That gentleman's forged papers were liable to come back any day and could, owing chiefly to his lack of caution, easily be traced back to me.

3. Officers and aspirants of the class which I had to forward over, namely the people, saddled me with a lot of criminals and blackmailers, whose eventual revelations were liable to bring about any day the explosion of the bomb.

4. Mr. Von Papen had repeatedly urgently ordered me to hide myself.

5. Mr. Igel had told me I was taking the matter altogether too lightly and ought to-for God's sake-disappear.

6. My counsel...had advised me to hastily quit New York, inasmuch as a local detective agency was ordered to go after the passport forgeries.

7. It had become clear to me that eventual arrest might yet injure the worthy undertaking and that my disappearance would probably put a stop to all investigation in this direction.

How urgent it was for me to go away is shown by the fact that, two days after my departure, detectives, who had followed up my telephone calls, hunted up my wife's harmless and unsuspecting cousin in Brooklyn, and subjected her to an interrogatory.

Mr. Von Papen and Mr. Albert have told my wife that I forced myself forward to do this work. That is not true. When I, in Berlin, for the first time heard of this commission, I objected to going and represented to the gentleman that my entire livelihood which I had created for myself in America by six years of labor was at stake therein. I have no other means, and although Mr. Albert told my wife my practice was not worth talking about, it sufficed, nevertheless, to decently support myself and wife and to build my future on. I have finally, at the suasion of Count Wedell, undertaken it, ready to sacrifice my future and that of my wife. I have, in order to reach my goal, despite infinite difficulties, destroyed everything that I built up here for myself and my wife. I have perhaps sometimes been awkward, but always full of good will, and I now travel back to Germany with the consciousness of having done my duty as well as I understood it, and of having accomplished my task.

"With expressions of the most exquisite consideration, I am, your Excellency,"

Very Respectfully,

/s/ Hans Adam von Wedell

Ruroede was tried, convicted and sentenced to three years in prison. The four reservists, pleading guilty, protested that they had agreed to return to Germany on false passports out of patriotism, were fined $200 each. As for von Wedell, the British took him off the Bergensfjord on the high seas off the coast of England but the British ship was torpedoed and von Wedell went down with the ship.

Heinrich Friedrich Albert[86]

On 27 July 1915 an ad appeared in the New York Evening Telegram. It read: "Lost on Saturday. On 3:30 Harlem Elevated Train, at 50th St. Station, Brown Leather Bag, Containing Documents. Deliver to G.H. Hoffman, 5 E. 47th St., Against $20. Reward." The ad was seeking to recover the lost briefcase of Heinrich Friedrich Albert, a German lawyer, who was serving as Commercial Attaché and financial advisor to the German Ambassador to the United States, Count Johann von Bernstorff. He was also the paymaster for the German sabotage operations in the United States.

To complement their sabotage operations, the Germans invented the idea of establishing a cover company to conduct a covert operation to induce labor unrest and encourage strikes by laborers at munitions companies in the United States. The conceived plan had three goals: the cover company was to purchase vital raw materials and manufacturing equipment and tools to keep them from reaching legitimate companies; to obtain armaments and powder contracts but not honor them; and to pay astonishing high salaries to its workers, causing other companies to do the same or face worker troubles. The plot called for the Bridgeport Projectile Company, the name selected for the cover company, to begin construction in Bridgeport, Connecticut in April 1915 and ready for operations in September that same year.

It was a bold plan that never came to fruition because of carelessness on the part of Albert. Albert was at the offices of the Hamburg-Amerika Line, at 45 Broadway in lower Manhattan. George Sylvester Viereck, the editor of the Fatherland, a pro-German publication, joined him there. Viereck was also under investigation by the Secret Service for violations of America's neutrality laws.

Before President Woodrow Wilson signed an Executive Order on 14 May 1915, authorizing surveillance of German Embassy personnel in the United States, the Secret Service was limited to watching clerks, technicians and errand boys for the Germans. After Wilson's order, William J. Flynn, chief of the Secret Service, immediately assigned a ten-man squad to keep the Germans under surveillance. Frank Burke, a young agent, was named head of this unit, located on the top floor of the Customs House at the Battery. Burke initiated coverage on all the significant people he knew involved in German activities, including Viereck.

Viereck, not a trained operative of the Germans, failed to notice that he was under surveillance. Secret Service agent, William H. Houghton, had followed him to the Hamburg-Amerika Line offices. After Viereck entered the building, Houghton telephoned the Custom House in New York and suggested to Frank Burke, that he should join him in case Viereck exited the site with another individual.

Burke and Houghton waited until mid-afternoon before Viereck and Albert came out of the building and proceeded to the uptown-elevated train station at Rector Street. The Germans sat in the middle of the car while Houghton sat opposite them and Burke sat behind them. The Secret Service agents did not know the identity of Viereck's companion at the time but suspected it might be Albert, a man they heard of but never saw before.

Albert was, indeed, an unknown individual to American counterintelligence. He was six-feet tall, heavy-set, and had crosscut saber scars on his right cheek, a dimpled chin and a stubby dark moustache. Every day, Albert rode the elevated train between his office at 45 Broadway and his Ritz-Carlton hotel room. He always carried his briefcase, which was stuffed with Berlin telegrams, communications from German agents, financial records and subordinate reports.

Viereck disembarked at the Thirty-third Street stop, trailed by Houghton. Burke remained on the train watching Albert, who was carrying a briefcase. A woman came on board the train and sat opposite Albert. As the train proceeded to the next stop, Albert closed his eyes and dozed off, his briefcase resting on the seat against the wall of the car.

When the train stopped at Fiftieth Street and was ready to move again, Albert suddenly awoke and realized it was his stop. He sprang from his seat and raced out the back door. The woman called to him about his briefcase but Burke picked it up and rushed out the front door. Albert realizing he left his briefcase on the train, reentered the train only to find it missing. He again ran out of the train looking for the person who took the briefcase.

Seeing Albert between him and the exit stairs, Burke partially covered the briefcase with his coat and using other passengers as cover, stood against a wall until Albert went down the stairs. Burke also made his way down the stairs behind Albert. When Burke reached the street, Albert spotted him and began to give chase.

Burke hopped on a streetcar heading uptown. He quickly told the conductor that a crazy fellow who had just caused a big scene on the elevated train was pursuing him. The conductor seeing Albert racing after the streetcar, arms flailing, told the motorman not to stop at the next corner. The streetcar continued on, leaving Albert waving helplessly behind.

Knowing he could not retrieve his briefcase, Albert proceeded to the German Club on Central Park West, where he held an impromptu meeting with German Embassy military attaché, Captain Franz von Papen, and naval aide, Captain Carl von Boy-Ed. Based on what Albert told them, they decided that a common thief had taken the briefcase and, after searching through the papers, would find nothing of value. The best way to get the papers back, they reasoned, was to place an ad in the newspapers offering a reward.

When Burke opened the briefcase and saw the papers, he notified Flynn. Flynn, in turn, contacted Secretary of the Treasury, William G. McAdoo, at his summerhouse in North Haven, Maine. Flynn took the briefcase to McAdoo, who with his aids decided that the contents proved beyond doubt that the German Embassy in the United States was violating the neutrality laws. McAdoo then took the papers to President Wilson.

The President asked McAdoo to consult with Col. Edward House, the president's closest advisor, and Secretary of State Robert Lansing. The United States government was in a bind because any use of the papers by the government would show that a government agency had stolen the papers of a fully accredited diplomat. Colonel House suggested that the contents of the papers be given to one of the newspapers to publish. The New York World was chosen and selected papers were given to the editor, Frank I. Cobb, who agreed to publish them without attribution in return for exclusive use of the documents.

The newspaper published the contents on page one and two succeeding pages 15 August 1915. The paper reported that Albert was the master German spy, who, along with van Papen, devised the Bridgeport Projectile Company operation and obtained approval for it from the German military general staff. According to the newspaper, it was their idea to divert legitimate orders from the British and French away from honest American munitions firms to their cover company with the intention of simply storing the gunpowder and shell casings. In fact, they hired an American industrialist, George Hoardley, to build and operate the plant so as to appear it was a genuine business.

The New York World also reported that the German government was financing Viereck's newspaper, The Fatherland. In letters between Viereck and Albert, published on the front page of the New York World, it showed that Albert was providing $1,500 monthly to Viereck. It further revealed that Albert was pushing for more say in how the paper was to be managed.

Post Civil War

He told Viereck that future payments were being held in abeyance until there was an understanding between them about the future direction of the paper's policy and that he, Albert, had a voice in its financial management.

Other newspapers picked up the story and were constantly hounding Albert for information. Albert, to try to calm the waters, gave the New York World a 2,500-word statement to print in its entirety. In his statement, he claimed that the press misinterpreted his papers. No one believed him and he was often mocked by being referred to as "the minister without portfolio."

Although Secretary of the Treasury, McAdoo wanted Albert recalled by the German government, no official U.S. action was taken against him. When the war began, Albert returned home to Germany where he was given responsibility for foreign assets in the country. When the war ended, he took charge of army surplus sales. In 1923, Chancellor Stresmann asked him to form a government in the Weimar Republic but he was unsuccessful in getting the agreement of the various parties. Instead, he left government to become a rich lawyer and advisor to foreign corporations in Berlin. During Hitler's Third Reich, Albert was on the sidelines, having no official role. After World War II be resumed his career in international business.

Paul Koenig

Paul Koenig

On 22 August 1914, von Papen designates Paul Koenig to recruit and supervise a gang of saboteurs. Koenig owned a small detective company, the Bureau of Investigation that handled requests from the Atlas Line, a subsidiary of the German shipping company, the Hamburg-Amerika Line. To accomplish this new assignment, he established a Secret Service Division within his company and instituted strict operational security methods. He prohibited his agents from meeting with him at his office. Instead, he used various locations, the identities of which were coded using a "safety block system." For example, a street indicated during a telephone conversation meant that the actual meeting would occur five blocks further uptown from the street mentioned.

Over the next year he began to put together his sabotage rings. Koenig selects the dock area as the logical place to recruit his members. However, his activities come to the attention of the New York City Bomb Squad. The Bomb Squad was initially organized to investigate crimes of violence but as time goes by, the Squad's attention increasingly focused on the Germans.

One day, members of the Bomb Squad noticed a man apparently working the docks. Inquiries determined that this individual is Koenig, who is employed by the German steamship line. What struck the Bomb Squad as unusual about Koenig's activities, was that they did not appear to be legitimate. The German steamship lines had attempted to send ships to sea under false cargo manifests in order to supply German naval raiders. Because of this violation of American neutrality, the entire steamship line was tied up in Hoboken for the duration of the war. With absolutely nothing to do, the Bomb Squad felt it odd for Koenig to be so busy. They launched an investigation into his activities.

During contact with the Department of Justice, the Bomb Squad was informed that Koenig had previously come to their attention but they eventually dropped their surveillance when they came to the conclusion that he was not worth the effort. The Bomb Squad felt otherwise. They surveilled Koenig to several popular German hangouts in the city; one of which was the German Club in Central Park West.

This same club also frequently hosted Albert, Boy-Ed and von Papen.

The Bomb Squad also determined that Koenig conducted much of his business out of his office. Knowing that any attempt to enter the building to collect information would probably come to Koenig's attention, the Bomb Squad placed a tap on his telephone. For some time nothing happened until one day they heard a person calling Koenig several unspeakable names during their conversation. Several days later, the same person called again, which allowed the Bomb Squad to identify the telephone number from which the person placed the call. It was a public telephone at a bar.

The Bomb Squad contacted the bartender who was able to provide a description of the individual using the telephone. The bartender did not know his name but thought he lived at a nearby address. Checks in the neighborhood allowed the Bomb Squad to identify the caller as George Fuchs. Fuchs was a distant cousin of Koenig who recruited Fuchs to spy on the Welland Canal. Later, Fuchs moved to New York City where Koenig hired him to work for $18 a week.

To make contact with Fuchs in a non-threatening way, a letter is sent to him by the Bomb Squad offering Fuchs a possible job. A meeting is later arranged and an undercover police officer, posing as the company representative, met with Fuchs. The undercover officer was able to gain Fuch's confidence. Fuchs confided to the officer the details of the Welland Canal and how he came to New York to work for Koenig. He told the officer that Koenig fired him because of his constant feuding with one of Koenig's operatives and his drinking and disorderly habits. Fuchs was also bitter because Koenig refused to pay him for one days work, a total of $2.57.

The Bomb Squad contacted the Bureau of Investigation and a few hours later, Koenig is arrested. A search of his house turned up his little black, loose-leaf book. In it, Koenig meticulously kept a record of all his agents and their assignments right up to the previous day.

Franz von Rintelen

On 3 April 1915, Franz von Rintelen arrived in New York City aboard the S/S Christianiafjord from Sweden. Before leaving for the United States, he attempted to secure an American passport from the American military attaché in Berlin, Major Langhorne, but was unsuccessful. Instead, he procured a Swiss passport, originally issued to Emily V. Gasche but altered the name to Emile V. Gasche.

Rintelen's mission was to prevent the shipment of munitions from the United States to the Allies. He claimed he was sent by the German Naval Ministry to replace Carl Boy-Ed, who was considered inefficient and unsatisfactory. He also claimed to have acted independently of Boy-Ed, von Papen and Ambassador Bernstorff. Instead of seeking assistance from the Hamburg-American line, which was used by Boy-Ed, von Papen and Bernstorff, he went to the German Lloyd line.

After his arrival, he probably conferred with Albert, the commercial attaché and sabotage financier, about the current situation in the large American munitions plants and to review financial information gathered by the Reichspress Bureau. He then met with von Papen to obtain the services of Walter Theodore von Scheele. Scheele was a major in the German Army and an intelligence agent. He came to the United States on an industrial espionage mission but was seconded to von Papen after the latter's arrival. Von Papen agreed to Rintelen's request and Scheele began

Franz von Rintelen

to build incendiary bombs for use abroad supply ships carrying food and munitions to the Allies.

Besides Scheele, Rintelen gathered about him a select group of recruits to carry out his operational plans. Within this group was an Executive Committee composed of Scheele; Eno Bode, a German citizen and superintendent of the Hamburg-American line; Erich von Steinmetz, also known as Captain Steinberg, Stein, H. Reichart, and Harold Rasmussen, who reported entered the United States disguised as a woman and carrying disease germs; and Otto Wolpert, a German citizen who was the pier superintendent of Atlas Lines. The Executive Committee met on Saturday afternoons at the Hofbrau House at 27th and Broadway in New York City.

Rintelen's plans called for fomenting strikes, firebombing shipping, instigating embargoes and pacifist propaganda, fomenting revolution in Mexico, purchasing munitions for the German government and shipping supplies to Germany. To finance his operation, Rintelen received funds from the Reichsbank through Richard A. Timmerscheidt, a naturalized U.S. citizen of German origin. Timmerscheidt was a partner in the bank of Ladenberg Thalmann & Co. He was also a German finance agent for espionage, propaganda and commerce. Scheele testified that Rintelen's expenditures of $10,000 and over were subject to approval by Albert. Most of the funds expended were not paid directly from Rintelen's bank account but rather was disbursed in certificates of deposit payable to bearer.

On 20 April 1915 Scheele delivered the first lot of 150 firebombs to Wolpert at a meeting at Carl Schimmel's office. Schimmel was responsible for obtaining information as to the exact sailing dates of vessels. Scheele had made the bombs in the engine room of the S/S Friederich der Grosse, NGL pier, in Hoboken. Scheele had constructed each incendiary device to look like a cigar-shaped tube. The tube was sealed at both ends. A thin copper disk separated two chambers within the tube. One of the chambers contained sulfuric acid and the other was filled with picric acid.

The first operation was planned for New Orleans. Steinberg had originally traveled there on 4 April to make arrangements for the distribution of the tetanus, foot and mouth and meningitis germ cultures that he had smuggled into the country. However, the cultures had lost their vitality and he was attempting to revive them but was unsuccessful.

Rintelen ordered Steinberg to return to New Orleans with Bode to recruit individuals to plant the firebombs on ships sailing from New Orleans. They recruited Maurice C. Conners, an American citizen. They offered Conners $25,000 cash for planting the bombs and $5,000 for each ship disabled. Before any activity took place, Rintelen canceled the contract, recalled Steinberg and Bode and sent Scheele to New Orleans. Scheele contacted Conners to renegotiate the contract and offered $5,000 in cash and $10,000 in notes. When Conners accepted the terms, Rintelen, using the alias Hansen, confirmed the arrangements in a telegram. Rintelen sent $5,000 to Scheele through Mechanics and Metals Bank in New York City to the Bank of New Orleans. Scheele withdrew the funds and paid Conners in cash.

Conners recruited two other individuals to help him and all three men traveled to New York. There they conferred with Steinberg, Bode and Scheele, who provided the three men with 80-90 firebombs. The three men returned to New Orleans but never carried out the plan. Conners sold the firebombs to a junk dealer.

Although the first sabotage attempt against shipping was a failure, Rintelen soon saw success. He persuaded a German-American woman he knew to write to the Russian military attaché in Paris, Count Alexis Ignatieff, who was an old friend of hers. In her letter, she informed the Count that she was acquainted with an American importer, E.V. Gibbons (in reality, Rintelen) who wanted to import some wine into the United States. The Count agreed to help and told the woman to have Gibbons use to his to make the purchase. Rintelen did so and promptly paid for the shipment.

Rintelen then wrote to the Count, offering the services of his import-export company to supply goods to Russia. The Count advised Rintelen to contact the Russian purchasing agents in New York and again lent his name to establish Rintelen's credentials.

The Russians awarded Rintelen's false company, E.V. Gibbons & Co. a large contract to deliver munitions and tin meat products. With the Russian contract in his pocket, Rintelen obtained a three million-dollar loan, which he deposited in a bank. Rintelen did no intent to fulfill the contract but the Russians contacted him to request a shorter delivery date and offered to pay a bonus.

Apprehensive that his intrigue might be exposed, Rintelen put together a partial shipment and had it loaded on the *Phoebus*. The Russians paid Rintelen his bonus at the docks. Unknown to them and to the guards that patrolled the decks of the ship with carbines at the ready to discourage pro-German rashness, anti-British stevedores had dropped at least six of Scheele's incendiary devices in hard-to-see crevices in the holds now piled tier upon tier with artillery shells for Russia.

Later *Shipping News* reported: Accidents. *S.S. Phoebus* from New York—caught fire at sea. Brought into port of Liverpool by *H.M.S. Ajax*.

The Russians did not suspect anything. Rintelen again offered his services and filled two large cargo vessels with material. To cover his plans and divert any suspicion from falling on him, Rintelen hired detectives to guard the vessels. After the ships left port, they met the same fate as the *Phoebus*.

The Russians continued to deal with Rintelen until several barges of ammunition suddenly sank as the barges were moved from the Black Tom Island terminal to ships waiting in the harbor. The Russians

Robert Fay's Suitcase

did not suspect Rintelen of any wrongdoing but demanded immediate delivery of the rest of their large order from him. Rintelen informed the Russians that he had no intention of honoring their order. Following his confrontation with the Russians, Rintelen moved quickly. He paid off his loan at the bank and liquidated his cover company. By the time the Russians obtained legal counsel, the firm of E.V. Gibbons no longer existed.

On 2 May 1915, the British freighter *Kirk Oswald* sailed from New York bound for Archangel, Russia but was diverted to Marseilles, France. On board the ship, French police discovered the incendiary devices and contacted the New York City Bomb Squad. The Bomb Squad began an investigation and pursued several dead end leads. They initially suspected that an individual or individuals had somehow placed the incendiary devices in the sugar bags as the bags were transported from small boats to the ships for loading. Their investigation failed to discover any saboteurs but they did find stealing of sugar by several of the barge captains.

The Bomb Squad had exhausted all their leads and their investigation was going nowhere until they received a telephone call from the French military attaché in New York. The attaché informed the Bomb Squad about a man who was believed to be involved in purchasing explosive material.

Officers from the Bomb Squad met with the man identified as Wettig. Wettig told his story and cooperated with the officers, who accompanied Wettig as he purchased the material and then delivered it to an address. A check by the officers revealed that the address was a delivery drop site. The actual destination for the package was a garage on Main Street in Weehawken, New Jersey. The officers also determined that the person to whom the package was destined was individual by the name of Fay.

The officers tried to deliver the package to Fay but he was out when the arrived. They left the package but placed surveillance on the garage. The Bomb Squad picked up Fay's trail and surveilled him and another individual along the Palisades where the two men stopped and disappeared into a wooded area. No attempt was made to follow them.

Surveillance continued on Fay for several days. Because the Bomb Squad had no arrest powers in New Jersey, the Bomb Squad contacted the Weehawken police and also the Secret Service. The three agencies agreed to cooperate and conducted joint surveillance on Fay. When Fay returned to the wooded area along the Palisades, surveillance team members followed them. Fay was arrested and confessed that he was a German agent but initially did not implicate anyone else. Later, he told the authorities that he had been waiting for word from von Papen or Boy-Ed to begin his sabotage operations. He said he never planted any incendiary bombs on any ships. He was tried, convicted and sentenced to eight years in prison. After a month in jail, Fay escaped and traveled to Baltimore where he met with Koenig who provided him with funds and instructed Fay to go to San Francisco. Fay, who feared that he would be killed, disobeyed and fled to Mexico and then to Spain, where he was finally captured in 1918.

The Bomb Squad was no closer to catching the saboteurs. A decision was made to send several German-speaking officers into the bars to strike up conversations with the customers. One officer got lucky when one of patrons asked the officer if he would like to be introduced to a man who was doing some work for the Germans. The officer, who used the cover story that he was a special agent for German Ambassador von Bernstorff, was subsequently presented to Captain Charles von Kleist.

Robert Fay being fingerprinted after his arrest.

At their first meeting, von Kleist never questioned the officer's bona fides but proceeded to tell the officer about an individual named Dr. Walter T. Scheele, who was using von Kleist in his laboratory in Hoboken. According to von Kleist, Scheele claimed to be a member of the German Secret service. Although the laboratory was ostensibly fabricating agricultural chemicals, von Kleist said its genuine operation was to manufacture incendiary devices. He provided further information on the other members involved in the operation and how the devices were assembled. The reason von Kleist unburdened his soul to the officer was his anger at Scheele because he was owed $134 in back pay and Scheele would not pay up.

The officer asked von Kleist if he would be willing to meet with a man, who was close to Wolf von Igel and in a position to get von Kleist his back pay if what he said was true. Without any hesitation, von Kleist agreed.

Several days later the Bomb Squad officer and one of his colleagues, posing as the man close to von Igel, met with von Kleist. Again von Kleist repeated his story and offered to show the two officers proof. He took them to the back yard of his house where he dug up one of the empty bomb containers.

The officers then proceeded to arrest von Kleist and took him to their headquarters. Thomas Tunney, the chief of the Bomb Squad, interviewed von Kleist, who repeated his story. After von Kleist was finished, Tunney stepped out of the room for several minutes. A workman was nearby repairing a light fixture and von Kleist, having heard the workman speak some English with a German accent, asked the workman if he would deliver notes to several people. The workman agreed.

Oblivious to the fact that he had been conned twice by two police officers pretending to be someone they were not, von Kleist readily accepted the workman as a legitimate workman. In fact, the workman was another police officer planted in the room. The police used the notes written by Von Kleist as calling cards.

Unfortunately, Scheele escaped arrest and fled to Cuba but was later arrested by the Havana police. The other members of Scheele's operation and von

Kleist were tried, convicted and sentenced to 18 months in jail.

In late April, Rintelen met David Lamar at the offices of Frederico Stallforth, a German citizen and financier, who provided funds to Poncho Villa. Lamar, a U.S. citizen, was formerly employed by J.P. Morgan & Co. but was dismissed and became a crooked stock manipulator known as the "Wolf of Wall Street." Rintelen and Lamar conceived a plan to foment strikes in munitions factories and shipping agencies. Their goal was to force an embargo on munitions by Presidential or Congressional action, hinder the manufacture and shipping of munitions by attacks on financial institutions and by litigation against pro-Ally business organizations, to create a peace sentiment in the country, and to crystallize pro-German sentiment.

Rintelen provided $300,000 to $400,000 to Lamar, who was considered to be the brains and the propelling force behind the conspiracy. Lamar's experience on Wall Street and his anti-trust agitation, his knowledge of conditions and individuals, his genius for manipulation and his lack of scruples, seemed an ideal fit for Rintelen's plan. However, Rintelen later realized that Lamar had swindled him.

Lamar's scam of Rintelen did not mean that the plan was not put into effect. The group hired Frank Buchanan, former President of the International Union of Structural Workers, who was serving in Congress as the representative of the Seventh District (Northern Chicago area). Buchanan was expected to introduce and lead the fight in Congress for embargo legislation. He served the cause well until he was paid; thereafter he went on a prolonged drunk and was useless.

Rintelen was now under intense investigation by American authorities. He decided to leave the United States. Having failed to procure an American passport, he used his Swiss passport in the name of Emile Gasche on which he had entered the U.S. He departed the United States on 3 August 1915 aboard the *Noordam*. When he arrived in Britain on 13 August, British port Control officers arrested him. The British interned him.

Rintelen and several others were indicted by a Federal Grand Jury in December 1915, under the Sherman Act for conspiracy to instigate strikes.

However, it wasn't until April 1917 that Rintelen was extradited to the United States from Great Britain. Rintelen was tried, convicted and sentenced to one year in prison. This was the first of several indictments of Rintelen. He was later indicted, tried and convicted of a conspiracy to obtain a U.S. passport by perjury, for a plot to destroy the ship S.S. *Kirk Oswald*, and for firebomb conspiracy.

In his jail cell in the Tombs, in New York City, Rintelen asked the Swiss Embassy to protest to the German government concerning his treatment and requested retaliation against members of the Allied Mission to Russia. The German government, through the Swiss Embassy, presented a note to the State Department regarding Rintelen. In the note, they stated that they have been unable to effect an improvement in the situation of Rintelen or his release and threaten reprisals. They proposed to exchange Rintelen for one Siegfried Paul London, who was condemned in Warsaw as a spy.

Secretary of State Robert Lansing answered the note, refusing to consider the release of Rintelen. He denied that reprisals in such a case would be legitimate and suggested that the German Government consider the large number of German subjects interned in the United States who could be made the subject of similar action.

Black Tom Island

The single, most important munitions and gunpowder assembly and shipping center in the United States to supply the Allies was located at Black Tom Island in New York harbor. Because of its importance, it became an obvious target for sabotage. For more than one year the German sabotage leaders, von Papen and Boy-Ed, focused on the facility and viewed it as a critically important target that had to be hit. Despite the recall of von Papen and Boy-Ed in 1915, the targeting of the Black Tom Island facility continued.

On Sunday, 30 July 1916 New York harbor "erupted in one of the greatest military explosions prior to the holocaust of Hiroshima nearly four decades later."[87] Several days after the explosion had destroyed the entire facility, federal officials and the media attributed the massive blast to carelessness not to sabotage. In fact, the investigation by the police departments of New York and New Jersey and by federal authorities, which lasted many years, failed to clearly determine how the tremendous blaze originated.

The Bayonne police department acquired the first lead when Anna Chapman contacted them to report her suspicions regarding a lodger at her boarding house. She told Captain John J. Rigney, chief of the police department that her lodger, Michael Kristoff, had returned to the house about 4 A.M. the morning of the explosion and proceeded to pace the floor for a long time. She further stated that she had noticed that whenever Kristoff was out-of-town there had been reported explosions or fires at those locations. She further added that one-day she observed a letter written by Kristoff to an individual, whose name was something like Graentnor, demanding large sums of money.

The Bayonne Police Department contacted the New York City Bomb Squad and the Department of Justice to brief them on Chapman's information. Surveillance of Kristoff began and for three weeks he was followed. The police eventually arrested him but no real evidence had been gathered to make the prosecution's case and he was released.

The Lehigh Valley Railroad hired the William J. Burns Detective Agency to investigate Kristoff. One of the detectives gained Kristoff's confidence by using the cover as an anarchist. Kristoff told the detective that he was responsible for the Black Tom Island blast. He also introduced the detective to David Grossman, who confirmed Kristoff's involvement in the Black Tom Island affair.

The Kingsland Site

Following the success of Black Tom Island, the next target selected by the German saboteurs was the Canadian Car and Foundry Company at Kingsland. The company had been contracted by the Russians to manufacture artillery shells. The company executives decided not to take any chances with security for their plant. They constructed a six-foot fence around the plant and hired security guards to conduct 24-hour patrols around the perimeter and to screen each worked as they entered the plant.

The group of saboteurs operated under the direction of Frederick Hinsch. Hinsch recruited a German national Curt Thummel, who changed his name to Charles Thorne. Hinsch instructed Thorne to obtain employment at the Kingsland site. Thorne is hired as assistant employment manager. In this position he facilitated the hiring of several operatives sent by Hinsch to infiltrate the factory. One of the men hired is Theodore Wozniak.

Unknown to the saboteurs, a British spy informed the British Secret Service that an individual by the name of Wozniak is a German or Austrian agent. According to the British source, Wozniak has obtained employment with a company located in Kingsland. Fortunately for the saboteurs, the British ignored the information.

After the Kingsland plant is completely destroyed, police and federal investigators uncovered the source of the fire. It started at Wozniak's workbench in Building 30. Like the Black Tom Island explosion, there is no conjecture that sabotage caused the destruction.

Executives of the company launched their own investigation and it pointed to Wozniak. They engaged the services of private detectives to follow Wozniak but he slipped away from them and disappeared.

When the United States declares war on Germany, the German Ambassador von Bernstorff returned home. Three days later, on 17 February 1917, three Germans are arrested for attempting to sabotage the Black Tom Island facility, which had been rebuilt. Under a wartime situation, sabotage was no longer an option since the penalty was death to anyone caught in the act. With the ringleaders gone, the other German saboteurs fled the United States.

Department Of State And Counterintelligence[88]

Shortly after the Office of the Chief Special Agent in Washington was created in 1916, Joseph "Bill" Nye was appointed the first chief special agent. Nye, who also held the title of special assistant to the Secretary of State, reported directly to Secretary of

State, Robert Lansing. The office worked out of two locations, Washington and New York, and operated on confidential funds from the Secretary's Office.

There was no formal reporting of the Office's activities and there was no listing of the Office in the Department's organization or telephone book. The size of the Office was never mentioned, but there were a handful of agents plus some "dollar-a-year" men who had volunteered their services-businessmen, lawyers and from other professions. They covered the entire United States in their operations, and some were sent overseas on special missions.

In 1916, as the United States entry in World War I loomed on the horizon, Secretary Lansing directed Nye to tap the telephones of the German embassy in Washington and report directly to him, daily. Who made the actual telephone tap installation was never mentioned but it was quite clear that the Office of the Chief Special Agent performed the monitoring operation.

One important result of the tap pertained to the Zimmerman Telegram. Nye was able to report in advance to the Secretary why the German ambassador was going to call on him at 4 p.m. on January 31, 1917. At that meeting, the ambassador advised Lansing that the German government would launch unrestricted submarine warfare in the Atlantic the next day. Nearly four weeks later, President Woodrow Wilson addressed Congress, asking for a declaration of war.

Each morning at 8 the chief special agent placed on the Secretary's desk a memorandum summarizing information developed during the proceeding 24 hours. Many projects were apparently assigned or approved directly by the Secretary and were reported back only to him.

After World War I, the scope of the Office's special activities diminished greatly. Robert C. Bannerman replaced Nye in 1920. The dollar-a-year men departed, leaving a few agents working out of the New York office, with only the chief special agent left in Washington. In 1927 the chief special agent began reporting to the assistant secretary for administration, Wilbur Carr. However, he still retained his title of special assistant to the Secretary and did report directly to him on sensitive matters.

From 1920 to 1940, jurisdiction for investigation of passport and visa frauds was unclear. Neither Justice, the FBI nor Immigration claimed absolute authority. The Office began to do passport and visa fraud investigations, working with the U.S. attorneys in various cities to obtain prosecutions. In many of these cases, the passport aspect was incidental to a much larger problem-Soviet and German espionage. The investigation of passport frauds in New York led to the discovery of a Soviet intelligence network and succeeded in exposing for the first time the existence of such Soviet operations. In addition, a ring of professional gamblers who operated on the Atlanta run of most steamship lines was broken up through prosecutions on passport frauds.

The accomplishments through the turbulent years of 1920-1940 were carried out by a minimal staff of special agents; at times no more than six. In 1936, when Robert L. Bannerman entered on duty with the Office of the Chief Special Agent in New York City, the New York office had a special agent-in-charge and four special agents. The Washington office

Secretary of State, Robert Lansing

consisted of his father and four clerks; no agents were assigned there.

Some of the duties included passport and visa frauds; special inquiries on behalf of consular officers abroad; various inquiries on individuals and organizations of interest to the Department of State; liaison with all Federal agencies in New York, particularly Immigration and Customs; liaison with the police in New York and the Royal Canadian Mounted Police; arranging port courtesies for visiting foreigners; and providing protective arrangements in the U.S. for visiting heads of state.

All investigations were handled in person; none was conducted by correspondence. Each agent handled about 30 to 40 cases per month. For cases outside New York, the agents would share the travel.

From Robert Lansing, With Enclosure

Private and Confidential

My Dear Mr. President:
Washington November 20, 1915

There has been an unfortunate and probably unavoidable lack of coordination between the different Departments of the Government charged with investigation of violations of law, growing out of the activity of agents of the belligerent Governments in this country. It seems to me that it would be advisable to have a central office to which results of investigations could be reported day by day and the proper steps taken to continue such investigations in the most efficient way. With the idea in view I submit to you a memorandum on the subject. This Department is not anxious to assume additional duties but, unavoidable, all these investigations-or at least the majority of them-have an international phase which should be not only considered but, I think, should control the action of other Departments.

The memorandum rests primarily on the idea that the Counselor for this Department should be the clearing house for the secret reports of the various Departments, and he could-if it seems advisable, and I think it does-furnish duplicates of his information day by day to the Secretary of the Treasury and the Attorney General, who are especially interested in these investigations.

I should be pleased to receive your views upon the subject, or any suggestion which you may have as to a better plan of coordination of work.

Faithfully yours,

Robert Lansing
Enclosure

It is understood that the attached memorandum deals only with the preliminary collection of information and investigations for the purpose of determining the importance of the information received. As soon as it appears that any laws have been violated or apparently violated the case would be turned over to the Department of Justice in the regular and orderly way.

The intent of the plan proposed is to keep this preliminary investigation free from delays and centralized in such a way as to keep the scattered threads together. It is also intended to keep the President accurately informed from day to day and the State Department constantly in touch with what is going on. The daily reports as summarized for the Counselor for the State Department should be forwarded in duplicate to the Secretary of the Treasury and the Attorney General.

Confidential: Memorandum

A great amount of information, some of it important, much of it trivial and a considerable part of it, misleading or absolutely untrue, is coming to various departments of the Government regarding the activities of people throughout the United States, who are alleged to be endangering the friendly relations of this Government with other governments by undertaking unneutral enterprises, some of which are criminal and some of which are merely indiscreet. Almost all of the acts reported, if true, require careful consideration from the viewpoint of our relations with other nations before this Government's action in the matter is determined.

The information may be divided roughly into information as to acts violating a law and for which the offenders can be prosecuted in the courts, and acts which are not technical violations of law but which are calculated to place the United States in the position of permitting violations of neutrality if they are not stopped. Under the latter may properly come certain acts of accredited representatives of foreign governments. Some of these matters can only be handled by confidential representatives to the accredited heads of the foreign governments involved that such acts are distasteful to our Government and must be discontinued.

There is another class of acts committed by citizens of the United States, either entirely on their own initiative or through influences which cannot be definitely traced and which can only be stopped by publicity, and in some cases the matters involved would be of such a delicate nature as to make it inadvisable even to call attention to them in an official way.

This information is at present coming to the Department of State, the War Department, the Navy Department, the United States Secret Service and the Department of Justice. Doubtless other Departments, such as Commerce, Post Office, and even Interior, receive or could gather information as well. It is seldom that information received is sufficiently definite even to warrant investigation and it is only by piecing together information from a number of sources that any practical lead can be obtained. At present there is no assurance that the various scattered scraps of information which when put together make a clear case will go to the same place. For instance, one item may be received by the Secret Service, the Navy may receive other information-all of which, when put side by side, makes a fairly clear case, but none of which when scattered through the different Departments seems of importance. It is evident that a single office where all this information must be instantly transmitted without red tape is absolutely necessary to an effective organization.

In view of the diplomatic questions involved it seems obvious that the receiving office should be under the Department of State. Otherwise grave errors may be made by well meaning but misdirected efforts. After this information has been received there are at present three ways in which it may be taken care of: The Department of Justice, the Secret Service and the Post Office Inspectors. The Department of Justice is charged with the gathering of evidence by which the Attorney General may proceed to prosecute for a definite crime; the Secret Service is charged with the protection of the President and the protection against counterfeiting and customs frauds; the Post Office Department is charged with watching for violations of the United States mail. None of these Departments is legally or by organization fitted to handle these matters alone and efficient cooperation without a central directing force with authority to supervise their operations and to assign them their respective work cannot be accomplished practically. There is the further objection that a case turned over by the State Department to any one of these investigating departments or bureaus is lost sight of and its daily developments are unknown for weeks and sometimes months.

To cure this situation, it is suggested:

That an Executive Order be issued placing all these matters under the authority of the Department of State, directing all Government officials and Departments to transmit immediately to the Department of State any information received along these lines and to collect at the request of that Department any information asked for. The Order should also direct that the Post Office Department, the Secret Service and the Department of Justice place their men when requested at the disposal of the Department of State for the purpose of investigating these matters.

It is suggested that the Department of State should assign the Counselor, as being able to decide the legal questions which sometimes arise, without waiting for reference, as the head of the system, acting, of course, always under the Secretary of State and, through him, under the President himself.

It is not thought that any additional force for the Department of State would be required beyond possibly a thoroughly trustworthy stenographer, and if the work is unusually heavy a filing clerk, as it will be absolutely necessary to maintain a card index and to keep each case separate and up to day.

From Robert Lansing

Personal and Private
My dear Mr. President:
Washington November 29, 1915

I feel that we cannot wait much longer to act in the cases of Boy-Ed, von Papen, and von Nuber. I believe we have enough in regard to the activities of these men to warrant us to demand of the German Government the recall of the first two named and to cancel the exequatur of von Nuber, giving notice to the Austro-Hungarian Government that we have done so.

The increasing public indignation in regard to these men and the general criticism of the Government for allowing them to remain are not the chief reasons for suggesting action in these cases, although I do not think that such reasons should be ignored. We have been over-patient with these people on account of the greater controversies under consideration for several months and did not wish to add to the difficulties of the situation by injecting another cause of difference. In my opinion action now cannot seriously affect the pending negotiations, and it would be well to act as expeditiously as possible.

In case you agree with me as to the action which should be taken would you favor informing Bernstorff orally that his attaches are *personae non gratae* or make a formal written statement to that effect without telling him in advance?

In the von Nuber case I would suggest that the Austrian Charge be told that we intend to cancel the *exequatur* of von Nuber.

As you know, I believe that we will soon have to go even higher up in removing from this country representatives of belligerents who are directing operations here. It would appear that these higher officials consider our patience to be cowardice. If this is so, the removal of subordinates would indicate our earnest purpose and would, I believe, help rather than hinder the progress of present negotiations.

I hope a decision can be reached speedily in this matter, as it should in my judgment be done, if at all, before Congress meets.

I enclose memoranda on German and Austrian officials here, among which you will find statements regarding the three mentioned.

From Walter Hines Page

London, Feb. 24, 1917,
5747. My fifty-seven-forty-six,
February 24, 8 a.m.

Confidential, For the President and the Secretary of State.

Balfour has handed me the text of a cipher telegram from Zimmermann, German Secretary of State for Foreign Affairs, to the German Minister to Mexico,[89] which was sent via Washington and relayed to Bernstorff on January nineteenth. You can probably obtain a copy of the text relayed by Bernstorff from the cable office in Washington. The first group is the number of the telegram, one hundred and thirty, and the second is thirteen thousand and forty-two, indicating the number of the code used. The last group but two is ninety-seven thousand five hundred and fifty-six, with Zimmerman's signature. I shall send you by mail a copy of the cipher text and of the de-code into German and meanwhile I give you the English translation as follows:

"We intend to begin on the first of February unrestricted submarine warfare. We shall endeavor in spite of this to keep the United States of America neutral. In the event of this not succeeding, we make Mexico a proposal of alliance on the following basis: make war together, make peace together, generous financial support and an understanding on our part that Mexico is to reconquer the lost territory in Texas, New Mexico, and Arizona. The settlement in detail is left to you. You will inform the President of the above most secretly as soon as the outbreak of war with the United States of America is certain and add the suggestion that he should, on his own initiative, invite Japan to immediate adherence and at the same time mediate between Japan and ourselves. Please call the President's attention to the fact that the ruthless employment of our submarines now offers the prospect of compelling England in a few months to make peace. Signed, ZIMMERMAN."

The receipt of this information has so greatly exercised the British Government that they have lost no time in communicating it to me to transmit to you, in order that our government may be able without delay to make such disposition as may be necessary in view of the threatened invasion of our territory.

The following paragraph is strictly confidential.

Early in the war, the British Government obtained possession of a copy of the German cipher code used in the above message and have made it their business to obtain copies of Bernstorff's cipher telegrams to Mexico, amongst others, which are sent back to London and deciphered here. This accounts for their being able to decipher this telegram from the German Government to their representative in Mexico and also for the delay from January nineteenth until now in their receiving the information. This system has hitherto been a jealously guarded secret and is only divulged now to you by the British Government in view of the extraordinary circumstances and their friendly feeling towards the United States. They earnestly request that you will keep the source of your information and the British Government's method of obtaining it profoundly secret but they put no prohibition on the publication of Zimmermann's telegram itself.

The copies of this and other telegrams were not obtained in Washington but were bought in Mexico.

Zimmerman Telegram

I have thanked Balfour for the service his Government has rendered us and suggest that a private official message of thanks from our Government to him would be beneficial.

I am informed that this information has not yet been given to the Japanese Government but I think it not unlikely that when it reaches them they may make a public statement on it in order to clear up their position regarding the United States and prove their good faith to their allies.

President Woodrow Wilson discussing his dilemma at the time of the Zimmerman Telegram:

You have got to think of the President of the United States as the chief counsellor of the Nation, elected for a little while but as a man meant constantly and every day to be the Commander in Chief of the Army and Navy of the United States, ready to order them to any part of the world where the threat of war is a menace to his own people.

And you cannot do that under free debate. You cannot do that under public counsel. Plans must be kept secret.

Knowledge must be accumulated by a system which we have condemned, because it is a spying system. The more polite call it a system of intelligence.

You cannot watch other nations with your unassisted eye. You have to watch them with secret agencies planted everywhere.

Let me testify to this my fellow citizens, I not only did not know it until we got into this war, but did not believe it when I was told that it was true, that Germany was not the only country that maintained a secret service. Every country in Europe maintained it, because they had to be ready for Germany's spring upon them, and the only difference between the German secret service and the other secret services was that the German secret service found out more than the others did, and therefore Germany sprang upon the other nations unaware, and they were not ready for it.

Counterintelligence: Pre-World War I

The first federal domestic counterintelligence program originated shortly before the United States entered World War I in 1917. The initial threat perceived by federal officials was the activity of German agents, including sabotage and espionage directed at the United States in the period before America entered the war. Although the neutrality laws were on the books, no federal statue made espionage or sabotage a crime. Attorney General Thomas W. Gregory proposed such legislation in 1916, but Congress took no action before American entry into the war. Nonetheless, the Executive Branch went ahead with development of a domestic security intelligence capability.

Several federal agencies expanded their operations. The Secret Service, which was established in the Treasury Department to investigate counterfeiting in 1865, had served as the main civilian intelligence agency during the Spanish American War. With $50,000 in War Department funds, the Secret Service had organized an emergency auxiliary force to track down Spanish spies, placed hundreds of civilians under surveillance, and asked the Army to arrest a number of alleged spies.[90] After the assassination of President William McKinley by an anarchist in 1901, the Secret Service was authorized to protect the President. Its agents were also assigned to the Justice Department as investigators until 1908 when Congress forbade the practice. In 1915 Secretary of State William Jennings Bryan decided that German diplomats should be investigated for possible espionage and he requested and received President Woodrow Wilson's permission to use the Secret Service.[91]

The military had performed extensive security intelligence functions during the Civil War, although operations were largely delegated to commanders in the field. When the military discontinued its surveillance programs after the War of Northern Aggression, as the South refers to the Civil War, Allan Pinkerton, who had worked for the War Department under President Abraham Lincoln founded a private detective agency. The Pinkerton agency and other private detective forces served both government and private employers in later years, frequently to spy upon labor organizing activities.[92] In the year immediately before American entry into World War I, military intelligence lacked the resources to engage in intelligence operations. Therefore, preparation for war rested largely with the Secret Service, and it main competitor, the Justice Department's Bureau of Investigation.

The Justice Department's investigative authority stemmed from an appropriation statue first enacted in 1871, allowing the Attorney General to expend funds for "the detection and prosecution of crimes against the United States."[93] The Attorney General initially employed several permanent investigators and supplemented them with either private detectives or Secret Service agents. When Congress prohibited such use of Secret Service personnel in 1908, Attorney General Charles J. Bonaparte issued an order authorizing creation of the Bureau of Investigation. There was no formal Congressional authorization for the Bureau, but once it was established, its appropriations were regularly approved by Congress. Members of the House Appropriations Committee debated with Attorney General Bonaparte over the need for safeguards against abuse by the new Bureau. Bonaparte emphasized, "The Attorney General knows or ought to know, at all times what they are doing." Some Congressmen thought more limits were needed, but nothing was done to circumscribe the Bureau's powers.[94]

A Navy Spy

On 5 May 1917, George Roenitz, ex-chief clerk of the Commandant, Naval Station, Pearl Harbor, was arrested and charged with espionage. Rather than stand trial, Roenitz plead guilty to a charge of unlawful possession of documents pertaining to the Naval Station and received a one year prison sentence and a fine of $250. Because he was discharged from the military in February 1917, Roenitz could not be courts-martial and was sentenced in civilian court. There was no information that he had passed the information on to a foreign power but he was suspected of being a German spy.

Passage of the Mann Act and other federal statues prohibiting interstate traffic in stolen goods, obscene materials, and prizefight films soon expanded the criminal investigative responsibilities of the Justice Department and its Bureau of Investigation.

By 1916 Attorney General Gregory had expanded the Bureau's personnel from 100 to 300 agents, primarily to investigate possible violations of the neutrality laws. The Attorney General objected to the Secret Service's investigations of activities which did not involve actual violations of federal laws. However, when President Wilson and Secretary of State Robert Lansing expressed continued interest in such investigations, Attorney General Gregory went to Congress for an amendment to the Justice Department's appropriations statute which would allow the Bureau to do what the Secret Service had already begun doing. With the agreement of the State Department, the statute was revised to permit the Attorney General to appoint officials not only to detect federal crimes, but also "to conduct such other investigations regarding official matters under the control of the Department of Justice or the Department of State, as may be directed by the Attorney General."

This amendment to the appropriations statute was intended to be an indirect form of authorization for investigations by the Bureau of the Investigation, although a State Department request was seen as a prerequisite for such inquiries.[95]

Under the direction of A. Bruce Bielaski, the Bureau concentrated at first on investigations of potential enemy aliens in the United States. According to the authorative history of the Justice Department:

The Bureau of Investigation made an index of aliens under suspicion. At the end of March 1917, just before the entrance of the United States into the war, the chief of the Bureau submitted a list of five classes of persons. One class, ninety-eight in number, should be arrested immediately on declaration of war. One hundred and forty should be required to give bond. Five hundred and seventy-four were strongly suspected. Five hundred and eighty-nine had not been fully cleared of suspicion. Three hundred and sixty-seven had been cleared of specific offenses. Others, after investigation, had been eliminated from the lists.[96]

In 1885 the Executive Office Building, then known as the State, War and Navy Building in Washington, D.C., was the first home of Army Intellegince.

Theoretically, the threat of dangerous aliens was the responsibility of the Immigration Bureau in the Labor Department. As early as 1903 Congress had enacted legislation requiring the deportation within three years of entry of persons holding anarchist beliefs or advocating "the overthrow by force or violence of the Government of the United States."[97] In early 1917 the immigration laws were amended to eliminate the three year limit and require deportation of any alien "found advocating or teaching the unlawful destruction of property...or the overthrow by force or violence of the Government of the United States."[98] Nevertheless the Immigration Bureau lacked the men, ability, and time to conduct the kind of investigations contemplated by the statute.[99]

As the United States entered World War I, domestic security investigations were the province of two competing civilian agencies-the Secret Service and the Bureau of Investigation-soon to be joined by military intelligence and an extensive private intelligence network called the American Protective League.

The American Protective League

The American Protective League (APL) was a voluntary association of patriotic citizens acting through local branches which were established in cities and counties throughout the country to operate under the control of a National Board of Directors. The league was formally created on 22 March 1917, two weeks before the American declaration of war,

Bruce Bielaski

and, on that same date, became designated as an auxiliary to the Bureau of Investigation of the Department of Justice.[100] The orginal idea for such an organization had been conceived by *A.M. Briggs* of Chicago, who then continued to function as Chairman of the National Board of Directors. The two other members of this national triumverate were *Victor Elting* and *Charles Daniel Frey*. The league itself was ultimately composed of some 250,000 male citizens, representing "every commercial, industrial, professional, social and economic level in American life."[101] Moreover, its members were provided with credentials in the form of a membership card and badge showing that the holder was connected with the Department of Justice.[102] These cards were actually issued in certain circumstances by the military intelligence division.

Although strongly supported during its entire career by Attorney General Thomas W. Gregory, the APL was never free from violent criticism. In June 1917, for example, Secretary of the Treasury William G. McAdoo, who was always on the alert to prevent any unauthorized use of the words "secret service" by an agency other than his own Secret Service of the United States, not only wrote to Gregory to register a complaint[103] but also to President Wilson himself in order to lodge a general protest against the whole organization. For the President, McAdoo even chose to compare the APL with the Sons of Liberty of the American Revolution "through which many injustices and abuses resulted."[104] This historical comparison by McAdoo is neither cogent nor valid. A more fitting description of the prejudicial side of the APL would be the New York Bar Association Report of 1919 which discussed vigilante associations in World War I:

> *"...These associations did much good in awakening the public to the danger of insidious propaganda but no other one cause contributed so much to the oppression of innocent men as the systematic and indiscrimate agitation against what was claimed to be an all pervasive system of German espionage."*

Defending the league, however, Gregory was able to answer McAdoo:

> *"...you state that your attention has been called to this association and that it seems to you it would be dangerous to have such an organization operating*

in the United States, and you ask if there is any way which we could stop it...Briefly stated, the American Protective League is a patriotic organization, composed of from eighty to one hundred thousand members, with branches in almost six hundred cities and towns, was organized with my approval and encouragement, and has been tremendously helpful in the work of the Bureau of Investigation of the Department of Justice. It has no official status and claims none. Its members serve without the slightest expense to the Government, and not a single officer or member receives compensation from any source."[105]

Beyond any question, the APL did provide the military security officials of the War Department with a tremendous amount of invaluable assistance in the conduct of their many difficult investigative chores. It was found convenient during November 1917, therefore, after the headquarters of the league moved from Chicago to Washington, to commission Charles Daniel Frey, one of the three national directors, as an Army captain. While still remaining a league official, he was then assigned to the departmental military intelligence agency for the express purpose of processing all cases requiring APL action. This task soon assumed such proportions that a regular APL liaison group was established and, in April 1918, made a separate subsection of MI.3. The civilian chief of this new group was Urban A. Lavery, who continued to act in that role until September 1918, when he was replaced by Captain John T. Evans. By the time of the Armistice, the APL subsection was using the services of 39 clerks, stenographers and typists.

Counterintelligence In World War I

Shortly after the declaration of war, Congress considerably strengthened the legal basis for federal investigations by enacting the Espionage Act of 1917, the Selective Service and Training Act, and other statutes designed to use criminal sanctions to assist the war effort. But Congress did not clarify the jurisdiction of the various civilian and military intelligence agencies. The Secretary of War established a Military Intelligence Section under Colonel Ralph Van Deman, who immediately began training intelligence officers and organizing civilian volunteers to protect defense plants. By the end of 1917 the MIS had branch offices throughout the United States to conduct investigations of military personnel and civilians working for the War Department. MIS agents cooperated with British intelligence in Mexico, with their joint efforts leading

American Protective League Publication

National Directors, American Protective League (l-r) Charles Frey, Albert Briggs, Victor Elting.

to the arrest of a German espionage agent during the war.[106]

A major expansion of federal intelligence activity took place with the formation of the American Protective League, which worked directly with the Bureau of Investigation and military intelligence. A recent FBI study recounts how the added burdens of wartime work led to the creation of the League:

To respond to the problem, Attorney General Thomas W. Gregory and then Bureau Chief A. Bruce Bielaski, conceived what they felt might suffice to answer the problem. The American Protective League (APL) composed of well-meaning private individuals, was formed as a citizen's auxiliary to "assist" the Bureau of Investigation. In addition to the authorized auxiliary, ad hoc groups too it upon themselves to "investigate" what they felt were un-American activities. Though the intentions of both groups were undoubtedly patriotic and in some instances beneficial, the overall result was the denial of constitutional safeguards and administrative confusion. To see the problem, one need only to consider the mass deprivation of rights incident to the deserter and selective service violator raids in New York and New Jersey in 1918, wherein 35 agents assisted by 2,000 APL operatives, 2,350 military personnel, and several hundred police rounded up some 50,000 men without warrants of sufficient probable cause for arrest. Of the 50,000 arrestees, approximately 1,500 were inducted into the military service and 15,000 were referred to draft boards.[107]

The FBI study also cites the recollection of an Agent of the Bureau of Investigation during World War I regarding the duplication of effort:

How did we function with relation to other agencies, both federal and state? In answering this query, I might say that while our relationship with the Army and Navy Departments was extremely cordial at all times, nevertheless there was at all times an enormous overlapping of investigative activities among the various agencies charged with winning the war. There were probably seven or eight such active organizations operating at full force during the war days and it was not an uncommon experience for an Agent of this Bureau to call upon an individual in the course of his investigation, to find out that six or seven other government agencies had been around to interview the party about the same matter.[108]

The Secret Service opposed the utilization of American Protective League volunteers and recommended, through Treasury Secretary McAdoo, establishment of a centralized body to coordinate domestic intelligence work. The Treasury Department's proposal was rejected in early 1918, because of the objections of Colonel Van Deman, Bureau Chief Bielaski, and the Attorney General's Special Assistant for war matters, John Lord O'Brien. Thereafter the role of the Secret Service in intelligence operations diminished in importance.[109]

During World War I the threat to the nation's security and the war effort was perceived by both government and private intelligence agencies as extending far beyond activities of enemy agents. Criticism of the war, opposition to the draft, expression of pro-German or pacifist sympathies, and militant labor organizing efforts were all considered dangerous and targeted for investigation and often prosecution under federal or state statutes. The federal Espionage Act forbade making false statements with intent to interfere with the success of military, attempting to cause insubordination, and obstructing recruitment of troops.[110] With little guidance from the Attorney General, the United States Attorneys across the country brought nearly 2,000 prosecutions under the Espionage Act for disloyal utterances.[111] Not until the last month of the war did Attorney General Gregory require federal prosecutors to obtain approval from Washington before bringing Espionage Act prosecutions. John Lord O'Brien, the Attorney General's Special Assistant, recalled "the immense pressure brought to bear throughout the war upon the Department of Justice in all parts of the country for indiscriminate prosecution demanded in behalf of a policy of wholesale repression and restraint of public opinion."[112]

In addition to providing information for Espionage Act prosecutions, intelligence operations laid the foundation for the arrest, of which some 2,300 were turned over to military authorities for internment and the remainder released or placed on parole.[113]

War Department General Order

26 August 1918

This order reestablished the Military Intelligence Division (MID), General Staff when it re-formed the General Staff into four divisions designated: Operations; Military Intelligence; Purchase, Storage and Traffic; and Plans. Appointed to head the reestablished MID was Col. Marlborough Churchill. The functional assignment then given to the new Division was:

This division shall have cognizance and control of military intelligence, both positive and negative, and shall be in charge of an officer designated as the director of military intelligence, who will be an assistant to the Chief of Staff. He is also the chief military censor. The duties of this division are to maintain estimates revised daily of the military situation, the economic situation, and of such other matters as the Chief of Staff may direct, and to collect, collate, and disseminate military intelligence. It will cooperate with the intelligence section of the general staffs of allied counties in commection with military intelligence; prepare instructions in military intelligence work for the use of our forces; supervise the training of personnel for intelligence work; organize, direct, and coordinate the intelligence service; supervise the duties of military attaches; communicate direct with department intelligence officers and intelligence officers at posts, camps, and stations; and with commands in the field in matters relating to military intelligence; obtain, reproduce and issue maps; translate foreign documents; disburse and account for intelligence funds; cooperate with the censorship board and with intelligence agencies of other departments.

The term "negative" intelligence fell into gradual disgrace following World War I and was replaced by "counterintellugence."

From Albert Sidney Burleson

Dear Mr. President:
(Washington) November 30, 1918

I am this moment in receipt of your letter of date November 27th in which you express the opinion that the mail censorship is no longer performing a necessary function. I thoroughly concur in the view expressed and shall accept your letter as a direction to me to bring same to an end.

On the same day you wrote me I received a letter from Mr. Swagar Sherley, Chairman of the Committee on Appropriations, advising me that "it is the purpose of the Committee on Appropriations of the House of Representatives to begin hearings next Monday with the view of returning to the Treasury such appropriations and the cancellation of such authorizations, or parts thereof, granted in connection with the prosecution of the war, as no longer may be required under present conditions" and requesting me to take immediate steps to furnish him "the available information" upon which the Committee could base action looking to the accomplishment of its purpose. I will make known to the Chairman of the Committee on Appropriations the action which has been take in connection with mail censorship and also advise him that I have reduced the clerical force used in connection with the enforcement of Espionage and Trading with the Enemy Acts in so far as they relate to the Postal Establishment to the lowest possible basis. These are the only activities carrying appropriations which

Gen. Marlborough Churchill

Post Civil War

have been imposed on the Post Office Department during the progress of the war.

Faithfully yours,

A.S. Burleson

From Newton Diehl Baker

Dear Mr. President:
Washington, December 27, 1918

It is suggested that in view of the armistice, it would be advisable to modify the Executive Order of September 26, 1918, concerning the censorship of submarine cables, telegraph and telephone lines as far as it affects the telegraphic and telephonic censorship.

The pressure of military necessity is removed, and the activities of the German agents in Mexico are no longer of a sort to require so elaborate and expensive an organization for their observation or control.

Pursuant to the Freedom of Information Act, 5 U.S.C. §552B(4), the article: "The Witzke Affair: German Intrigue On The Mexican Border", pp.114-122, has been redacted at the request of the author.

This page intentionally left blank.

Post Civil War

This page intentionally left blank.

This page intentionally left blank.

Post Civil War

This page intentionally left blank.

This page intentionally left blank.

Post Civil War

This page intentionally left blank.

This page intentionally left blank.

Post Civil War

The Espionage Act
May 16, 1918

Be it enacted, That section three of the Act...approved June 15, 1917, be...amended so as to read as follows:

Section 3. Whoever, when the United States is at war, shall willfully make or convey false reports or false statements with intent to interfere with the operation or success of the military or naval forces of the Unites States, or to promote the success of its enemies, or shall willfully make or convey false reports or false statements, or say or do anything except by way of bona fide and not disloyal advice to an investor...with intent to obstruct the sale by the United States of bonds...or the making of loans by or to the United States, or whoever, when the United States is at war, shall willfully cause...or incite... insubordination, disloyalty, mutiny, or refusal of duty, in the military or naval forces of the United States, or shall willfully obstruct...the recruiting or enlistment service of the United States, and whoever, when the United States is at war, shall willfully utter, print, write, or publish any disloyal, profane, scurrilous, or abusive language about the form of government of the United States, or the Constitution of the United States, or the military or naval forces of the United States, or the flag...or the uniform of the Army or Navy of the United States, or any language intended to bring the form of government...or the Constitution...or the military or naval forces...or the flag...of the United States into contempt, scorn, contumely, or disrepute...or shall willfully display the flag of any foreign enemy, or shall willfully...urge, incite, or advocate any curtailment of production in this county of any thing or things...necessary or essential to the prosecution of the war...and whoever shall willfully advocate, teach, defend, or suggest the doing of any of the acts or things in this section enumerated and whoever shall by word or act support or favor the cause of any country with which the United States is at war or by word or act oppose the cause of the United States therein, shall be punished by a fine of not more than $10,000 or imprisonment for not more than twenty years, or both...

From Edward Mandell House

Paris Nov 12, 1918

Number 99. Secret for the President. Referring further to our number 61, I beg to suggest the following:

The whole problem of securing political intelligence, establishing an adequate counter espionage organization and providing protection for you and for the personnel, papers, and property of the American representatives at the Peace Conference should be dealt with, I believe along the following lines:

I. *Political Intelligence*

At the present time the United States officials in Europe charged with considering political and economic questions presented by the termination of the war are receiving practically no dependable information concerning political and economic conditions in the following countries: Poland, Bohemia, Ukraine, Austria, Servia (including Yugo-Slavia), Hungary, Bulgaria, Albania and Turkey. From Roumania and Greece some information is obtained but it is very incomplete. I consider it essential that we at once set up instrumentalities in these localities which will furnish us with information concerning political conditions in these countries and that this information concerning political conditions in these countries and that this information should come to us through American eyes. I do not think it will be difficult promptly to set up an organization for this purpose and I suggest that I be authorized to proceed along the following lines:

A. After conferring with Hoover and learning his plans for relief, to select men from among the United States military and naval forces now in Europe and from any other available sources, who shall be appointed for the time being agents of the Department of State. These men to constitute the basis of a "political intelligence section" of the American delegation to the Peace Conference.

B. To dispatch the men so selected as soon as practicable to do so, to points such as Warsaw, Lemberg, Posen, Prague, Bern (Moravia), Budapest (and some point in Transylvania), Kiev, Serejevo, Scutari, Constantinople, and Odessa. One agent should be sent to each place and he should take with him one code clerk with codes, one stenographer and if necessary one interpreter. A courier service also will shortly have to be established to operate between the United States and individual agents and their base from which messages could be forwarded by telegraph to Paris.

C. These agents so selected not to be in any sense accredited to the countries in which they are located. The military and naval men will of course not wear their uniforms. So far as possible the Governments in the localities to which they are sent will be requested to give them assistance in the conduct of their work. These men would work in close cooperation with any relief (arrangements?) (agencies) set up by Hoover.

D. To set up at some point in the Balkans, such as possibly Bucharest, a central office to which these agents can forward (probably for the President by courier only) their reports for transmission to the United States via Paris.

E. To establish at Paris for the assistance of the American delegation at the Peace Conference a "political intelligence section" under the direction of Grew and such other persons as the State Department may send to help him to which would be forwarded all reports from these agents and from other agents of the Department of State already constituted in European countries.

II. *Counter Espionage Organization*

I have conferred with General Nolan the head of the United States Military Intelligence in Europe and I believe that this work should be handed over to him and I suggest that a civil official of the Department of State who has an appreciation of the duty of work desired done should be associated with him.

III. *The protection of the President and of the American delegation at the Peace Conference and their papers and property.*

I suggest that the most practical method of handling this problem is through the use of the military authorities working under the direction of General Nolan who is entirely familiar with the peculiar conditions presented by this kind of work in France.

Almost all of the personnel to do the work outlined in paragraph one can be obtained here in Europe. I should very much appreciate an expression of your views respecting this important matter. If the plan as outlined is promptly approved it can be put into operation before the Peace Conference is called.

Edward House

The Red Scare Period

The end of the war in 1918 did not bring about the termination of counterintelligence operations. The Bureau of Investigation shifted its attention from critics of the war to the activities of radical and anarchist groups. The new threat was dramatized vividly by a series of terrorist bombings in 1919, including one explosion on the doorstep of Attorney General A. Mitchell Palmer's residence. Congress responded with calls for action, although the applicable provisions of the Espionage Act had expired at the end of the war and no new federal criminal statute was enacted to replace it. Instead, state statutes and the deportation provisions of the Immigration Act became the basis for the federal response.

Attorney General Palmer authorized two major revisions in Justice Department counterintelligence operations in 1919. First, he established a General Intelligence Division in the Justice Department, headed by J. Edgar Hoover, who had served during the war as head of the Department's program for compiling information on enemy aliens. At the same time, Palmer appointed William J. Flynn, former head of the Secret Service, as Director of the Bureau of Investigation.

Less than two weeks after the GID was established, Flynn ordered a major expansion of Bureau investigations "of anarchistic and similar classes, Bolshevism, and kindred agitation advocating change in sedition and revolution, bomb throwing, and similar activities." Since the only available federal law was the deportation statute, Flynn stressed that the investigations "should be particularly directed to persons not citizens of the United States." Nevertheless, he also directed Bureau agents to "make full investigations of similar activities of citizens of the United States with a view to securing evidence which may be of use in prosecutions under the present existing state or federal laws or under legislation of that nature which may hereinafter be enacted." The instructions discussed the provisions of the recent amendments to the Immigration Act, which expanded the grounds for deportation to include membership in revolutionary organizations as well as individual advocacy of violent overthrow of the government.[156] Director Flynn concluded by urging Bureau agents to "constantly keep in mind the necessity of preserving the cover of our confidential informants."[157]

The results of these investigations were reported to the Department's General Intelligence Division for analysis and evaluation. Overall direction of the work of the GID under Hoover and the Bureau under Flynn was placed in the hands of an Assistant Attorney General Francis P. Garvan, who had been a division chief in the New York district attorney's office before the war.[158]

Historians have documented fully the tremendous pressures placed on Attorney General Palmer, not just by his subordinates, but by public opinion, other members of President Wilson's cabinet, and the Congress to act decisively against the radical threat in 1919. For example, Secretary of State Lansing declared in a private memorandum written in July, "It is no time to temporize or compromise; no time to be timid or undecided; no time to remain passive. We are face to face with an inveterate enemy of the present social order." The Senate unanimously passed a resolution demanding that Palmer inform it whether he had yet begun legal proceedings against those who preached anarchy and sedition. According to his biographer, after passage of the Senate resolution, Palmer decided that the "very liberal" provisions of the Bill of Rights were expendable and that in a time of emergency there were "no limits" on the power of the government "other than the extent of the emergency."[159]

The principal result of the Justice Department's counterintelligence activities, in coordination with Immigration Bureau investigations, was the infamous "Palmer raids" on the night of January 2, 1920. Bureau of Investigation and Immigration Bureau agents in thirty-three cities rounded up some ten thousand persons believed to be members of the Communist and Communist Labor Parties, including many citizens and many individuals not members of either party. A summary of the abuses of due process of law incident to the raids includes "indiscriminate arrests of the innocent with the guilty, unlawful

Attorney General A. Mitchell Palmer.

seizures by federal detectives, intimidating preliminary interrogations of aliens held incommunicado, highhanded levying of excessive bail, and denial of counsel."[160] Apart from the unavoidable administrative confusion in such a large-scale operation, these abuses have been attributed to several crucial decisions by federal officials.

The first was Director Flynn's instructions to Bureau agents that, in order to preserve "the cover of our confidential informants," they should "in no case...rely upon the testimony of such cover informants during deportation proceedings."[161] Consequently, Flynn's assistant Frank Burke, advised the Immigration Bureau that informants should not be called as witnesses and that immigration inspectors should "make an effort to obtain from the subject a statement as to his affiliations." The success of eliciting incriminating admission depended, in turn, upon decisions which made possible the prolonged detention and interrogation of arrested persons without access to counsel. In previous deportation proceedings, defense attorneys had urged aliens to remain silent. Therefore, it was necessary to amend the immigration regulation which allowed "attorneys employed by the arrested persons to participate in the conduct of hearings from their very commencement."[162] The head of the Justice Department's General Intelligence Division, J. Edgar Hoover, reiterated this request for a modification of immigration procedures.[163] Three days before the raids the regulation was revised to permit hearings to begin without the presence of counsel.

Another barrier to effective interrogation was the alien's right to bail. Three weeks after the round-up, J. Edgar Hoover advised the Immigration Bureau that to allow aliens out on bail to see their lawyers "defeats the ends of justice" and made the revision of immigration regulations "virtually of no value."[164] Hoover later told immigration officials that since the purpose of the raids was to suppress agitation, he could not see the sense of letting radicals spread their propaganda while out on bail.[165] He also urged the Immigration Bureau to hold all aliens against whom there was no proof on the chance that evidence might be uncovered at some future date "in other sections of the country."[166] However, despite the Justice Department's pleas, the Secretary of Labor ordered a return to previous policies after the raids, once again allowing detained aliens access to legal counsel and admission to bail if hearings were delayed.[167]

An advantage of the amended Immigration Act had been that aliens could be deported simply for membership in a revolutionary group, without any evidence of their individual activity. J. Edgar Hoover urged literal application of the law to all members regardless of the individual's intent or the circumstances involved in his joining the organization.[168] Nevertheless, the Labor Department refused to deport automatically every Communist Party alien, instead adopting a policy of differentiating between "conscious" and "unconscious" membership, declining to deport those who membership in the Socialist Party had been transferred to the Communist Party without the member's knowledge and those whose cases were based on self-incrimination, without counsel or illegally seized membership records. Assistant Secretary of Labor Louis F. Post, who strongly opposed the Justice Department's position, also defied Congressional threats of impeachment in his vigorous defense of due process of law.[169]

During the months following the "Palmer raids," a group of distinguish lawyers and law professors prepared a report denouncing the violation of law by the Justice Department. They included Dean Roscoe Pound, Felix Frankfurter, and Zechariah Chafee, Jr. of the Harvard Law School, Ernest Freund of the University of Chicago Law School, and other eminent lawyers and legal scholars. The committee found federal agents guilty of using thrid-degree tortures, making illegal searches and arrests, using agent provocateurs, and forcing aliens to incriminate themselves. Its report described federal counterintelligence operations in the following terms:

We do not question the right of the Department of Justice to use its agents in the Bureau of Investigation to ascertain when the law is being violated. But the American people have never tolerated the use of undercover provocative agents or "agents provocateurs" such as have been familiar in old Russia or Spain. Such agents have been introduced by the Department of Justice into radical movements, have reached positions of influence therein, have occupied themselves with informing upon or instigating acts which might be declared criminal, and at the express direction of Washington have brought about meetings of radicals in order to make possible wholesale arrests at such meetings.[170]

The initial reaction of the head of the Justice Department's General Intelligence Division to such criticism was to search the files, including military intelligence files, for evidence that critics had radical associations or beliefs.[171]

The work of the General Intelligence Division was summarized by J. Edgar Hoover in a report prepared later in 1920. Even though federal criminal statutes were "inadequate to properly handle the radical situation," Hoover stressed the "need in the absence of legislation to enable the federal government adequately to defend and protect itself and its institutions (from) not only aliens within the borders of the United States, but also American citizens who are engaged in unlawful agitations." Therefore, in addition to providing intelligence for use in the deportation of aliens, the General Intelligence Division (GID) supplied information to state authorities for the prosecution of American citizens under the broad state sedition laws.

The GID also had expanded "to cover more general intelligence work, including not only the radical activities in the United States and abroad, but also the studying of matters of an international nature, as well as economic and industrial disturbances incident thereto." Hoover described the GID's relationship to the Bureau of Investigation:

While the General Intelligence Division has not participated in the investigation of the overt acts of radicals in the United States, its solo function being that of collecting evidence and preparing the same for proper presentation to the necessary authorities, it has however by a careful review system of the reports received from the field agents of the Bureau of Investigation, kept in close and intimate touch with the detail of the investigative work.

The GID developed an elaborate system for recording the results of Bureau surveillance:

In order that the information which was obtained upon the radical movements might be readily accessible for use by the persons charged with the supervision of these investigations and prosecutions, there has been established as a part of this division a card index system, numbering over 150,000 cards, giving detailed data not only upon individual agitators connected with the radical movement, but also upon organizations, associations, societies, publications and social conditions existing in certain localities. This card index makes it possible to determine and ascertain in a few moments the numerous ramifications of individuals connected with the radical movement and their activities in the United States, thus facilitating the investigations considerably. It is so classified that a card for a particular city will show the various organizations existing in that city, together with their membership rolls and the names of the officers thereof.

The report said little about any tangible accomplishments in the prevention of terrorist violence or the apprehension of persons responsible for specific acts of violence. Instead, groups and individuals were characterized as having "dedicated themselves to the carrying out of anarchistic ideas and tactics"; as "urging the workers to rise up against the Government of the United States"; as having "openly advocated the overthrow of constitutions, governments and churches"; as being "the cause of a considerable amount of the industrial and economic unrest"; as "openly urging the workers to engage in armed revolt"; as being "pledged to the tactics of force and violence"; as being "affiliated with the III International formed at Moscow" and under "party discipline regulated by Lenin and Trotsky"; and as "propagandists" appealing directly to "the negro" for support in the revolutionary movement.

The only references to particular illegal acts were that one group had participated in an "outlawed strike" against the railroads, that one anarchist group member had assassinated the king of Italy, and that Communists had smuggled diamonds into the United States to finance propaganda. The head of the GID did not claim to have identified terrorists whose bombings had aroused public furor. Instead, Hoover reported that the mass arrests and deportations "had resulted in the wrecking of the communist parties in this country" and that "the radical press, which prior to January 2nd had been so flagrantly attacking the Government of the United States and advocating its overthrow by force and violence, ceased its pernicious activities." State sedition prosecutions had served to protect "against the agitation of persons having for their intent and purpose the overthrow of the Government of the United States." Finally the GID's work had :enabled the government to study the situation from a more intelligent and broader viewpoint."[172]

Parallel to the Justice Department and Immigration Bureau operations, military intelligence continued its wartime surveillance into the post-war era. After a temporary cut-back in early 1919, the Military Intelligence Division resumed investigations aimed at strikes, labor unrest, radicals, and the foreign language press. The American Protective League disbanded, but its former members still served as volunteer agents for military intelligence as well as for the Bureau of Investigation. While the military did not play a significant role in the "Palmer raids," troops were called upon in 1919 to control race riots in several cities and to maintain order during a steel strike in Gary, Indiana, where the city was placed under "modified martial law." Following the 1920 round-up of aliens, J. Edgar Hoover arranged for mutual cooperation between the GID and military intelligence. Reports from the Bureau of Investigation would be shared with the military, and investigations conducted at military request. In return, military intelligence agreed to provide Hoover with information from foreign sources, since the State Department had refused to do so and Hoover was prohibited from having agents or informants outside the United States.[173]

The domestic intelligence structure as finally established in 1920 remained essentially intact until Attorney General Harlan Fiske Stone took office in 1924. Under the Harding Administration and Attorney General Harry Daugherty, the GID was made a part of the Bureau of Investigation under Director William J. Burns, with J. Edgar Hoover becoming an Assistant Director of the Bureau. Although the deportation program was strictly limited by Labor Department policies, the Bureau still supplied results of its surveillance operations to state authorities for the prosecution of Communists.[174] Hoover also prepared a lengthy report for the Secretary of State on Communist activities in the United States. The State Department submitted the information to the Senate to back up its opposition to a resolution to grant diplomatic recognition to the Soviet Union.[175] During this period, the Bureau spelled out its domestic intelligence activities in annual reports to Congress, including summaries of investigation findings on the role of Communists in education, athletic clubs, publications, labor unions, women's groups, and Negro groups. Radical propaganda was "being spread in the churches, schools, and colleges throughout the country." The Bureau also told the Congress that it was furnishing information for prosecutions under state laws punishing "criminal syndicalism and anarchy."[176]

Military Intelligence Division

Neglect of Military Intelligence 1919

Prior to our declaration of war with Germany this essential general staff agency which is charged with gathering, collating, and disseminating the military information necessary as a basis for correct military decisions existed only in a rudimentary form. In April, 1917, it consisted of a section of the War College Division comprising a total personnel consisting of two officers and two clerks and supplied with only $11,000 by congressional appropriation for the performance of duty vital to the interests of the Army and the Nation. Every other army of importance was provided with a far-reaching military intelligence service directed by a well-equipped general staff agency recognized as a par with agencies charged with military plans, operations, and supplies. As a result of our neglect of this service, the valuable information gathered by the officers whom we had attached to European armies during the first year and a half of the war was never properly used. We were also without accurate data as to the powerful and insidious espionage , propaganda, and sabotage methods with which Germany at once attempted to thwart our military effort.

Organization of Military Intelligence Division

On July 1, 1918, the Military Intelligence Section, War College Division, General Staff, had been reorganized as the Military Intelligence Branch, Executive Division, General Staff, and consisted of 173 officers, 23 noncommissioned officers, and 589 clerks in Washington, as well as representatives in the more important cities of the United States, in all important foreign countries, and an extensive field force made up of specially chosen and instructed personnel in each military unit at home and overseas. This service had already rendered Gen. Pershing great assistance by supplying him with the required intelligence funds, with competent, loyal interpreters, agents, code and cipher experts, and other special intelligence personnel, with the material peculiarly adapted for intelligence needs.

The Staff reorganization, effected by General Orders, No 80, War Department, August 26, 1918, made the Military Intelligence Service a coordinate division of the General Staff and placed it on a par with similar services of general staffs of other nations of the world. The additional authority and prestige thus provided made it possible for this division to deal with other governmental agencies and with the intelligence services of our allies much more expeditiously and effectively than was possible under the previous imperfect organization. At the time of the armistice the Military Intelligence Division in Washington was made up of a highly specialized personnel consisting of 282 officers, 29 noncommissioned officers and 948 civilian employees, there field force had been greatly improved and enlarged, the assistance furnished the intelligence section of Gen. Pershing's staff was becoming daily more direct and more valuable, as was the staff was becoming daily more direct and more valuable, as was the cooperation with State Department, the Treasury Department, the Department of Justice, the Post Office Department, Naval Intelligence, the War Trade Board, the War Industries Board, and the National Research Council.

Since the signing of the armistices the Military Intelligence Division, in spite of the necessary rapid demobilization of its civilian and temporary commissioned personnel, had contributed much valuable information to the American commission to negotiate peace, for which over 20 officer-specialists were furnished, and with which was effectively linked the military attaché system and the intelligence service of the American Expeditionary Forces. Investigation of alleged cases of enemy activity and disloyalty within the civil population in the United States which had been necessary during the period of actual hostilities terminated November 30, 1918, but the enormous financial interests of the United States involved in the cancellation of war contracts and the salvage of surplus stores has made necessary the continuance of a small bureau in this division for the investigation of alleged graft and fraud in connection with such matters. The gathering and effective use of military information is, however, held to be primary function of the Military Intelligence Division in time of peace; and it is upon this principle that the business of this division is now being conducted.

The duties assigned to Military Intelligence Division by General Orders, No. 80, War Department, 1918, are:

This division shall have the cognizance and control of military intelligence, both positive and negative, and shall be in charge of an officer designated as the Director of Military Intelligence, who will bean assistant to the Chief of Staff. He is also the chief military censor. The duties of this division are to maintain estimates revised daily of the military situation, the economic situation, and of such others matters as the Chief of Staff may direct, and to collect, collate, and disseminate military intelligence. It will cooperate wit the intelligence section of the general staffs of allied countries in connection with military intelligence; prepare instructions in military intelligence work for the use of our forces: supervise the training of personnel for intelligence work: organize, direct, and coordinate the intelligence service: supervise the duties of military attaches: communicate direct with department intelligence officers and intelligence officers at posts, camps, and stations, and , and with commands in the field in matters relating to military intelligence: obtain, reproduce, and issue maps: translate foreign documents: disburse: and account for intelligence funds: cooperate with the censorship board and with intelligence agencies of other departments of Government.

In order to perform the duties thus assigned it the Military Intelligence Division has been organized into an Administrative Section and 12 other sections, grouped according to the nature of their functions into three branches, Positive, Geographic, and Negative. The magnitude, importance, and variety of the work of this division can best be shown by a summary of the activities of its various sub-divisions.

The Negative Branch

This branch collects, collates, and disseminates information upon which may be based measures of prevention against activities and influences tending to impair our military efficiency by other than armed force.

This branch was created on August 18, 1918, by uniting four existing sections. The sections so united were the Foreign Influence Section, the Army Section, the News Section, and the military morale Section. In September, 1918, the Travel Section and the Fraud Section were added. On October 19, 1918, the Military Morale Section became the Military Morale Branch of the General Staff. The organization at the time of the cessation of hostilities, when the branch had reached its highest point of development, consisted of five sections, as follows: Foreign Influence (M.I. 4); Army (M.I. 3); News (M.I. 10); Travel (M.I. 11); Fraud (M.I. 13).

At its maximum the branch employed the services of 202 officers, 60 enlisted men (Corps of Intelli-gence), 65 volunteers (candidates for commissions), and 605 clerks. It directed the activities of thousands of officers and enlisted men in the field and through this organization did the War Department's share in completely foiling the well-laid plans of the enemy to impede our military program. In which aggregate more than the entire appropriation for Military Intelligence.

A consideration of the functions of the several subdivisions of the branch gives a comprehensive view of its activities, which included the handling of cases during the current year in number closely approximating half a million.

The Foreign Influence Section (M.I.4), is the present section from which grew the Negative Branch. As delimited by the diversion of specialties to other sections, the duty of this section in general is the study of espionage and propaganda directed against the United States or against its allies, and also the study of the sentiments, publications, ad other actions of foreign language and revolutionary groups both here an abroad, in so far as these matters have a bearing upon the military situation. The activities of a the section were carried on through seven subsections, as follows:

The Executive Subsection apportioned, supervised and coordinated the work of the section, determined questions of policy and represented the section in its relations ,important officials.

The Departmental subsection studied the intelligence situation in the territories embraced within the several geographical military departments of United States. It investigated enemy espionage activities and channels of communication, the financing of enemy activities and particular cases of enemy influence.

The Propaganda subsection studied and collated information on dissemination by the enemy of doctrines and false rumors aimed to create confusion of thought and so impair our military efficiency. It also studied and suggested methods for meeting and overcoming this imponderable mode to attack.

The Foreign Subsection studied the intelligence situation abroad and , in cooperation with the corresponding agencies of allied powers, determined the nature and extent of enemy secret activity and formulated methods for overcoming its effect.

The Legal and Liaison Subsection maintained liaison with the various Government agencies in Washington through officers familiar with the various departments. Specific recommendations of measures for fire prevention. It organized watch and guard systems for plants engaged in Government work and provided watchmen where necessary. It also devised plans and furnished agents for detecting and preventing sabotage or other malicious interference with the production. In addition, it systematically studied legislation, enacted or pending, proclamations, executive orders, and legal decisions affecting the Intelligence Service.

The Research Subsection took over from other subsections, cases which appeared to have reached unusual significance or importance, summarized all material information available a prepared such cases for final disposition.

The Labor and Sabotage Subsection handled all matters relating to the prevention or delay of deliveries of war materials by immobilization of resources, control of factories, or raw materials, subversion or intimidation of labor or physical damage to plants or products.

The Army Section (M.I.3) — The Functions of this section is the organization, instruction and supervision of the Negative Intelligence Service within the Military Establishment: more specifically it protects the Army by the prevention and detection of enemy and disloyal activity among the military, including civilian personnel under military authority and in volunteer auxiliary associations. It supervises and coordinates the work of the Negative Intelligence officers stationed with each military unit and promulgates instructions for the operation and maintenance of the Negative Intelligence Service in the field.

The Executive Subsection coordinated the work of the section, assigned personnel and issued the bulletins and instructions which determined policy for the field organization. It also handled a variety of special and miscellaneous matters which did not fall within the province of another subsection. Among such specialties were the observation of conscientious objectors and of foreign church organizations and pacifist religious bodies operating among troops. The intelligence problems arising through there presence in the American Army of large bodies of Negro troops were studied in this subsection and much valuable information was secured and digested.

The Line Subsection cooperated with intelligence officers in line units in the field in investigating cases of disloyalty, sedition or enemy activity, either among troops or at points where troops were stationed. It also investigated and reported upon the antecedents and personal character for loyalty and integrity of candidates for commissions in the line of the Army. The duties of this section included not only the observations of dangerous tendencies or incidents arising within military units, but also those which operated from without directly upon the Army personnel.

Three other subsections performed for the technical and administrative corps and departments duties identical with those which the Line Subsection handled for the line of Army. This work was grouped as follows: (a) General Staff, Judge Advocate General's Office, Adjutant General's Office, Corps of Engineers, Ordnance Department, Quartermaster Corps, and Motor Transport Corps. (b) Medical, Dental, and Veterinary Corps and the Chemical Warfare Service. (c) Signal Corps ad Air Service.

The Personnel Subsection served all other subsections by conducting preliminary investigations of candidates for commissions and other persons under investigation, and so from further consideration all whose character for loyalty and integrity proved to be questionable. This subsection also performed a valuable service in detecting applicants for commissions in technical branches who had previously been rejected or discharged for cause from other branches of the service. One result of the investigations of this group was to prove the utter unreliability of letters of recommendation in estimating the fitness of individuals. Approximately 15,000 cases were handled during the emergency.

The Statistical Subsection, by means of maps and indexes, kept records of all military units in the United States and of the Intelligence organization of each; of the various cooperating agencies and of the status of the field service in general. It had custody of all literature issued by the section and attended to the mailing of circulars, bulletins, and instructions. It coordinated the administrative work of the field and the office. This subsection maintained liaison with statistical offices of other branches of the War Department.

The Instruction Subsection, studied the development of the Negative Intelligence system, evolved general principles and specific policies of general application and promulgated the result for the improvement of the service. It developed a well-considered plan for the personal instruction of Negative Intelligence officers, and prior to the signing of the armistice conducted schools for two groups of officers brought in from the field instruction.

The Plant Protection Bureau.–This was a civilian organization which originated in the Air Service as a measure of protection for the airplane production program. It was taken over by Military Intelligence and its scope enlarged to include the protection of Government plants and construction projects as well as all private plants engaged in war work. This bureau systematically studied and inspected fire risks and made recommendations of measures for fire prevention. It organized watch and guard systems for plants for engaged in Government work and provided watchmen where necessary. It also devised plans and furnished agents for detecting and preventing sabotage or other malicious interference with the production of war material. Approximately 5,000 plants were under the inspection of this bureau, which employed and operative force of 373 and supervised the activities of thousands of guards and watchmen. Offices were maintained at Boston, Springfield, New Haven, Bridgeport, New York, Albany, Syracuse, Buffalo, New ark, Philadelphia, Baltimore, Nitro, Atlanta, Nashville, Pittsburgh, Cleveland, Dayton, Indianapolis, Detroit, Chicago, Milwaukee, Minneapolis, Davenport, St. Louis, Fort Worth, San Francisco, and Los Angeles.

An important by-product of the activities of this bureau arose from its intimate knowledge of the operation of plants working on Government contracts whereby it was in a position to frustrate false claims and overcharges. No account was kept from which an accurate statement can be made of the total savings effectuated in this way. One item amounted to $600,000. and the total is estimated as $2,000,000.

Liaison with American Protective League: American Protective League was a volunteer civilian organization of 3000,000 members, operating under the supervision of the Department of Justice, and thoroughly covering the United States. By special arrangement with the Department of Justice this agency of information was placed at the disposal of Military Intelligence Division, and to facilitate communication directly with the various local branches of the league a Liaison Subsection was created under the direction of an officer of Military Intelligence, who was also an officer of the American Protective League.

The News Section (M.I.10)–On June 11, 1918, the Director of Military Intelligence was appointed to represent the War Department on the Censorship Board and the work incidental to this additional duty was at first handled in several sections of the Negative Branch. On August 16, 1917, the Director of Military Intelligence assumed the duty of Chief Military Censor and this section, which was originally called the Censorship Section, was created to handle increased volume of work entailed.

Censorship–In practice it was found that much of the organization necessary to examine publications and communications for censoring served equally well for collecting and digesting current news in a manner which proved to be of great value to the War Department. As time progressed these informational functions became more and more important and when, with the close of hostilities, the censorship became unnecessary, this feature of the section, now called the News Section, was continued. At its maximum the section had 15 subsection, as follows:

The Executive Subsection coordinated and supervised the work of the section, handled necessary administrative details, together with miscellaneous matters which did not fall within the province of any other subsection, and maintained liaison with the boards of experts in other departments.

The Legal Subsection advised on the legal aspects of the censorship and recorded the precedents established upon rulings obtained from the staff of technical experts organized in the various bureaus of the War Department to cooperate with the Chief Military Censor.

The Postal Subsection maintained liaison with the Post Office Department and handled those matters which arose through the duties of the Chief Military Censor as War Department member of the Postal Censor ship Board.

The Prisoner of War Subsection censored all mail to or from prisoners of war held by the United States in the several war prison camps and coordinated the work in this country with that done abroad.

The Telegraph and Telephone Subsection conducted the censorship of telegraph and telephone messages to Mexico during the period that the regulation were in force.

The Radio Subsection supervised the interception of radio messages originating in Mexico and through this service obtained much invaluable information regarding the activities and intentions of the enemy.

The Official Photograph Subsection censored all official motion and still pictures and made appropriate recommendations to the Signal Corps, the Historical Branch, an the Committee on Public Information.

The Commercial Motion Picture Subsection surveyed the private motion picture field for harmful propaganda or indiscreet revelations and in conjunction with Customs Intelligence censored the importation and exportation of films.

The Photographic Permit Subsection in cooperation with the Committee on Public Information handled the matter of official permits to make photographs on or about military camps and reservations.

The Press Subsection examined newspapers and periodicals to detect violations of the voluntary press censorship, advised the press regarding the suppression of information which might be of military value to the enemy, and attended to the accrediting of war correspondents.

The Foreign Language Press Subsection examined publications in foreign languages published in the United States land foreign language material entering this country.

The Book Subsection examined books, pamphlets, posters and all publications other than newspapers and periodicals, reported on such as were contrary to the interests of the United States, and recommended repressive measures where necessary.

The Propaganda Subsection examined periodicals and publications clearly engaged in propaganda activities for the purpose of ascertaining if their teachings are inimical to the interests of the United States.

The Digest Subsection prepared a daily news summary, a semi-weekly digest of editorial opinion for transmission to France, and a weekly press review for the Secretary of War.

The Clipping Bureau maintained a newspaper and magazine clippings service for all of the Military Intelligence Division and several other branches of the General Staff.

The Signal Intelligence Service was housed in this building from 1929 to 1942. The building was located on Constitution Avenue in Washington, D.C.

Post Civil War Bibliography

Allensworth, W.H. and W.G. Spottswood. *The Cipher of the War Department*. Washington, DC: GPO, 1902.

Aston, George G. *Secret Service*. New York: Cosmopolitan, 1930.

Bernstorff, Johan Heinrich, Graf von. *Memoirs of Count Bernstorff*. New York: Random House, 1936.

Brownrigg, Admiral Sir Douglas. *Indiscretion of the Naval Censor: Counterintelligence and Economic Warfare*. New York: George H. Doran, 1920.

Bywater, Hector, and Ferraby, H.C. *Strange Intelligence: Memoirs of Naval Secret Service: Naval Intelligence*. London: Constable, 1931.

Deakin, F.W., and Storry, G.R. *The Case Of Richard Sorge*. New York: Harper and Row, 1966.

Doerries, Reinhard R. *Imperial Challenge: Ambassador Count Bernstorff and German-American Relations*. Chapel Hill: University of North Carolina Press, 1989.

Dorwart, Jeffrey M. *The Office of Naval Intelligence: The Birth of America's First Intelligence Agency, 1865-1918*. Annapolis, Md.: Naval Institute Press, 1979.

Dunn, Robert W. *The Palmer Raids*. Labor Research Association, International Publishers, New York, 1948.

Friedman, William F., and Charles J. Mendelsohn, *The Zimmerman Telegram of January 16, 1917 and its Cryptographic Background*. Laguna Hills, CA: Aegean Park Press, 1976.

Goltz, Horst von der. *My Adventures as a German Agent*. New York: Robert M. McBride. 1917

Grant, Hamil. *Spies and Secret Service: the Story of Espionage, Its Main Systems and Chief Exponents*. New York: Frederick Stokes, 1915.

Harris, Charles H. III and Louis R. Sadler, Louis R. *The Border and the Revolution*. Center for Latin American Studies/Joint Border Research Institute. New Mexico State University, Las Cruces, New Mexico. 1988

Jeffreys-Jones, Rhodri. "The Montreal Spy Ring of 1898 and the Origins of 'Domestic Surveillance' in the United States." *Canadian Review of American Studies* 5 (Fall 1974): 119-134.

Jones, John P. and Paul M. Hollister. *The German Secret Service in America, 1914-1918*. Boston, Small, Maynard, 1918.

Katz, Friedrich. *The Secret War in Mexico: Europe, the United States, and the Mexican Revolution*. Chicago: U. Chicago Press, 1981.

Landau, Henry. The Enemy Within: *The Inside Story of German Sabotage in America*. New York: Putnam's, 1937.

LeCaron, Henri, pseud. (Thomas Miller Beach). *Twenty-five Years in the Secret Service: The Recollections of a Spy*. London: William Heinemann, 1892.

O'Toole, G.J.A. "Our Man in Havana: The Paper Trail of Some Spanish War Spies," *Intelligence Quarterly*, 2:2 (1986): 1-3.

Pannunzio, C.M. *The Deportation Cases of 1919-1920*. A Report Published for the Federal Council of Churches of Christ of America, Chapter III, 1920.

Powe, Marc B. *The Emergence of the War Department Intelligence Agency: 1885-1918*. Manhattan, KS: Military Affairs, 1975.

Testimony of U.S. Attorney General A. Mitchell Palmer's to the House of Representatives Committee on Rules, Hearings, 66th Congress, 2nd Session, on charges made against the Dept of Justice by Louis F. Post and others. pages 157-158, Quotations from Palmer 171-173, 1919.

Tuchman, Barbara W. *The Zimmerman Telegram*. New York: Dell, 1958.

US Secret Service Division, *Annual Reports of the Chief of the Secret Service Division*, Washington, DC: GPO, 1907-1911.

Willert, A. *The Road to Safety: A Study in Anglo-American Relations*. London: Derek Verchoyle, 1952.

Witcover, Jules. *Sabotage at Black Tom: Imperial Germany's Secret War in America, 1914-1917*. Chapel Hill, NC: Algonquin Books of Chapel Hill, 1989.

Woodward, P.H., *The Secret Service of the Post Office Department*, Hartford, CT: Winter, 1886.

IMPORTANT DATES AND COUNTERINTELLIGENCE EVENTS
POST CIVIL WAR TO WORLD WAR I, 1866-1919

1871	1 July	Department of Justice is established.
1876		U.S. Supreme Court issues Totten Decision, affirming that the President has the power to appoint "Secret Agents" and pay them from the Contingent Fund.
1882	23 March	Office of Naval Intelligence (ONI) established within the Bureau of Navigation.
1884	6 October	Navy War College is established at Newport, Rhode Island.
1885	October	The War Department establishes the Bureau of Military Intelligence (Military Information Division -MID) at the Adjutant Generals Office.
1889	27 February	Army institutes the Military Attaché system that was approved by Congress in 1888.
1898	15 February	U.S. battleship *Maine* destroyed by an explosion in Havana Harbor.
	21 April	The Spanish-American War begins. The War ends almost four months later on 13 August.
	10 December	ONI overseas networks demobilized at the conclusion of the Spanish American War.
	10 December	Treaty of Paris signed. Spain granted Cuba its freedom and ceded Guam, Puerto Rico, and the Philippines to the United States.
1901	6 September	President William McKinley assassinated by Leon Czolgosz, an anarchist.
	6 September	Secret Service tasked with Presidential Protection.
1902	18 June	Separate Military Intelligence Division (MID) established in Division of the Philippines, later absorbed by the MID.
1903	14 February	G-2 for military intelligence created with the designation of General Staff Corps.
1908	24 June	G-2 and G-3 merged.
	26 July	Attorney General Charles Bonaparte appoints a force of special agents.

IMPORTANT DATES AND COUNTERINTELLIGENCE EVENTS
POST CIVIL WAR TO WORLD WAR I, 1866-1919

1908	30 June	Secret Service, which fulfilled a counterintelligence function during the Spanish American War, stripped of all but investigations of treasury violations and presidential protection, and is prohibited from investigating members of Congress.
1909	16 March	The special force in the Department of Justice becomes the Bureau of Investigation.
1910	26 March	Congress amends the Immigration Act of 1907 to prohibit criminals, paupers, anarchists and diseased persons from entering the US.
1911	7 March	President Taft dispatches 20,000 troops to the Mexican border as fighting in the Mexican Revolution occurs close to US territory.
	26 October	General Bernardo Reyes' conspiracy to use Texas as a base of operations to overthrow the Mexican government is stopped.
1914	September	First successful U.S. aerial reconnaissance by airplane.
	9 April	An unarmed group of sailors from the USS *Dolphin*, patrolling in Mexican waters, is arrested in Tampico, Mexico after they accidentally enter a restricted area while seeking to secure supplies.
	21 April	American forces bombard Vera Cruz, Mexico and occupy the city to prevent a German ship from landing arms there.
	28 June	Serb nationalist at Sarajevo, Bosnia, assassinates Archduke Franz Ferdinand, heir to the Austrian throne. Incident leads to World War I.
	7 July	Berlin summons its Ambassador, Johann von Bernstorff, home from the United States.
	18 July	Congress authorizes Formation of an Aviation Section within the Army Signal Corps.
	30 July	German Military Attaché Franz van Papen leaves Mexico for the United States.
	August	Russian Navy reportedly finds a German naval code book, which is given to British Naval Intelligence.
	2 August	Von Bernstorff returns to the United States with sabotage instructions and funds to finance them.

IMPORTANT DATES AND COUNTERINTELLIGENCE EVENTS
POST CIVIL WAR TO WORLD WAR I, 1866-1919

1914	4 August	President Wilson issues a proclamation of neutrality on outbreak of World War I.
	22 August	German Military Attaché to U.S., Franz von Papen, tasks Paul Koenig to form an intelligence and sabotage ring in New York.
	September	Horst von der Goltz fails to blow up the Welland Canal.
	2 November	German General Staff issues directive to military attaches in neutral countries to recruit anarchists for sabotage operations.
	15 December	Von Bernstorff receives cable from German Foreign Office instructing him to target Canadian Railways for destruction.
1915	1 January	Roebling wire and cable plant in Trenton, New Jersey is blown up.
	26 January	Von Bernstorff and von Papen urged to recruit Irish agitators for sabotage by German Foreign Office.
	28 January	A German ship sinks an American merchant ship carrying wheat to Britain.
	2 February	Werner Horn captured attempting to blow up the Vanceboro Bridge.
	April	Germans covertly establish a munitions plant, the Bridgeport Projectile Company, in Connecticut to divert U.S. war materials destined for its enemies.
	2 April	Doctor Walter Scheele forms a front company in New Jersey to manufacture incendiary devices for German sabotage operations.
	3 April	Captain Franz von Rintelen and Robert Fay arrive in U.S. with sabotage assignments.
	7 May	Lusitania torpedoed by German U-boat off Irish coast.
	15 May	Unexploded bombs found in ship docking at Marseilles; devices traced to von Rinetelen operation.
	2 July	U.S. Capital bombed.
	3 July	Financier J.P. Morgan shot by protester.

IMPORTANT DATES AND COUNTERINTELLIGENCE EVENTS
POST CIVIL WAR TO WORLD WAR I, 1866-1919

1915	15 July	Doctor Heinrich Albert leaves portfolio with plans to foment labor unrest, other German schemes on subway. A Secret Service agent, following Albert, takes the portfolio.
	13 August	Von Rintelen captured by British at Dover as he was attempting to return to Germany.
	30 August	Documents of Austro-Hungarian Ambassador Constantin Dumba, which included instructions for subversion and implicating Von Papen and Captain Karl Boy-Ed, seized by British; President Wilson demands recall of Dumba.
	24 October	Robert Fay arrested, further implicates Von Papen and Boy-Ed in German sabotage operations.
	1 December	President Wilson demands recall of Von Papen and Boy-Ed.
	28 December	Von Rintelen indicted for fomenting strikes in American munitions plants.
1916	January	Director of ONI complains that Secretary of the Navy Franklin D. Roosevelt is forming his own secret intelligence bureau separate from ONI.
	16 February	Key meeting at Section 3B, German General Staff takes place to plan sabotage and use of new incendiary devices in U.S.
	9 March	Pancho Villa raids Columbus, a New Mexico border town, killing 17 American soldiers and civilians.
	15 March	President Woodrow Wilson dispatches a Punitive Expedition under Brigadier General John J. "Blackjack" Pershing against Villa.
	May	House of Representatives defeats anti-espionage legislation proposed by the Attorney General.
	21 June	US troops in Mexico are attacked at Carrizal.
	9 July	German merchant submarine *Deutschland* arrives in Baltimore; provides front for Captain Frederick Hinsch's sabotage activities.
	30 July	German agents blow up Black Tom Island, a munitions transfer point between New York and New Jersey. The explosions killed two and caused $20 million in damage.

IMPORTANT DATES AND COUNTERINTELLIGENCE EVENTS
POST CIVIL WAR TO WORLD WAR I, 1866-1919

1916

10 August	Hilken pays $2,000 to Hinsch for the Black Tom sabotage.
29 August	Council of National Defense is formed to coordinate war preparedness efforts in American industry.
4 November	Secretary of State Robert Lansing creates the Bureau of Secret Intelligence, funded with confidential funds, much of which comes from American businessmen.

1917

11 January	Fire destroys the Kingsland Plant.
1 February	Germany launches unrestricted submarine warfare.
3 February	President Wilson breaks off diplomatic relations with Germany; sends Von Bernstorff home.
5 February	General Pershing's Punitive Expedition withdraws from Mexico.
24 February	The British give The Zimmerman Telegram to Walter Hines Pages, the U.S. Ambassador to Great Britain.
22 March	American Protective League established to support the government in its domestic investigations of "radicals."
31 March	Attorney General, Thomas W. Gregory, without congressional authority, authorizes Bureau of Investigations to investigate German espionage in the United States.
3 April	Most German saboteurs leave U.S. because, under declaration of war, anyone committing sabotage can be sentenced to death.
6 April	U.S. declares war on Germany.
13 April	Fred Herrman, German saboteur, writes Paul Hilken, German sabotage paymaster, invisible message requesting funds to blow up Tampico oil fields.
14 April	First wartime Executive Order dealing with the broad subject of censorship issued by President Wilson.
28 April	Secretary of War given wartime censorship control over telegraph and telephones leading out of the United States.

IMPORTANT DATES AND COUNTERINTELLIGENCE EVENTS
POST CIVIL WAR TO WORLD WAR I, 1866-1919

1917	3 May	Col. Ralph Van Deman, head of Military Intelligence, initiates unauthorized secret intelligence efforts, contrary to orders of the Chief of Staff.
	3 May	Military Intelligence Section of the U.S. Army War College is created.
	18 May	Selective Service Act is passed.
	10 June	Van Deman hires Herbert O. Yardley to head the Code and Cipher Bureau (MI-8), thus beginning the US government's special effort to decipher foreign coded communications.
	15 June	Espionage Act passed.
	13 August	Corps of Intelligence Police officially established.
	31 August	General Pershing creates the Intelligence Section, General Staff.
	6 October	Trading with Enemy Act passed which authorizes president to place an embargo on imports, forbids trade with enemy nations, and allows the government to censor the mail.
	12 October	President Wilson creates the National Censorship Board.
	12 November	First Signal Corps intercept station in World War I operational at Souilly, France.
	25 November	Corps of Intelligence Police arrived in St. Nazaire, France.
	20 December	Bolsheviks create the Cheka, the Soviet forerunner of the KGB, now the SVRR.
1918	1 February	Lothar Witzke arrested crossing into U.S. and confesses role in Black Tom Island sabotage but later recants.
	22 February	Radio Intelligence Service created in MID to intercept and record all messages originating in Mexico.
	28 August	Negative Branch (counterintelligence) officially created in Military Intelligence Division.
	16 May	The Sedition Act, an amendment to the Espionage Act, is passed.
	17 August	Witzke convicted and sentenced to hang; only man thus sentenced in U.S. in World War I. Sentenced later commuted and he is eventually freed.

IMPORTANT DATES AND COUNTERINTELLIGENCE EVENTS
POST CIVIL WAR TO WORLD WAR I, 1866-1919

1918	14 September	Eugene Debs, Socialist Party, is found guilty of making seditious statements that impede recruitment efforts and is sentenced to 10 years in prison under the Espionage Act of 1917.
	16 October	The Deportation Act passed by Congress; provided for the deportation of aliens who were anarchists.
	11 November	Armistice ending World War I signed.
1919	January	MID orders all civilian investigations to cease; MID personnel to confine investigations to military reservations.
	2 June	A bomb explodes in front of Attorney General Palmer's townhouse in Washington, D.C. The bomber was killed, but leaflets found on the body suggest foreign involvement.
	13 June	Soviet Representative Marten arrested and deported in 1920.
	12 August	J. Edgar Hoover appointed Head of the General Intelligence Division.
	7 November	The General Intelligence Division, headed by J. Edgar Hoover, raided the offices of the Union of Russian Workers, a labor society.
	22 December	Attorney General A. Mitchell Palmer initiates a series of raids against communists, anarchists and other radicals.

CHAPTER 4

Counterintelligence Between The Wars

Introduction

The "war to end all wars" was over and the United States was poised on the threshold of world leadership, when the American people retreated into a period of isolationism. They wanted to forget the war, and its destructive influence on the nation's psyche, and forget the world's problems. Americans wanted to be happy and enjoy life.

Enter the "Roaring Twenties." Depicted in movies by speakeasies, gangsters, dapper college boys and flapper girls dancing to the new, electrifying jazz, it displayed an era of happy, carefree Americans enjoying a materialistic lifestyle. That image disguised the many problems facing the nation. Most Americans still harbored deep-rooted bias against foreigners immigrating to the United States. To them, these refugees from abroad were undercutting their dreams of a good life by willing to work for low wages. They also brought the evils associated with the Old World and the new evil of communism.

A "Red Scare" began to sweep the country. American business leaders alleged that there was more to the growing strikes across the nation than workers desiring higher pay. They accused the foreign "Reds" and anarchists, Bolsheviks, Communists and Socialists of plotting to destroy the American way of life. Hysteria increased. Government leaders said that unless these anarchists were stopped, a Red revolution would subvert America.

In June 1919 a bomb exploded outside the home of Attorney General, A. Mitchell Palmer, which killed the bomber. A search of the body found leaflets, which suggested a foreign conspiracy. Almost six months later, Palmer, using the Bureau of Investigation and citizen volunteers, launched a series of raids on "radical" meetings. Thousands of people were arrested without cause. Palmer was a hero but as the raids and the abuses committed by the raiders continued, American public opinion shifted. In the end, Palmer and the Bureau of Investigation were rebuked.

There were cries that the Bureau of Investigation be stripped of its investigative authority and that the Secret Service be given this role. Instead, a new Attorney General, Harlan Fiske Stone, decided that the Bureau was needed but had to operate under strict legal guidelines. Stone fired William Burns, chief of the

Bureau, and abolished the General Intelligence Division, headed by J. Edgar Hoover. Hoover was then made acting director and later director of the Bureau.

Further, after World War I ended, the military did not want to terminate its cryptographic and decoding activities. Working with the Department of State, a Cipher Bureau was established in New York with secret funds provided by State. This bureau became known as the "Black Chamber." Using cooperative liaison contacts in Western Union Telegraph Company and the Postal Telegraph Company, the Black Chamber was given access to diplomatic cable traffic. The Chamber operated until the new Secretary of State, Henry Stimson, withdrew State Department's funding in 1929. The military then transferred the Chamber's functions to the Army Signal Corps.

In the early 1930s, a special committee, led by New York Congressman Hamilton Fish, was authorized by the House of Representatives to investigate communism. After almost a year of study, the committee concluded that the federal intelligence community had no authority to deal with the growing problem of communist activity. The committee recommended that the Department of Justice severely crackdown on communists but the recommendation fell on deaf ears.

In 1934 Congress granted the Bureau of Investigation the power to make arrests but required the Bureau to obtain a warrant from the Judiciary prior to making the arrest. To obtain the warrant, the Bureau was required to show reasonable grounds for suspecting the person to be arrested and the Judiciary had to agree with the grounds.

In 1938, Texas Congressman Martin Dies, who headed a special committee to investigate subversion in the United States, continued to shove the Roosevelt Administration and the FBI to be more active in the investigation of communists and Nazis. The FBI informed Congressman Dies and his committee that it had commenced "building up a system of internal security" since early 1935.

There was an ardent desire by the counterintelligence community to counter this newly perceived threat but the old arguments surfaced as to what government entity would be in charge. President Roosevelt, also feeling the heat from the Dies Committee, directed the creation of the modern federal counterintelligence system. He temporarily solved the mistrust and discord that plagued the counterintelligence community in a series of presidential directives that gave the FBI the mantle of lead agency to investigate and conduct domestic surveillance against individuals and organizations posing a threat to the United States.

Having gained the advantage over the Army's Military Intelligence Division and Navy's Office of Naval Intelligence, Hoover would never waive his primary role. This would have serious consequences when the Office of Strategic Services is formed during World War II and the Central Intelligence Agency is created in 1947.

The Corps Of Intelligence Police From 1917 To World War II

During World War I the Intelligence Section, American Expeditionary Force, recommended and the War College Division sanctioned the establishment of the Corps of Intelligence Police. Authority for such action was contained in the provisions of Section II of an Act of Congress (approved 18 May 1917) giving the President the power to increase the Army to meet the national emergency. This Corps of fifty men in the rank of sergeant of infantry was to report for counterespionage duty under the Commanding General, American Expeditionary Force. On 13 August 1917, War Department General Orders officially established the Corps of Intelligence Police.

A French-speaking officer with experience in police work was given the mission of recruiting the men. He traveled to New Orleans and New York City where he advertised in the local newspapers for men who could speak French to do intelligence work in France. He accepted all candidates who could pass the Army physical examination and answer a few simple questions in French.

On 25 November 1917, the Corps of Intelligence Police, fifty strong, arrived in St. Nazaire, France. Some were sent to British Intelligence at Le Havre for further training. The others were assigned to the rear area under the control of General Headquarters or were merged with divisional intelligence sections. The Le Havre Detachment worked at copying British suspect lists and counterespionage summaries and began indexing these lists. This training continued until a short while before the Armistice.

In January 1918, the Corps opened its office in Paris and began work on its central card file, securing names from British, French, and American sources. At the end of the war this file contained some 50,000 names.

The first actual counterespionage work was done at St. Nazaire where enemy agents were reported to be active. Agents apprehended by the Corps of Intelligence Police were immediately turned over to French authorities for disposition. Civilians were screened, travelers checked, and passports examined. In addition to work of a counterespionage and security nature, the Corps of Intelligence Police also did investigative work for the Department of Criminal Investigation by conducting fraud and graft investigations. Members of the Corps of Intelligence Police were assigned to the American Peace Delegation in Paris. One detachment was assigned to guard President Wilson's residence while he was in France.

In January 1918, authorization was granted to increase the Corps gradually to an eventual strength of 750 men. One year later, there were 405 agents on duty with the American Expeditionary Force. However, the allotted 750 vacancies were never filled because of the Armistice and demobilization of the Corps.

Meanwhile, during the years 1917-1918, the work of the Corps of Intelligence Police in the continental United States was carried out under the Chief of the War College Division, General Staff. On 28 November 1917, the Corps was increased to 300 men, 250 of whom were to work within the United States. In March 1918, with the abolition of the War College Division of the General Staff, the Corps of Intelligence Police was transferred to the control of the Military Intelligence Branch of the Executive Division of the General Staff.

The next increase in strength came in an order from The Adjutant General dated 4 September 1918. This was deemed necessary because of the rapid increase in the number of investigations being conducted throughout the United States and the territorial departments.

However, these goals were never reached, for by January 1920, of a total of 600 men who had been on duty in the Corps of Intelligence Police, only 18 remained. This caused serious concern among those who saw the menace of failing to provide a permanent place for the Corps of Intelligence Police in the organization of the Army. Many saw the necessity for such personnel, in New York, Washington, and the Western and Southern Departments for investigation and guard duties of a strictly confidential nature. Therefore, authority was requested to detail not more than 24 sergeants of the duly authorized organizations of the Army for intelligence service. These were to be evenly divided among the Eastern, Western, and Southern Departments, and the District of Columbia. The Adjutant General granted the authority for such action on 7 February 1920. These men were to be subject to the orders of the Department Commander in whose territory they were assigned, except for the six men on duty with the Western Department who were to be subject to the orders of the Director of Military Intelligence. However, this order did not create a permanent status for the Corps of Intelligence Police in the organization of the Army.

A series of memoranda, prepared by the Director of Intelligence, pointed out the necessity for such a body of men, requested a permanent organization for the Corps of Intelligence Police, and set forth the quotas for the Corps Areas and Departments. The quota of 45 sergeants allotted by the resultant order was not as great as had been desired by the various Corps Areas and Departments, but it did give the Corps of Intelligence Police a permanent foothold in the organization of the Army.

Duties of the Corps of Intelligence Police were outlined by the War Department in the spring of 1921. All individuals who might be suspected of operating against the Military Establishment were to be closely observed. In addition, the Corps of Intelligence Police was directed to report on radical activities in political and industrial fields. This was a tremendous assignment for a handful of men whose number was reduced to a mere 30 in 1922 when the Army was cut to 125,000 men.

The policy of isolationism that swept the country at that time made it impossible to increase the Army in general and the Corps of Intelligence Police in particular. Although there was important work for the Corps, the policy of the Army prohibited the Corps of Intelligence Police from growing large enough to control subversive activity or directly affecting the Military Establishment. However, in 1926, when it became clear that the Corps of Intelligence Police would have to expand rapidly in an emergency, a "Mobilization Plan" for the Corps was drawn up. The initial strength of the Corps was set at 250 men with provision for increments as the mobilization progressed. The functions of the personnel were outlined more clearly, and a promotion plan formulated.

Despite the best intentions of the men who were aware of the real value of the Corps of Intelligence Police, a further decrease occurred in 1926, which brought the total to 28; and in November 1933, strength was decreased to 15. This curtailment of essential personnel was effected as an economy move in the days of the depression. It was argued that the grades held by the men were too high for the clerical duties they were performing. It was even suggested that other military personnel or civilian employees replace the Corps of Intelligence Police in certain localities. To this, the Philippine Department answered:

> "This Department presents a special case in that its distance from the homeland, its close proximity to World Powers, its heterogeneous mixture of foreigners, and the uncertainty of the future, all tend to emphasize the importance of keeping the Commanding General fully informed at all times. In order to perform this important duty, the scope of the organization charged with its execution is wide and varied...All of the present members of the Corps of Intelligence Police are men of proven ability, loyalty, and experience... Were any of these agents replaced by civilians or military personnel, it would confront this office with the necessity of building a new organization and discarding one which has reached its present state of efficiency after years of intelligence effort and experience."

From 1934 to 1939, with but a single increase of one man authorized for work in the Philippine Department, the Corps of Intelligence Police existed precariously with its small quota. Meanwhile, continued reports indicated that Japanese and Nazi activity were on the upswing in the Panama, Hawaiian, and Philippine Departments. Finally, in June, 1939, President Franklin D. Roosevelt issued a proclamation which stated that the control of all matters of an espionage, counterespionage, and sabotage nature would be handled by the Federal Bureau of Investigation of the Department of Justice, the Military Intelligence Division of the War Department, and the Office of Naval Intelligence of the Navy Department. The Directors of these three agencies were ordered to function as a committee to coordinate their activities.

One year later, the chiefs of the three agencies involved drew up an agreement as to jurisdiction, with particular emphasis given to foreign operations. Further revision of this agreement, defining clearly the work to be handled by each agency, was made in February 1942. This has become known as the Delimitations Agreement of 1942.

Expansion of the Corps began almost immediately. In June 1940, authorization was granted to bring in an additional 26 men. In December 1940, the allotment was increased to 188 men. Although some difficulty was experienced in recruiting, because of a lack of definite standards of qualifications, it was soon established that only men of the highest integrity with a high school education or better would be selected. On 20 February 1941 a total of 288 men was reached. A total of 18 agents was allotted to the important Panama Canal Department. By 31 May the over-all total swelled to 513, and by 17 February 1942 the Panama Canal Department alone could count 59 men on duty there.

In January 1941, the office of the Chief of the Corps of Intelligence Police-Sub-Section, Investigating Section, Counter Intelligence Branch, Military Intelligence Division, was established. On 24 February 1941, the Corps of Intelligence Police Investigators School became operational in the Army War College and, after two classes, was moved to Chicago. By April, Technical Manual 30-215 (Tentative) was published, thereby creating a definite and consistent procedure of training for all personnel in the Corps.

On 6 December 1941, the eve of Pearl Harbor, the Corps of Intelligence Police was a permanent organization of the Army, organized under the direction of the Assistant Chief of Staff, G-2, General Staff. It had authorization for 513 enlisted men, and had begun the task of expanding its work under the policies set forth in the Delimitations Agreement. Suddenly the days of begging for men and money had come to an end. The problem was now to grow as rapidly as possible, procure and train men, and do a professional job simultaneously.

Memo to Director of Naval Intelligence

United States Asiatic Fleet
U.S.S. Huron, Flagship
Manila, P.I.
24December 1923

From: Commander in Chief
To: Director of Naval Intelligence
Subject: Orange[1] Radio Code

1. Information has been received from a reliable military source that considerable progress has been made in the Department of Military Intelligence, Washington, in breaking certain Orange Radio Codes.

2. If the above information is true, the Commander in Chief considers it of vital importance that all such data be available in his SECRET files prior to any emergency that may arise.

3. Should the above information be sent to the Commander in Chief, and if the Director of Naval Intelligence considers it advisable, the mailing envelope will be kept sealed and the seal unbroken until such conditions arise that make it advisable to open it.

4. In connection with the above, it is considered highly desirable that an officer who has completed the Orange language course be made available for duty in the Asiatic Fleet. One such officer is at present on duty on board the flagship, but he is at present under orders to the United States, and his departure will leave no one who is able to speak or translate Orange language.

Thos. Washington
Army's Domestic Intelligence

Under the terms of the National Defense Act of 1920, the six territorial departments of the Army within the continental limits of the United States, were superceded for purposes of administration, training and tactical control by nine corps areas. Likewise, for inspection, maneuvers, war mobilization and demobilization, these same corps areas were further grouped into three larger army areas with the commanding officers and staffs for them to be named from time to time only as necessity arose. The overseas territorial commands, however, continued to remain officially designated as departments.

Subsequent War Department orders also required that there should be an "Assistant Chief of Staff for Military Intelligence" included on the staff of the Commanding General of each Corps Area and Department. This, of course, would have been a particularly appropriate time for the War Department authorities to describe in detail the specific duties assigned to these Corps Area and Department Military Intelligence officers, as well as to establish beyond any doubt their precise relationship to the Assistant Chief of Staff G-2 in Washington. Unfortunately for all concerned, though, these two important steps were not properly taken.

Both the MID officials and the Corps Area Intelligence officer soon felt the need for additional information to provide the latter with effective guidance in the conduct of their assigned duties. It was finally decided, therefore, to furnish each Corps Area and Department Headquarters with six hastily revised copies of a pamphlet that had been prepared during 1918 for use by the field intelligence offices in order to form a divisional intelligence service. This obsolete wartime pamphlet was given the new title of "Provisional Instructions for the Operations of the Military Intelligence Service in Corps Areas and Departments" but it still contained a number of references to approved wartime methods for investigating individuals and groups who might become involved in domestic disorders within the United States. Its issuance under peacetime conditions thus plainly presaged future difficulties for the departmental military intelligence agency.

Following the conclusion of World War I, most of the experienced intelligence personnel within the War Department felt strongly that MID should continue to follow the growth of all significant radical movements either at home or abroad, so as to discharge fully its basic military intelligence responsibilities.[2] This action appeared to be even more essential in view of the possible need for a sudden commitment of Federal troops in the event of major domestic disturbance[3] and because of the constantly increasing efforts by various extremist groups to subvert members of the armed forces. There was no desire on the part of these same officials; however, to examine in any way the political beliefs or other private opinions held by military personnel.[4] That was one reason why an agreement had been concurred in calling for the War Department to relinquish all previous activities connected with military graft and fraud investigations and to turn the entire function without delay over to the Department of the Justice.[5]

Despite every possible effort by the department intelligence authorities to execute their domestic intelligence responsibilities in a manner calculated to avoid outside criticism, they were steadily forced on the defensive. Important segments of the American public were in no mood to countenance any military intelligence activities which they could construe as being an intrusion into their own private affairs, while left wing socialist and pacifist organs remained constantly on the alert to publish in sensational style whatever evidence that came to light point toward military intelligence involvement in such matters.[6] In the MID annual report for the fiscal year ending 30 June 1921, the military security mission assigned to the Negative Branch was most carefully defined as consisting only of the following non-operational tasks:

> 1. Observation of movements within the United States whose object is the overthrow by violence of the government of the United States, or the subversion of the loyalty of the personnel of the military establishment.
>
> 2. Observation of the activities based on foreign countries the object of which is the overthrow of the United States by force.
>
> 3. Study of the measures necessary for carrying out the counter-espionage service in the military establishment in time of war."[7]

The problem of how best to acquire needed information on important radical movements in the United States during peacetime, without stirring up a public furor or encroaching upon the established authority of the Department of Justice, continued to remain an exceedingly vexatious one for the military intelligence authorities to solve. It already had become clearly evident that it no longer be practicable for MID to perform any actual investigations of

American individuals engaged in radical activities, even though their activities were closely related to military subversion or might bear directly upon the possible use of Federal troops in domestic disturbances.[8] The only practicable course of action appeared to lie in working out some sort of an arrangement wherein MID could regularly receive from the Department of Justice "sufficient information on individuals to enable it to have full knowledge of radical and interracial movements" developing within the United States. Necessary steps were taken toward the end of 1920, to initiate a series of conferences between the responsible officials of MID and the Department of Justice on domestic intelligence matters.[9] When these exploratory talks proved to be successful, a formal agreement was jointly signed by Maj. W.W. Hicks, Chief, MI4 and J. Edgar Hoover, which said:

> 1. The Department of Justice will transmit to MID eleven additional copies of its General Intelligence Bulletin, for distribution to each of the Corps Area and Department Intelligence Officers of the Army. Also, after having been officially designated to the Department of Justice by MID, these same Corps Area and Department of Intelligence officers will be granted full access by the Divisional Superintendents of the Department of Justice to their field reports. Such reports, however, are to be examined at the Department of Justice field offices and not removed therefrom by the military intelligence personnel.
>
> 2. MID will furnish to the Division of Investigation enough extra copies of its "G-2 Weekly Situation Survey" for distribution to the nine Divisional Superintendents of the Department of Justice in the field.[10]

Upon completing this noteworthy agreement with the Army intelligence authorities, Hoover took the occasion to declare:

> *"I sincerely hope that the plan which we have devised for a more thorough and effective cooperation will be satisfactorily carried out and if there is any matter which should arise in connection with the arrangements do not hesitate to bring the same to my attention as I am particularly desirous of establishing a thorough cooperation between our two services."*[11]

Although the MID officials did manage in this way to remain for the time being comparatively well-informed regarding the domestic intelligence situation, problems of an extremely embarrassing nature kept coming up on the subject at frequent intervals. These problems were derived principally from the fact that many of the Corps Area G-2's were still conducting undercover investigations along the lines described in their previously issued "Provisional Instructions for the Operation being of the Military Intelligence Service in Corps Areas and Departments." Since activities of this type had already caused a large amount of adverse public comment to be directed against the United States Army, the Director of Military Intelligence, in June 1922, secured permission from the Office of the Chief of Staff to rescind that offending pamphlet. At the same time, the Corps Area Commanders were specifically instructed, as follows:

> The Assistant Chiefs of Staff, G-2 of Corps Areas should be charged with such of the specific duties of the Military Intelligence Division enumerated in paragraph 9, AR 10-15, as are applicable within their respective boundaries. They should be required to make studies from an opponent's point of view of possible operations on the frontier contiguous to their areas, as such studies are necessary for the formulation of mobilization and defense plans. In general, except for the supervision of all activities concerning Military Topographical Surveys and Maps, the collection of information pertaining to our own territory is a function of staff sections or branches other then G-2.[12]

This noticeably vague letter describing the duties of the Corps Area G-2's fell far short of constituting a suitable official directive for delimiting their operations within the domestic intelligence field. Questionable intelligence practices continued in most of the Corps Areas, especially because all the higher tactical headquarters of the Army were still being required to maintain an up-to-date emergency plan covering the possible commitment of their troops in local civil disturbances.[13] It was finally considered necessary, therefore, to dispatch another letter on the same subject to the Corps Area Commanders, in December 1922 as follows:

> *The Secretary of War is much concerned at reports from time to time of the activities of intelligence officers in the United States. It is obvious that the*

American people are very sensitive with regard to any military interference in their affairs. Harmless and even readily justifiable inquiries arouse suspicion and opponents of the Army are very apt to quote such acts as forms of Russian or Prussian military supervision. During the World War it became necessary to investigate individuals, groups and corporations.... All investigations ceased shortly after the Armistice but the general idea was kept alive by the seeking of information preparatory to the drafting of the various local War Plans White. The result is that in the minds of civilians and those of many officers as well, the word "intelligence" is associated with the investigations and inquiries mentioned above.[14]

While this more strongly worded communication seemed to put across the desired point effectively to the Corps Area G-2's themselves, it failed to solve the problem of curbing activities of the more enthusiastic intelligence officers at post, camps and stations, or members of the Military Intelligence Section of the Officers Reserve Corps (M.I. Reserve) who were sponsoring semi-private investigations of radical groups on their own. As long as these individuals kept operating, it probably would be only a matter of time when one of them would undertake some embarrassing project and put military intelligence right back on the front pages of the so-called liberal press. An incident of this sort did take place, derived from a circular letter written by 1st Lt. W.D. Long, Post Intelligence Officer, Vancouver Barracks, Washington, and addressed to all "County Sheriffs of the State of Oregon."[15]

Sent out on his own initiative and without the knowledge or sanction of his commanding officer, the letter contained the following highly explosive statements:

The Intelligence Service of the Army has for its primary purpose the surveillance of all organizations or elements hostile or potentially hostile to the government of this country, or who see to over-throw the government by violence.

Among organizations falling under the above heads are radical groups such as the I.W.W., World War Veterans, Union of Russian Workers, Communist Party, Communist Labor Party, One Big Union, Workers International Industrial Union, Anarchists, Bolsheviki, and such semi-radical organizations as the Socialists, Non-partisan League, Big Four Brotherhoods, and the American Federation of Labor.[16]

As might well be expected, when this circular letter was reproduced in such news organs as *The Nation* and *The Labor Herald*, a violent storm erupted. The affair not only received prominent editorial coverage throughout the country but also caused a deluge of protesting letters to reach the President and Secretary of War, many of them signed by politically influential labor leaders.[17] Secretary of War John W. Weeks ordered the immediate relief of Lt. Long from his military duties[18] and instructions dispatched to all Corps Area Commanders for them to take whatever steps were necessary to insure that no intelligence officer would be appointed in the future at any post, camp or station unless the assignment was specifically prescribed under an existing table of organization.[19] Furthermore, whenever a table of organization did call for the assignment of such an intelligence officer, his responsibilities were to be limited strictly to training troops in their combat intelligence duties.[20]

Still remaining at hand, however, was the ticklish problem of curbing unofficial investigative activities on the part of individual M.I. Reserve officers. This matter was soon handled by addressing a War Department letter to all listed members of the M.I. Reserve and forwarding it to them through their respective Corps Area Commanders. The letter first emphasized that the mere fact of an appointment in the M.I. Reserve did not automatically give the individual permission to perform military security investigations and then went on to forbid the actual conduct of any operations of such type unless they had been directly authorized by the War Department. It also warned each M.I. Reserve officer against taking any personal advantage of his military commission to promote some unofficial investigation in which he might be privately engaged.[21]

These various strictures on domestic intelligence activities were originally applied with equal force both within the overseas Departments and the Corps Areas. It was not long, though, before the intelligence officials of the overseas departments started to complain that they were being seriously hindered by them in the execution of their primary missions. For example, on 16 February 1924, the Assistant Chief of Staff G-2, Hawaiian Department, protested that owning to the peculiar racial conditions existing throughout his area and the absence of any other governmental agency capable of keeping him properly informed about the domestic situation, it was necessary for him to carry out investigations similar to those described in the recently rescinded War Department countersubversive pamphlet. He requested permission, therefore, to continue maintaining "the close watch and supervision that is now being kept on our alien and other racial groups" in Hawaii.[22] Despite the admitted special conditions in his area, the MID authorities chose to reply to him most indefinitely as follows: "You must appreciate that both the letter and spirit of the recent instructions are opposed to investigation activities by military authorities and contemplate them only when absolutely necessary in the interest of national defense or when civilian agencies do not function."[23]

The G-2's of the Panama Canal and Philippine Departments likewise expressed themselves as being thoroughly dissatisfied with the new domestic intelligence situation. The former commented that "a G-2 should be able to give warning of approaching trouble and not wait until trouble starts to find out what it is all about," while the latter felt that in the Philippine area it was "essential that the G-2 be fully informed of the political situation at all times and to do this it is necessary to carry on a modified form of espionage.[24]

On 8 March 1924, the Assistant Chief of Staff G-2, Sixth Corps Area, finally made the rather telling point that he could hardly be expected to devise a suitable counterespionage system for his command under the existing War Department Mobilization Plan unless he was granted access to some effective form of official guidance in the matter. When he further requested that the rescinded provisional instruction pamphlet be reissued to him for such purpose, the action was approved by the Deputy Chief of Staff but only with the proviso that all the returned copies would be clearly stamped "To Be Used Solely in the Preparation of War Plans."[25]

A discouraging climax to the entire postwar domestic intelligence effort occurred early in April 1925. By the time it had become completely apparent to Col. (later Brig. Gen.) James H. Reeves, the Assistant Chief of Staff G-2, War Department General Staff[26], that MID was not receiving enough information under the approved system to fulfill its assigned military security responsibilities for developing the War Department General Mobilization Plan. He believed that the Corps Area Commanders should again be required to forward periodic reports to the War Department "relative to groups and organizations which might be involved in internal disorders or in aiding an enemy." To accomplish this action, he had a letter drafted in MID for dispatch to all the major unit commanders that slightly modified the restrictions that were already in force covering the collection of such information. When this proposed letter was submitted to the Chief of Staff for his approval, it came back with the following unfavorable notation inscribed on it:

> **DISAPPROVED:** *G 2 in liaison with Department of Justice should keep in good touch with general situation without calling on Corps Area Commanders.*
>
> *By order of the Secretary of War*
>
> */s/ D.E. Nolan*
>
> D.E. NOLAN
> *Major General*
> *Deputy Chief of Staff*[27]

A marked deterioration in the performance of basic counterintelligence responsibilities within MID was now plainly evident, with irresistible pressures generated by a hostile public opinion having forced the departmental military intelligence authorities to adopt an essentially negative approach to the whole problem. During 1927, 1928, and 1929, therefore, with reference to domestic intelligence, the following carefully worded paragraph appeared as a regular part of the G-2 Annual Report:

The collection of information by G-2 regarding the radical situation in the United States is confined to that which appears in the public press. The information collected is studied in connection with the possible effect of the radical situation upon the execution of any existing or proposed war plans. It is also studied in connection with the effect upon the efficiency of the Army of the United States at the present time, especially with reference to the military training in schools, colleges and activities of pacifists and radicals.[28]

It was during this particular period that M/Sgt. John J. Mauer, Corps of Intelligence Police, was put in personal charge of all MID activities bearing upon Communist activities and the subversion of Army personnel. He continued to supervise these operations until 18 January 1943, when he was finally forced to transfer to an inactive reserve status "by reason of physical disqualification." His duties were considered to be so ultra-secret that even many members of his own MID branch had no true idea of who was or what he was actually doing. Under his efficient direction, the cellular organization commencing at company level, which had been introduced into the Army in World War I to detect subversives, was first reestablished and then revitalized.

During 1929, in compliance with a provision of the War Department General Mobilization Plan, the MID Operations Branch completed a new "Regulations for Counter Espionage in Time of War." These regulations were promptly approved by the Chief of Staff but with the stipulation that they would be issued only to key field commanders who might have a definite need for them in the appropriate development of their respective mobilization plans.

Early in 1931, with the Nation already in the midst of a severe economic depression and the threat of serious domestic disturbances mounting daily, Brig. Gen. A.T. Smith, the new Assistant Chief of Staff G-2[29], decided to reopen once more the sensitive question of MID shortcomings in not being able to maintain an effective surveillance over radical activities in the United states. On 19 February 1931, he submitted a relevant study to the Chief of Staff, which strongly recommended the lifting of all restrictions in regard to corps area and other field intelligence officers investigating such matters. Even though this recommendation had been formally concurred in by the G-1, G-3, G-4, and the Chief of the War Plans Division, it was disapproved by the Chief of Staff, Gen. Douglas MacArthur, who declared "it is not believed advisable at this time to initiate this procedure."[30] Unfortunately for the departmental military effort, this adverse decision was made just when the first bonus marches were being organized throughout the country for the avowed purpose of converging upon the District of Columbia and intimidating the United States Government. Six months later, though, permission was finally obtained on a temporary basis to have the Corps Area Commanders forward to the War Department a monthly report covering subversive activities detected within their own areas.

After the initial bonus marcher groups had actually started to undertake a mass descent upon Washington, the Assistant Chief of Staff G-2, was belatedly instructed by higher authority to follow their detailed progress. Accordingly, on 25 May 1932, a secret War Department memorandum was sent out to all Corp Area Intelligence Officers directing them to investigate and report regularly concerning "bonus demonstrations by veterans." At the same time, MID commenced to forward a daily memorandum to the Chief of Staff describing the current status of the bonus marcher situation within the Nation's capital.[31] Because of this intensified intelligence effort, the antisubversive files of the departmental intelligence agency soon grew to be richly productive in valuable information and personnel data covering the large number of Communist agitators who were operating with the Bonus Expeditionary Force (BEF).[32]

The principal sources utilized by MID in collecting information on subversive individuals within the ranks of the bonus marchers were through direct observation by departmental military intelligence personnel, civil police[33] and press reports, and interviews held with cooperative BEF members. Alerted United States Army troop units stationed in or near the District of Columbia also executed a number of special reconnaissance missions and notified MID of the results obtained. The departmental agency thus soon found itself actually acting as an operational intelligence center, with Sergeant Mauer in direct charge. Oddly enough, in this same connection, when the Assistant Chief of Staff G-2, Second Corps Area, queried a local representative of the Division of Investigation of the Department of Justice on the subject of bonus marcher activities, he was told that "the Bureau has no jurisdiction over communistic or radical activities and cannot engage in any inquiry concerning same."[34]

Even after the remarkably successful eviction, on 28-29 July 1932, of the original bonus marcher expedition from the District of Columbia by United States Army elements without firing a single shot, the threat of further domestic disturbances along similar lines continued to remain dangerously acute.[35] As a mater of fact, radical elements had recently launched a concerted subversive drive among the ranks of the Civilian Conservation Corps, which was then in the process of being organized as an antidepression measure by the national administration. Communist-inspired efforts to stir up discontent of major proportions not only continued throughout the life of that particular corps but also were later coupled with a companion effort aimed at personnel of the National Guard.[36]

The United States Army now stood in obvious need of an active and efficient counterintelligence organization centered about MID but it was not long before the powerful influences which were constantly trying to limit activities along such lines again became controlling. Effective 19 March 1934, for example, "in order to relieve the Corps Area G-2's of the burden of preparing monthly subversive reports, that profitable requirement was abruptly terminated.[37] Nevertheless, to overcome the effects of this unfavorable development, an informal practice shortly grew up wherein the Corps Area Assistant Chief of Staff G-2's continued to forward to MID a series of unofficial monthly "Notes on the Subversive Situation."[38] They were severely handicapped in this irregular enterprise, however, since they did not dare to engage in any open investigative activity to support it.

During early 1934, with Japanese-American relations rapidly worsening, both the President and the War Department began to receive a large number of letters claiming information to the effect that the Panama Canal was in immediate danger of sabotage. As might well be expected, these warnings proceeded to set off a complicated train of events involving the departmental military intelligence agency. After a high-level conference on the subject, attended by representatives of the War, Navy and State Departments, the Secretary of War addressed a letter to the Commanding General, Panama Canal department, with information copy to the Governor of the Canal Zone, directing that "no effort be spared to maintain the safety of the Canal from any type of sabotage."[39] A corresponding conference was then held within the Panama area, which mainly resulted in a request to Washington for additional counterespionage funds and the assignment of a qualified specialist to coordinate and advise the Governor relative to military security matters. The Secretary of War duly approved these two requests on 11 April 1934.

In searching for a counterintelligence expert to assist the Governor of the Canal Zone as requested, Brig. Gen. A.T. Smith first consulted with J. Edgar Hoover and W.H. Moran, Chief of the United States Secret Service, hoping that one of these key internal security officials might be able to recommend an acceptable civilian for the position. When neither of them seemed willing to do so, he was then forced to turn to the Officer Reserve Corps list in order to find a qualified person with suitable military intelligence background. After careful reviewing the considerable number of applications he had received, General Smith finally selected Maj. Harry A. Taylor, Infantry Reserve, for the assignment. Major Taylor was directed to report to Panama without delay, to become the "Intelligence Specialist for the Governor of the Canal Zone."[40]

Under the existing "Joint Cooperative Plan for the Defense of the Panama Canal," the G-2 Office, Panama Canal Department, was designated as the "coordinating agency for protective information gathered by the Canal Administration, Army and Navy." Although the American Legation in Panama had not formed a part of this early collection arrangement, the MID officials felt that it should now be brought into the regional intelligence picture just as soon as possible. Hence, the Secretary of War was prevailed upon to direct the Governor of the Canal Zone to reach an agreement with the American Administer in Panama City, which would serve to link the Legation in security matters with the three other parties concerned and thereby insure a maximum coordination of effort for collecting information on Canal Zone protection. The eventual result was the creation of a four-member

Interdepartmental Intelligence Liaison Board to accomplish that particular purpose, composed of appropriate local intelligence representatives from the Canal Zone Administration, American Legation in Panama, Naval District and Army Department.

The pressures caused by that particular sabotage scare not only served to improve the conduct of counterintelligence operations throughout the Panama Canal area measurably but also helped the Assistant Chief of Staff G-2, War Department General Staff, gain requisite authority to reopen the American military Attaché Office in Columbia, which had been closed in 1932 as an economy measure. On the other hand, similar requests for reopening inactive military posts in Peru and Venezuela failed to obtain like approval until 1939 and 1940, respectively.

During the same general period, MID received numerous reports from a wide variety of more or less reliable sources claiming to describe the operations of Japanese intelligence agents both in the United States and its overseas territories. Additionally, the Army Signal Corps succeeded in intercepting and translating a significant volume of Japanese governmental and commercial coded messages. There was, therefore, a gradual but notable resurgence of counterintelligence activity within the War Department that finally culminated on 17 April 1939, in the establishment of a separate MID Counterintelligence Branch.

This new Counterintelligence Branch was purposely designed to achieve a better functional concentration for military security activities than had been obtainable under the earlier catchall Operations Branch. For that reason, it was given the more aptly descriptive name of "counterintelligence" in denoting its activities, instead of the less adequate terms of "negative intelligence" or "counterespionage." Initially allocated an officer complement of only one colonel, one lieutenant colonel and one major, the branch was called upon to accomplish the following specific tasks:

1. Plans and regulations for both national and military censorship.
2. Plans and regulations for counterespionage and passport control.
3. Domestic intelligence information.
4. Safeguarding of military information.
5. Plans and regulations for espionage.[41]

One of the immediate effects of the improved counterintelligence situation in MID was to place a greatly increased emphasis upon issuing proper security instructions for use by the United States Army. This was a most important matter because the current instructions were not only in obvious need of re-codification but also often in actual conflict with each other. The first AR 380-5 "Safeguarding Military Information," dated 19 June 1939, therefore, sought to combine all of the existing rules and regulations on that complicated subject into one concise document. A new counterintelligence field manual was then promptly prepared, which later formed an integral part of the BFM 30 (Military Intelligence) series that was issued to the Army commencing in 1940.

Because the War Department Mobilization Instructions for 1938 had stressed that all subordinate mobilization plans must provide for the immediate institution of military censorship in case of an emergency, the new counterintelligence manual included detailed instructions covering the establishment of such censorship in the field.[42] Censorship planning at the departmental and national level was also expedited in order to complete a joint (Army-Navy) censorship plan by early 1941, which was then approved by the President. While most of the activity within the censorship field continued to remain only in the planning stage prior to the end of the peacetime period, several selected officer-specialists were sent to Bermuda for the purpose of observing British censorship methods and an informal lecture course in military censorship for "certain key officers" was opened at Clarendon, Virginia. Finally, effective 1 September 1941, a separate Censorship Branch was created in MID.

Along with the rest of MID, the Counterintelligence Branch was being sorely handicapped at this time by a constant lack of insufficient and qualified personnel. During June 1940, though, after the assignment of three recent graduates from the Army War College, it was reorganized on a much sounder basis and placed in a better position to conduct an orderly expansion if and when more funds might become available. Early in 1941, the branch also managed to establish a school for the express purpose of training counterintelligence agents. Instructors for this school were selected from among former FBI agents and civilian detectives holding ORC commissions. Its initial graduates all had to be utilized directly by MID in attempting to uncover subversives working at Army arsenals or plants executing government contracts but it was later possible to assign some of them to tactical units in the field.[43]

There were several other important counterintelligence developments just before Pearl Harbor, as follows:

1. Shortly after the Counterintelligence Branch was formed, the problem of satisfying the basic requirements for establishing suitable security measures in industrial plants working on manufacturing projects for the Army became acute. Since the FBI had already started to make lengthy surveys along such lines[44], there was also a compelling need for devising more effective coordination procedures among the many different government agencies involved. Any new system adopted would have to be extended without delay in order to cover the numerous plants and arsenals still operating directly under military control. In October 1939, therefore, Maj. (later Brig. Gen.) W.E. Crist, received instructions from the Assistant Chief of Staff G-2, War Department General Staff, to form a "Plant Protection Section." His new section then promptly commenced to compile pertinent security data with reference to civilian manufacturing facilities engaged in classified or sensitive government contracts, as well as for all military installations handling critical items.

2. In June 1940, MID issued a revised confidential pamphlet entitled "Countersubversive Instructions" to all Army, Corps Area, Department and GHQ Air Force Intelligence Officers. The Chief purpose of this security pamphlet was to clarify earlier instructions regarding the formation of a cellular countersubversive control organization within their respective commands starting at the company level. The new instructions were optimistically intended to achieve a high degree of lateral coordination between this undercover security system and the normal chain of command, a most desirable goal but one which had never before been satisfactorily attained.

3. In view of the impressive combat successes that had recently been gained throughout Western Europe by the German Army, the Assistant Chief of Staff G-2 became gravely concerned early in 1940 with the problem of providing appropriate security in the rear areas of American military forces operating in the field. He felt that under currently accepted defense doctrines a serious "fifth column" threat could easily develop within these areas, occasioned either by a major domestic disturbance or a full-scale attack from without. For this reason, he had already directed the preparation in MID of a "War Department Counter Fifth Column Plan." This plan, which was submitted to the Chief of Staff on 6 October 1940,[45] not only described the effective organization of a rear area defense without any important commitment of combat troops but also contemplated the timely accumulation of sufficient counterintelligence information in the United States and possessions to cover all areas where such a defense might become necessary. It was given prompt official approval and forwarded to the Corps Area and Department Commanders on 22 October 1940.[46]

4. Early in January 1941, Brig. Gen. (later Maj. Gen.) C.H. Bonesteel, Commanding General, Sixth Corps Area, addressed a letter to the War Department calling attention to certain military steps which should be taken without further delay to insure the security and continued operation of the canal and locks situated near Sault Ste. Marie, Michigan. Both the Director, FBI, and the Transportation Commissioner of the Advisory Commission for the Council of National Defense had previously written personnel letters on this same subject to the Secretary of War.[47] The matter was far from simple, though, because one of the locks was located on Canadian territory and there were two international bridges crossing the canal area. Brig. Gen. (later Maj. Gen.) Sherman Miles, the Acting Assistant Chief of Staff G-2, had displayed an active interest in the problem and MID was already preparing a detailed intelligence study pertaining to it. When finished, this study recommended the immediate institution of more than twenty new security procedures at critical defense plants and the transfer of an infantry battalion from Camp Custer to Fort Brady, Michigan, so as to give such points more substantial military protection. It also recommended stationing a Coast Artillery unit with the general area. Eventually, the War Department created, effective 15 March 1941, a special "District of Sault Sainte Marie" defense sector in the Sixth Corps Area for the announced purpose of "safeguarding and protecting the St. Mary's Falls Canal and Great Lakes Waterway from Whitefish Bay to Lake Huron."[48]

5. On 10 June 1941, in view of the national emergency,[49] the Assistant Chief of Staff G-2 was finally granted permission to instruct the Corps Area and Department Commanders to "maintain a digest of subversive situation which will be kept in such form that a brief estimate of the situation, with conclusions, may be submitted promptly by telephone, radiogram, or otherwise, upon request of the War Department." These same commanders were again cautioned, however not to allow any unauthorized investigative activities by their intelligence personnel in accomplishing this newly assigned mission.

6. The President, on 14 November 1941, directed the Secretary of State, to set up a "comprehensive system for the control of all persons, citizens and aliens alike, entering or leaving the United States and its possessions." In compliance, the Secretary of State soon requested the War Department to provide proper representation on several visa committees and one seaman's passport committee, which were being established. MID was naturally called upon to furnish this representation, so the departmental military intelligence agency once more commenced to take part in handling passport and visa control matters for the United States Government.

Hence, after undergoing an abrupt shrinkage immediately following the conclusion of World War I, domestic intelligence operations for the United States Army were soon committed to a lengthy period of enforced inactivity. This unfavorable situation was dictated principally by a public opinion that remained consistently hostile to any form of military intelligence activities along such lines. The handicaps stemming from such outside pressure were somewhat overcome in 1932, though, when the Government was confronted with a series of threatening domestic disturbance caused to a large extent by economic unrest but also conveniently exploited throughout by Communist and other radical elements. These same events likewise served to focus the attention of the national authorities upon the prompt necessity for uncovering Communist attempts to subvert members of the Civilian Conservation Corps and the National Guard. A rapid succession of espionage and sabotage scares pointing toward an alarming increase in foreign agent activities, especially Japanese, against the United States, further contributed to this delayed recognition of the seriousness of the domestic intelligence problem.

Even though the creation of a separate Counterintelligence Branch, within the MID in April 1939, resulted in a more effective domestic intelligence program, this branch, along with the rest of the departmental agency, continued to suffer from a persistent lack of personnel and funds. As a matter of fact, it was not until after the President had issued his limited emergency proclamation in September 1939 that these crippling conditions were permitted slightly to ease. They gradually did improve, however, to the extent that during the last year before Pearl Harbor, there was a marked increase in all phases of Army counterintelligence operations. By 7 December 1941, the Counterintelligence Branch of MID had progressed to the point where it was relatively well-prepared to perform most of its major functional responsibilities and to participate actively in the crucial military security problems which were about to face the Nation.

ONI Message

From: Director of Naval Intelligence
To: Pacific Coast Communication Superintendent
Subject: Japanese Government Radio Traffic
Reference: (a) Letter 1651 24 of 25 January 1924

1. Reference (a) addressed to the Chief of Naval Operations was referred to this office. The letter itself has been referred to the Director of Naval Communications so far as the traffic problem is concerned.

2. The enclosures have been examined in this office and they are all from Japanese officials in this country to Japanese Government offices, principally to the Ministry of Foreign Affairs.

3. The copies enclosed have been sent to the Cryptographic Section of the Code & Signal Section, where they are accumulating a file of all Japanese code messages and it is noted that code and English and code and Japanese have been mixed which us a valuable aid in cryptography.

4. This office also picked up one or two names from Buenos Aires that are interesting from the espionage standpoint and the message regarding

Loomis shows his standing as a propagandist in the Japanese Government.

5. It is believed highly desirable that copies of all Japanese messages in code and all Japanese messages in plain Japanese addressed to government offices in Japan or in the United States be sent to this office for examination and later to be sent to the Code & Signal Section for cryptographic work. It is requested if practicable that this be done. It is impossible to get from the telephone companies or cable companies any Japanese messages, government of otherwise.

/s/ Henry H. Hough

Attorney General Harlan Stone's Reforms

In April 1924, a new Attorney General took charge of a scandal-ridden Department of Justice. Harlan Fiske Stone, former Dean of the Columbia Law School, had been appointed by President Calvin Coolidge to replace the late President Warren Harding's political crony Harry Daugherty. Stone confronted more than simply corruption in the Justice Department when he took office. The Department's Bureau of Investigation had become a secret political police force. As Stone recalled later, "The organization was lawless, maintaining many activities which were without any authority in federal statutes, and engaging in many practices which were brutal and tyrannical in the extreme."[50]

Attorney General Stone asked for the resignation of the Bureau Director William J. Burns, former head of the Burns Detective Agency, and directed that the activities of the Bureau "be limited strictly to investigations of violations of the law, under my direction or under the direction of an Assistant Attorney General regularly conducting the work of the Department of Justice." Stone also ordered a review of the entire personnel of the Bureau, the removal of "those who are incompetent and unreliable," and the future selection of "men of known good character and ability, giving preference to men who have had some legal training."[51] The Attorney General chose the young career Bureau official, J. Edgar Hoover, as Acting Director to implement these reforms, largely because of Hoover's reputation within the Justice Department as an honest and efficient administrator.[52]

A principal problem Stone faced was the Bureau's domestic intelligence operation. He was vividly aware of the violations of individual rights committed in the name of domestic security at the time of the 1920 "Palmer raids." He had joined a committee of protest against Attorney General Palmer's round up of radical aliens for deportation and had urged a congressional investigation. When a Senate Judiciary Subcommittee began hearings in 1921, its first order of business was a letter from Stone calling for "a thoroughgoing investigation of the conduct of the Department of Justice in connection with the deportation cases."[53]

In considering *J. Edgar Hoover* for the position of permanent Director of the Bureau of Investigation, Attorney General Stone was aware that he had played a major role in the "Palmer raids" as head of the Justice Department's General Intelligence Division. Roger Baldwin of the American Civil Liberties Union told Stone that he was skeptical of Hoover's ability to reform the Bureau.

With the Attorney General's knowledge, Baldwin met with Hoover to discuss the future of the Bureau. Hoover assured Baldwin that he had played an "unwilling part" in the activities of Palmer, Daugherty, and Burns. He said he regretted their tactics but had not been in a position to anything about them. He intended to help Stone build and efficient law enforcement agency, employing law school graduates, severing connections with private detective agencies, and not issuing propaganda. Most important from the American Civil Liberties Union's point of view, the Bureau's "radical division" would be disbanded. Baldwin wrote Stone, "I think we were wrong in our estimate of his attitude," and announced to the press that the ACLU believed the Justice Department's "red-hunting" days were over.[54]

When Attorney General Stone arrived in 1924, he requested a review of the applicability of the federal criminal statutes to Communist activities in the United States. Various patriotic organizations had urged that Communists be prosecuted under the federal sedition conspiracy law, but the courts had ruled that this Civil War statute required proof of a definite plan to use force against the government.⁵⁵ Justice Department lawyers also rejected prosecution under the Logan Act, enacted in the 1790s to punish hostile communications between American citizens and a foreign country.⁵⁶ These conclusions buttressed the Attorney General's decision to abolish the Bureau's domestic intelligence operations, although Stone told Roger Baldwin of the ACLU that he had no authority to destroy the Bureau's intelligence files, without an Act of Congress.⁵⁷

Attorney General Stone may also have contemplated the possibility of future investigations under Congress's prewar revision of the Justice Department appropriations statute. He asked Acting Director Hoover whether the Bureau would have the authority to investigate Soviet and Communist activities within the United States for the State Department in connection with the question of recognition of the Soviet government. Hoover replied that the appropriations act did allow such investigations, upon formal request by the Secretary of State and approval of the Attorney General. The Acting Director stressed that such investigations "should be conducted on an entirely different line than previously conducted by the Bureau of Investigation" and that there should be no publicity "because any publicity would materially hamper the obtaining of successful results."⁵⁸

After 1924, the Bureau of Investigation continued to receive information volunteers to it about Communist activities, and Bureau field offices were ordered to forward such data to headquarters. But the Bureau made "no investigations of such activities, inasmuch as it does not appear that there is any violation of a Federal Penal Statute involved."⁵⁹ Military intelligence officers still had a duty, under an Army emergency plan, to gather information "with reference to the economical, industrial and radical conditions, to observe incidents and events that may develop into strikes, riots, or other disorders and to investigate and report upon the industrial and radical situation."

However, by 1925 the military lacked adequate personnel and requested the Bureau of Investigation to provide information on "radical conditions."⁶⁰ J. Edgar Hoover replied that the Bureau had discontinued "general investigations into radical activities," but would communicate to the military any information received from specific investigations of federal violations "which may appear to be of interest" to the military.⁶¹

Despite the curtailment of federal intelligence operations, it would be misleading to say that domestic intelligence operations ceased in the United States after 1924. The efforts of state and local authorities to investigate possible violations of state sedition laws continued in many parts of the country. Moreover, private industry engaged the services of detectives and informers to conduct surveillance of labor organizing activities. These industrial espionage programs reached their peak in the early 1930's.

A Senate committee investigations in 1936 exposed these tactics and influenced at least one private detective firm, the Pinkerton Agency, to discontinue its anti-labor spying. The Senate inquiry documented the efficient techniques developed by labor spies for destroying unions. They wreaked havoc on union

John Edgar Hoover

locals, generating mistrust, inciting violence, and reporting the identities of union members to hostile employers.[62]

On one major occasion early in the Depression, military intelligence was reactivated temporarily. Army Chief of Staff Douglas MacArthur ordered corps area commanders in mid-1931 to submit reports on subversive activities in their areas. When the "bonus marchers" began arriving in Washington in 1932 to demand veteran benefits, military intelligence agents investigated Communist influence with the help of American Legion officials, reserve officers, and other volunteers.

Military intelligence reports exaggerating the threat of "insurrectionists" among the veteran protestors contributed to the decision to use troops in a mass assault to clear the demonstrators out of Washington. Criticism of this operation led military authorities to instruct that intelligence officers be more discreet although they continued to gather intelligence on civilian groups.[63]

Therefore, while Attorney General Stone had stopped the Justice Department's intelligence efforts in 1924, safeguards did not exist against state, private or military intelligence operations. Moreover, the Bureau of Investigation retained its massive domestic intelligence files from the 1916-1924 period, as well as the vague legal authority under the appropriations act to conduct investigations going beyond the detection of federal crimes if a future Attorney General and a Secretary of State should direct it to do so.

Nevertheless, when Congressman Hamilton Fish and members of a Special House Committee to Investigate Communist Activities in the United States proposed legislation authorizing the Bureau of Investigation to investigate "Communist and revolutionary activity" in 1931, Director Hoover opposed it. He told Congressman Fish that it would be better to enact a criminal statute and not expand the Bureau's power beyond criminal investigation, especially since the Bureau had "never been established by legislation" and operated "solely on an appropriation bill."[64]

Hoover advised the Attorney General a year later,

The work of the Bureau of Investigation at this time is...of an open character not in any manner subject to criticism, and the operations of the Bureau of Investigation may be given the closest scrutiny at all times...The conditions will materially differ were the Bureau to embark upon a policy of investigative activity into conditions which, from a federal standpoint, have not been declared illegal and in connection with which no prosecution might be instituted. The Department and the Bureau would undoubtedly be subject to charges in the matter of alleged secret and undesirable methods...as well as to allegations involving charges of the use of "Agents Provocateur."

Hoover assumed that the Immigration Bureau with jurisdiction to deport Communist aliens conducted such investigation and, if it did not, "would be subject to criticism for its laxity along these lines." Thus, the Director's position was not based on opposition to the idea of domestic intelligence itself, but rather on his concern for possible criticism of the Bureau if it were to resume "undercover" activities which would be necessary "to secure a foothold in Communistic inner circles" and "to keep fully informed as to changing policies and secret propaganda on the part of Communists."[65]

Letter Hoover to Lang

September 18, 1925

>Commander E.K. Lang
>Office of Naval Intelligence
>*Navy Department*
>*Washington, D.C.*

There has just come to my attention certain information which I thought might be of some interest and value to you. The son of a friend of mine in New York has succeeded in picking up Nijui Novgorod Soviet Government Radio laboratory on his short wave set. The transmission is now experimental, as announced by the operation of the Soviet station.

It has occurred to me that the Navy short wave station might probably be interested in this information and might be able to pick up some code which would be interesting to decipher. The set which the son of this friend of mine is using was made by him and I have no doubt but that other parties who really have an interest in getting information from Russia are operating sets that are receiving messages from the Soviet station. Knowing that the Soviets are still disseminating propaganda and are in touch with parties on this side, it occurred to me that the medium of the radio would be excellent to use in sending code messages.

Very truly yours,

/s/ J. Edgar Hoover
Director

Navy Department Memo

Navy Department
Office of Chief of Naval Operations
Washington
22 September 1925

From: Officer-in-Charge, Code and Signal Section
To: Lieut. Comdr. E.K. Lang, U.S.N.

SUBJECT: Messages from Nujui Novgorod Soviet Government Radio Laboratory

Reference: Letter from Mr. J. Edgar Hoover, of 18 September 1925

1. The Navy short wave receiving sets are all engaged in handling traffic or in experimental work and cannot be spared for the purpose of copying foreign traffic in which the State Department may be interested.

2. It is suggested that you request this amateur, through Mr. Hoover, to copy such traffic from the Nujui Novgorod Radio Laboratory as he can, and forward it direct to the Office of Naval Intelligence. This traffic will probably be in plain language (if for propaganda) and can be translated by your Translating Section.

3. Such parts of this traffic as may be in cipher can be forwarded to the Code and Signal Section.

/s/ D. J. Friedell

Special Committee To Investigate Un-American Activities

This committee was established in 1934 and chaired by Representative John W. McCormack from Massachusetts. The committee was charged with investigating activities by Communists, Nazis and Fascists. The committee concluded that communism was not sufficiently strong enough to harm the United States but its continued growth did represent a future danger to the country. The committee's report cited that attempts were being made from abroad and by diplomatic or consular officials to influence Americans. They also found that some efforts were being made to organize some of the citizens and resident aliens and said that constitutional rights of Americans had to be preserved from these "isms." They found Nazism, Fascism and Communism all to be equally dangerous and unacceptable to American interest.

To solve the problem, the Committee recommended that a law be enacted:

1. that required the registration of all publicity, propaganda, or public relations agents, or other agents who represent any foreign country;

2. that the Secretary of Labor have authority to shorten or terminate any visit to the United States by any foreign visitor traveling on a temporary visa if that person engaged in propaganda activities;

3. that the Department of State and Department of Labor negotiate treaties with other nations to take back their citizens who are deported;

4. that Congress make it unlawful to advise, counsel or urge any military or naval member, including the reserves, to disobey the laws and regulations governing such forces;

5. that Congress enact legislation so the U.S. Attorneys outside the District of Columbia can proceed against witnesses who refuse to answer questions, produce documents or records or refuse to appear or hold in contempt the authority of any Congressional investigating committee; and

6. that Congress make it unlawful for any person to advocate the overthrow or destruction of the United

States Government or the form of government guaranteed to the States by Article IV of the fourth section of the Constitution.

On the basis of the Committee's recommendation, Congress enacted the McCormack Foreign Agents Registration Act in 1938.

The FBI Intelligence Program, 1936-1938

Instructions were issued to FBI agents immediately after Director Hoover's meeting with the President and the Secretary of State. FBI field offices were ordered "to obtain from all possible sources information concerning subversive activities being conducted in the United States by Communists, Fascists, representatives or advocates of other organizations or groups advocating the overthrow or replacement of the Government of the United States by illegal methods."[66]

Theoretically, this directive included purely domestic matters besides the international Communist and Fascists movements. There is no indication; however, that the President or the Attorney General were advised of this order; and the communications between the FBI Director and his superiors made no mention of advocacy of overthrow of the government. Instead, the terms used in 1936 were "general intelligence" and subversive activities."

Following the Hoover-Roosevelt meetings, FBI officials also began developing a systematic organization for intelligence information "concerning subversive activities." The following general classifications were adopted:

Maritime Industry
Activities in Government Affairs
Activities in the Steel Industry
Activities in the Coal Industry
Activities in the Newspaper Field
Activities in the Clothing, Garment and Fur Industries
General Strike Activities
Activities in the Armed Forces of the United States
Activities in Educational Institutions

General Activities—Communist Party and Affiliated Organizations
Activities of the Fascists
Anti Fascists Movements
Activities in Organized Labor Organizations

Steps were also taken to determine whether certain individuals were "available for service in the capacity of an informant," to "index the material previously submitted," and to "prepare memoranda dealing individually with those persons whose names appear prominently at the present time in the subversive circles." The Director was to receive daily memoranda on "major developments in any field" of subversive activities.[67]

The President's instructions had dealt with relations between the FBI and other federal agencies. At this initial meeting with Hoover, the President said that the Secret Service "had assured him that they had informants in every Communist group," but Roosevelt believed this" was solely for the purpose of getting any information upon plots upon his life." He told Hoover that the Secret Service "was not to be brought in on this matter of protecting his life and the survey which he desired to have made with on a much broader field." In addition, the President suggested that Hoover "endeavor to coordinate any investigation along similar lines which might be made by the Military or Naval Intelligence Services."[68]

The Director told his subordinates that he had advised the Attorney General that he would "coordinate, as the President suggested, information upon these matters in the possession of the Military Intelligence Division, the Naval Intelligence Division, and the State Department.[69]

The FBI and the military intelligence proceeded along these lines in 1937-1938. The President designated Attorney General Cummings "as Chairman of a Committee in inquire into the so-called espionage situation" in October 1938, and to report on the need for "an additional appropriation for domestic intelligence." The Attorney General advised the President that a "well defined system" was functioning, made up of the FBI, the Military Intelligence Division, and the Office of Naval Intelligence, whose heads were "in frequent contact and are operating in harmony." He recommended that the appropriations be increased by $35,000 each for MID and ONI and by $300,000 for the FBI. He also submitted a plan prepared by Director Hoover in consultation with the military agencies. He observed that "no additional legislation to accomplish the general objectiveness seems to be required" and that "the matter should be handled in strictest confidence."[70]

The FBI Director's memorandum spelled out the reasons why legislation was considered undesirable. Hoover believed the FBI's expansion could "be covered" by the language in the appropriations statute relating to "other investigations" conducted for the State Department: [71]

> Under this provision investigations have been conducted in years pasts for the State Department of matters which do not in themselves constitute a specific violation of a Federal Criminal Statute, such as subversive activities. Consequently, this provision is believed to be sufficiently broad to cover any expansion of the present intelligence and counter espionage work which it may be deemed necessary to carry on....

In considering the steps to be taken for the expansion of the present structure of intelligence work, it is believed imperative that it be proceeded with, with the utmost degree of secrecy in order to avoid criticism or objections which might be raised to such an expansion by either ill-informed persons or individuals having some ulterior motive. The word "espionage" has long been a word that has been repugnant to the American people and it is believed that the structure which is already in existence is much broader than espionage or counterespionage, but covers in a true sense real intelligence values to the three services interested, namely, the Navy, the Army, and Justice. Consequently, it would seem undesirable to seek any special legislation which would draw attention to the fact that it was proposed to develop a special counter-espionage drive of any great magnitude.[72]

Hoover noted that Army and Navy Intelligence did not need additional legislation "since their activities...are limited to matters concerning their respective services."

The FBI Director reviewed the current and proposed future operations of each of the three intelligence agencies. The FBI had set up a General Intelligence Section to investigative and correlate information dealing with "activities of either a subversive or a so-called intelligence type."

Each FBI field office had "developed contacts with various persons in professional, business, and law enforcement fields" to obtain this information. The following was a break-down of the subject matter in the Intelligence Section: "Maritime; government; industry (steel, automobile, coal, mining, and miscellaneous); general strikes; armed forces; education institutions Fascists; Nazi; organized labor; Negroes; youth; strikes; newspaper field; and miscellaneous." All information "of a subversive or general intelligence character pertaining to any of the above" was reviewed and filed at FBI headquarters, with index cards on individuals which made it possible to identify the persons "engaged in any particular activity, either in any section of the country or in a particular industry or movement."

This index then included "approximately 2500 names...of the various types of individuals engaged in activities of Communism, Nazism, and various types of foreign espionage." In addition, the FBI had "developed a rather extensive library of general intelligence matters, including sixty-five daily, weekly, and monthly publications, as well as many pamphlets and volumes dealing with general intelligence activities." From both investigative sources and research, the FBI from time to time prepared "charts...to show the growth and extent of certain activities."[73]

The Office of Naval Intelligence and the Military Intelligence Division were concerned with "subversive activities that undermine the loyalty and efficiency" of Army and Navy personnel or civilians involved in military construction and maintenance; with sabotage of military facilities or of "agencies contributing o the efficiency:" of the military; and with "spy activities that may result in divulgence of information to foreign countries or to persons when such divulgence is contrary to the interests of our national defense." However, MID and ONI lacked trained investigators, and they relied on the FBI "to conduct investigative activity in strictly civilian matters of a domestic character." The three agencies exchanged information of interest o one another, both in the field and at headquarters in Washington.

For the future, all three agencies agreed that other federal agencies should be excluded from intelligence work since others were "less interested in matters of general intelligence and counter-intelligence." And because "the more circumscribed this program is, the more effective it will be and the less danger there is of its becoming a matter of general public knowledge." The FBI hoped to expand its personnel so that it could assign an agent specializing in intelligence to each of its forty-five field offices and could reopen offices in Hawaii, Alaska, and Puerto Rico. Additional funds would also be used to expand FBI facilities for "specialized training in general intelligence work."[74]

Director Hoover met with the President in November 1938 and learned that he had instructed the Budget Bureau "to include in the Appropriations estimate $50,000 for Military Intelligence, $50,000 for Naval Intelligence and $150,000 for the Federal Bureau of Investigation to handle counter-espionage activities." The President also said "that had approved the plan which (Hoover) had prepared and which had been sent to him by the Attorney General," except for the revised budget figures. [75]

The Search For Japanese Spies

The Office of Naval Intelligence (ONI) suspected that the Japanese naval attaché office at the Japanese Embassy in Washington, D.C. controlled their spy operations throughout the United States. Under ONI guidance, efforts were increased to cover Japanese activities, including surveillance of Embassy military officials and suspected Japanese naval officers posing as students at major American universities. Their efforts resulted in the expulsion of Japanese assistant naval attaché, Yoshiro Kanamoto, who was caught photographing the U.S. Navy's fuel oil reserve depot at Point Loma and sketching the North Island Naval Air Station.

William D. Puleston, ONI Director, took a personal interest in the so-called language students. "The personality and movements of Japanese language officers are matters of greatest interest to this office, because experience in the past has shown that they engage in illegal activities." ONI was able to confirm the Director's concerns about this perceived threat from deciphering Japanese coded radio messages.

In reviewing a Japanese message, a cryptoanalyst, Miss Aggie Driscoll, had marked a section with contained the word "TO-MI-MU-RA." Not knowing what it meant, Miss Aggie, as her colleagues called her, showed the message to a Japanese language expert. The expert initially said that the word could reflect a Japanese name but Miss Aggie did not buy that explanation. The expert next suggested that the part of the word "mura" means town but also has an alternate meaning of "son." By putting the first part of the word with "son," the word becomes "Tomison or Thompson. ONI now a lead to a possible spy.

The lead led to Harry J. Thompson, a clerk in the Navy, who was contacting his ex-shipmates on behalf of the Japanese. His case officer was Commander Miyazaki, who was in the United States under English language student cover. When the FBI arrested Thompson, Miyazaki suddenly left the United States for Japan. Thompson was convicted under the Espionage Act of 1917 and sentenced to fifteen years at McNeil Island.

The radio traffic also revealed another possible American spy, codenamed Agent K. ONI investigation resulted in identifying Agent K as John Semer Farnsworth.

John Semer Farnsworth was arrested on 14 July 1937 and charged with selling confidential papers of the U.S. Navy to an agent of the Japanese government. Farnsworth, a former Lt. Commander, was held on $10,000 bond and confined to the Washington, D.C. jail until his preliminary hearing.

The Japanese embassy depicted the charges as "astonishing" and stated that the first time they heard of Farnsworth was on the day before his arrest when someone called the embassy twice to ask for money in connection with a recent spy case. The spy case the embassy was referring to involved a former navy enlisted man, Harry T. Thompson, who was convicted and sentenced at Los Angeles, California for selling naval secrets to a Japanese agent.

FBI Director, J. Edgar Hoover, denied the arrest of Farnsworth was connected to the Thompson case. Thompson was the first man convicted of espionage since World War I. The U.S. Navy said that Farnsworth and Thompson are the only two such espionage cases in the history of the navy. Later years would see many more such cases.

Farnsworth, born 13 August 1893 in Chicago, Illinois, was appointed to the U.S. Naval Academy in 1911. The Naval Academy yearbook described Farnsworth as "daring and reckless." The writer of the account stated that if Farnsworth had resided in the days of the old navy, he "would have been famous for his desperate deeds and hairbreadth escapes." The writer closed his remarks with a quote from John Milton, "He can, I know, but doubt to think he will."

After his graduation in 1915, he was assigned to the Asiatic fleet, where in 1916 he went aboard the

Photograph of John Semer Farnsworth in the U.S. Naval Academy Yearbook.

S.S. Galveston. He returned to the United States in 1917 and was given the temporary rank of lieutenant. His next assignment was in 1920 when he took flight training at Pensacola Air Station. He completed his training in 1922 and received ratings on seaplanes and airships. Farnsworth returned to Annapolis for a post-graduate course and then on to Massachusetts Institute of Technology and a college in New York to complete his post-graduate studies.

He was assigned to duty with VO Squadron 6, Aircraft Squadron, Scouting Fleet. Farnsworth, considered to be one of the most brilliant of the navy's young officer, was court-martialed in 1927. He was dismissed from the service on 12 November 1927 for conduct "tending to impair the morale of the service" and for "scandalous conduct tending to the destruction of good morale. The official explanation for the dismissal of one of the Navy's bright future stars was that Farnsworth borrowed money from enlisted men and committed perjury in disclaiming indebtedness.

Farnsworth was under surveillance for two years by Office of Naval Intelligence (ONI) and FBI officers. Surveillance began after Farnsworth visited Annapolis where he was reported to have pushed the wife of a high-ranking navy officer to allow him to read official documents. The wife reported the incident to Navy authorities. Since the case concerned a former navy officer and navy equities, ONI and the FBI jointly worked the investigation.

Farnsworth was destitute and needed money. To try to solve his problem, he began to recontact former associates to solicit documents. The warrant for his arrest charged that "on or about May 15, 1935," Farnsworth sold to a Japanese agent a confidential Navy publication, "The Service of Information and Security." The warrant stated that Farnsworth, "did with intent and reason to believe that the same was to be used to the injury of the United States, and to the advantage of a certain foreign nation, communicate, deliver and transmit to an officer and agent of the imperial Japanese navy a certain document and writing relating to the national defense-to wit, a certain book entitled 'The Service of Information and Security,' a confidential publication of the U.S. Navy.

This publication was first issued in 1916 under the title, "Scouting and Screening," but the title was changed in 1917 to the present title. The publication contains plans for battle information and tactics that were gathered from actual fleet maneuvers and tested by high-ranking naval officials.

On 17 July 1937, Farnsworth admitted to a journalist that he did show photographs of U.S. Navy aviation equipment to a Japanese agent while he was negotiating employment with the Japanese Air Force. He said that the photographs were available to anyone from the U.S. Navy's Public Relations Office. He also said that he included with the official photographs, some of his own photos taken during his naval service. He was attempting to demonstrate to the Japanese his experience and knowledge by including the photographs with his employment application.

He told the journalist that he had accidentally sent the document, mentioned in the warrant, home with his personal affects when he left the navy. He said the document, along with other personal items, was destroyed by a fire at his house. He denied passing the document to the Japanese agent.

Three days later, Farnsworth informed a newsman that he did sell two articles or monographs on naval subjects to the Japanese agent for $1,000. He said the articles were not classified. One of the articles was on a London naval conference and the other on naval aviation training.

The case was given to a grand jury. During the grand jury testimony it was revealed that Farnsworth had telephoned the Japanese embassy twice on the day before his arrest. Lt. Commander Leslie G. Genhres testified that Farnsworth took the confidential study from his desk in the Navy Department on 1 August 1934. An employee of the navy photostat plant, Mrs. Grace Jamieson, said that Farnsworth made frequent visits to the plant to copy military documents.

Based on the evidence presented, the grand jury indicted Farnsworth on two charges. The first charge was that Farnsworth actually transmitted the confidential book to an agent of Japan and the second count alleges an attempt to transmit the volume.

At the upcoming trial, Farnsworth faced a maximum penalty of 20 years, authorized under the provisions of the law making it illegal in peacetime "to disclose information affecting the nation's defense. Farnsworth said he would base his defense on an aircraft accident he had when he was an aviation student at Pensacola Naval Air Station. The Navy said it had no record of such an accident but Farnsworth's parents insisted that their son had been "irresponsible: since the accident.

In November 1936, Farnsworth's lawyer asked the court-martial commission to have the American Consul General in Tokyo take depositions from the two Japanese naval officers with whom Farnsworth was alleged to have conspired. The two officers, Yosiyuki Itimiya and Akira Yamaki, both Lt. Commanders of the Imperial Japanese Navy, were formerly stationed at the Japanese embassy in Washington, D.C. as naval observers. Farnsworth's lawyer argued that since the two Japanese officers were no longer accredited to the United States as diplomats, they could freely testify and that their answers to defense questions were material to the case.

In December, Japan refused to authorize its naval officers to present testimony to any disposition in the Farnsworth case. The embassy noted that Japanese law could not compel its military officers to answer interrogations of foreign nations.

On 15 February 1937, Farnsworth changed his innocent plea to nolo contendere and threw himself on the mercy of the court. The prosecution had a list of fifty witnesses ready to testify against Farnsworth. The judge said he wanted to review the aspects of the case before pronouncing sentence. A few days later, Farnsworth requested to again change his plea from nolo contendere to not guilty. In his written request to the judge, he said that he made his decision without the advice of his counsel and it based on the publicity the case received. He claimed that his family suffered from the publicity and he was under the mistaken impression that his nolo contendere plea would not bring such adverse notoriety. The judge said that Farnsworth was in his rights to change his plea before sentencing and that he would hear Farnsworth's motion.

This was the first in a series of moves by Farnsworth to have his case dismissed. Farnsworth's lawyers withdrew from the case, and Farnsworth tells the judge that he will conduct his own defense. His next move was to file a writ of habeas corpus to get released from prison. He argued that the facts alleged in the indictment, under which he was convicted, did not constitute a crime. He claimed that he did not understand nolo contendere meant guilty and wanted to withdraw the plea but the court rejected it. The judge denied his writ and upheld the indictment.

Farnsworth was sentenced on 27 February 1937 to serve "not less than four years nor more than twelve years in prison."

In January 1938, Farnsworth again appealed the judge's decision in the writ of habeus corpus. He alleged that the court erred in holding a petitioner could not be released "from unlawful imprisonment" by habeas corpus proceedings; that the trial court did not have the jurisdiction in the case and that the court did not have the power to pronounce an indeterminate sentence. Farnsworth's sentence was upheld by the U.S. Fifth Circuit Court of Appeals for conspiracy to divulge military secrets to Japan. The court ruled that Farnsworth and others conspired "to communicate and transmit to a foreign government- to wit Japan- writings, code books, photographs and plans relating to the national defense with the intent that they should be used to the injury of the United States."

Special House Committee For The Investigation Of Un-American Activities

Martin Dies, a Texas Congressman, introduced a resolution on 21 July 1937 to create a special committee to investigate subversion in the United States. After prolonged debate the resolution passed on 26 May 1938. The committee, known as the Dies Committee after its chairman, was formed on 6 June but formal hearings did not begin until 12 August. The major target of the committee was organized labor groups, particularly the Congress of Industrial Organizations. A major tactic employed by Dies, and one that set a pattern for how the committee functioned until after World War II, was his meeting alone and secretly with friendly witnesses who accused hundreds of individuals of supporting Communist activities. The press sensationalized these accusations but only a few of the accused were given the opportunity to defend themselves.

Because the Dies Committee was a special committee, its mandate had to be renewed by the Congress every two years. This changed in 1945 when it was replaced by the permanent standing Committee on Un-American Activities. Over the next five years the committee originated investigations into the motion picture industry, hunting for communists. Their investigation resulted in the blacklisting of producers, writers and actors by Hollywood. But the committee's greatest fame was its investigation of Alger Hiss and his eventual perjury, which fixed internal communism as a leading political issue. As a major political force, the Committee used contempt citations as a major weapon against those who refused to testify by taking the Fifth Amendment right against self-incrimination. In 1950, for example, the Committee issued 56 citations out of the 59 citations voted by the House of Representatives.

In the 1950s, Senator Joseph McCarthy began his investigations into communists in government, which overshadowed the work of the committee. Being in the background, the committee did not suffer any affect from McCarthy's downfall. The committee continued to pursue communists and other un-American activities until the beginning of 1960. For the next two decades, the committee focused on the black militants, the anti-war movement, other radical youth groups and terrorism. In 1968 the committee was renamed the Committee on Internal Security. In 1975 the committee was abolished.

Defectors

Alexander Gregory Barmine

Alexander Gregory Barmine, born 16 August 1899, in Russia, joined the Red Army as a private and rose through the ranks to become a brigadier general. He was recruited by Soviet military intelligence (GRU) from his graduating class in the Soviet General Staff Academy in 1921.

Following three years of language study at the Oriental Institute, he joined the People's Commissariat of Foreign Trade. He served as a foreign trade specialists at several diplomatic posts in Europe. In addition, Barmine reported on his contacts to the GRU.

In 1937, while assigned as Soviet Charge d'Affaires in Athens, Greece, Barmine defected. He first fled to Paris as a political refugee. Three years later he entered the United States where he became a naturalized citizen in July 1943. During World War II he joined the US Army and later served with the Office Strategic Services (OSS) from 1943 until September 1944. He was dismissed from the OSS for absenteeism.

In October 1948, Barmine began work as a consultant with the Department of State. Prior to his retirement in the spring of 1972, he served as chief of the Russian Desk of the Voice of America.

In July 1951 he testified before the Senate Committee on Un-American activities. He wrote two books, *Memoirs of a Soviet Diplomat* (published in 1938 in London–translated by Gerard Hopkins) and *One Who Survived* (published in 1945 by Putnam) as well as occasional anti-Soviet magazine articles.

Ignace Reiss

Ignace Reiss, born January 1899 in Galicia, a part of the old Austro-Hungarian Empire. His true name was apparently Poretskiy. His mother was reportedly a Russian Jewess and his father a gentile. In 1922, while in the Soviet Union, Reiss married Else Bernaut, a student. The couple had one son, Roman Bernaut. Else kept her maiden name and, at times, Reiss used this surname operationally.

From 1921 to 1931 Reiss traveled throughout Europe where he engaged in political action operations for the COMINTERN and then in espionage for the GRU. In 1931 he was recruited by the Soviet Security Service and assigned to industrial espionage directed primarily against Germany. In the Soviet Security Service he was known as "Ludwig." After Hitler's rise to power, Reiss operated from countries bordering on Germany.

In the spring of 1937, Reiss, whose family was living in the West with him, decided to break with the Soviets because of the brutal purges then under way in the Soviet Union. During this time, he established contacts with Trotskiyites in Western Europe. On 17 July 1937, Reiss wrote a letter to the Central Committee of the Communist Party of the Soviet Union and delivered it to the Soviet Commercial Mission in Paris. In this letter he condemned the frightful excesses of Stalin and the Soviet Security Service. He then fled to Switzerland where his family was located.

Turning their full attention to the liquidation of Reiss, Soviet agents tracked him down in Switzerland. On 4 September 1937 Reiss was shot and killed by Soviet assassins and his bullet-ridden body dumped on the side of a road in Chamblandes outside Lausanne, Switzerland.

Reiss' wife identified the body bearing identity papers with the name Herman Eberhardt as that of Ignace Reiss. In later years after World War II, she was at time in contact with US intelligence about Soviet Security Service operations and personnel. She also wrote *Our Own People: A Memoir of Ignace Reiss and his Friends* (published in London in 1969). The book is a study of their involvement in pre-World War II Soviet operations in Europe. One of Reiss' friends mentioned in the book was the defector Walter Krivitsky.

An active participant in the Soviet operation against Reiss was Roland Abbiate, born 15 August 1905 in London, who lived at one time in the United States during the early twenties. Abbiate disappeared after the murder. Later, during World War II, he turned up again in the United States where he served as a Soviet diplomat, Vladimir Sergeyvich Pravdin.

Anatoli Golitsyn, another Soviet defector in the 1960s, also claimed that Pravdin was active in Austria after World War II, often passing as a Frenchman.

The French Ministry of Interior study, *A Soviet Counter-espionage Network Abroad – the Reiss Case*, published on 20 September 1951, stated "The assassination of Ignace Reiss on 4 September 1937 at Chamblandes near Lausanne, Switzerland, is an excellent example of the observation, surveillance and liquidation of a 'deserter' from the Soviet secret service."

Walter G. Krivitsky

Walter G. Krivitsky, born 28 June 1899 in Podwoloczyska, Russia, was a Soviet military intelligence officer who defected to the West prior to World War II. Krivitsky, whose true name was Samuel Ginsburg, spent nearly twenty years in Soviet intelligence.

At the age of thirteen, Krivitsky became active in the Russian working class movement and five years later, in 1917, he joined the Bolshevik Party. Shortly after the revolution, he entered the Red Army and was assigned to military intelligence.

In 1920, he was sent to Danzig, with orders to prevent the landing of French munitions being shipped to the Polish army. He was also instructed to organize strikes against arms shipments in other European cities. In 1922 Krivitsky, along with other Soviet officers, was dispatched to Berlin to mobilize elements of unrest in the Ruhr; to create the German Communist Party's intelligence service; and to form the nucleus of the future German Red Army.

By 1926, Krivitsky was chief for Central Europe in Soviet Military Intelligence. After several years in Moscow he was posted to The Hague in 1935 as Chief of Military Intelligence for Western Europe.

During this assignment, he provided Moscow with information about secret negotiations then taking place between Japan and Germany. In 1936, Krivitsky was instructed to create a system to purchase and transport arms to the Red forces fighting in the Spanish Civil War.

In September 1937, one of Krivitsky's closest colleagues and friends, Ignace Reiss, was murdered after having broken with the Soviets. Krivitsky feared that he too was doomed to be purged. In later years he claimed that his friend's death, coupled with Stalin's purges of the Old Bolshevik Guard, many of whom were his friends and colleagues, were key factors influencing his own decision to sever his connection with the Soviet government and the Communist Party of the Soviet Union in October 1937.

Krivitsky with his family were given asylum by the French government in October 1937. During the next year, while living in France and guarded by the French police, the Soviets tried unsuccessfully to assassinate him. In November 1938, Krivitsky, who planned to write a book, arrived in the United States for an extended visit. The following year he testified before the House Committee on Un-American Activities and was interviewed by British authorities.

Traveling from Canada, Krivitsky re-entered the United States in October 1940 in order to settle in New York under the name Walter Poref. On 10 February 1941 he was found shot to death in a hotel room in Washington, D.C. where he was in transit to New York. Questions still remain whether his death was a suicide or a Soviet liquidation.

Krivitsky's book *I Was Stalin's Agent*, was published in London in 1940. In it, he warned of high-level penetrations in Western governments.

Aleksandr Orlov

Aleksandr Orlov, whose true name was Leon Lazarevich Feldbin, was born on 21 August 1985 in Bobruisk, Russia. He was drafted into the Russian army and stationed in the Urals in 1916. The next year he joined the Bolshevik Party and graduated as a second lieutenant from the Third Moscow Military School.

By September 1920 he was with the 12th Red Army on the Polish front where he was in charge of guerrilla activity and counterintelligence. The successes of his work on the Polish front brought him to the attention of Feliks Dzerzhinskiy, chief of the Cheka, the Soviet State Security Service at the time. A year later, during a brief assignment to Archangel, Orlov was married.

With his wife, Orlov returned to Moscow in 1921 to become assistant prosecutor to the Soviet Supreme Court. While in this position, he worked on the formation of the Soviet criminal code and, at Dzerzhinskiy's request, investigated Soviet citizens accused of economic crimes. Soon thereafter Dzerzhinskiy brought Orlov into the Cheka as deputy chief of the Economic Directorate. He served in this position until 1925 when he became brigade commander of the border guards in Armenia. The following year Orlov was reassigned to the Foreign Department in a newly created headquarters unit that was to oversee and control Soviet foreign trade. Shortly thereafter, under the alias Leon Nikolayev, Orlov was transferred to the Paris representation as chief of Soviet intelligence operations in France.

From 1928 until 1931 he served at the Soviet Trade Delegation in Berlin where he again was concerned with economic intelligence. As deputy chief of the headquarters economic control component from 1933 to early 1936, Orlov traveled frequently to Europe, directing illegals in operations against Germany. While still assigned in Moscow, he served a year as deputy chief of the Department of Railways and Sea Transport in the Soviet State Security Service.

In 1936 Orlov was sent to Spain as Soviet liaison representative to the Republican Government for matters of intelligence, counterintelligence, and guerrilla warfare. Throughout Orlov's stay in Spain, tales mounted of secret trials, summary executions, and widespread terror in the Soviet Union.

In July 1938, Orlov was abruptly ordered to Paris. While in transit, he stopped to see his family, which was living in France not far from the Spanish border. Orlov discussed with his wife his growing suspicions and his moral revulsion, and then decided to break with Stalin and the Soviet Union. After first enlisting the aid of the Canadians, the Orlovs entered the United States on 13 August 1938. Eighteen years later they were granted permanent residence.

After Orlov's defection, he provided much information to US intelligence on pre-World War II personnel and operations of the Soviet State Security Service. With the publication of his book, *The Secret History of Stalin's Crimes* in 1953, the true history of the Soviet Union from 1934 to 1938 was revealed for the first time. In 1955 and again in 1957, Orlov appeared before the Senate Subcommittee on Internal Security. His second book, *The Handbook of Intelligence and Guerrilla Warfare*, was published in 1963.

In April 1973 Orlov died in the United States.

FBI Intelligence Authority And Subversion

There is no evidence that either the Congress in 1916 or Attorney General Stone in 1924 intended the provision of the appropriations statue to authorize the establishment of a permanent domestic intelligence structure. Yet Director Hoover advised the Attorney General and the President in 1938 that the statute was "sufficiently broad to cover any expansion of the present intelligence and counter-espionage work which it may be deemed necessary to carry on."[76] Because of their reluctance to seek new legislation in order to keep the program secret, Attorney General Cummings and President Roosevelt did not question the FBI Director's interpretation. Nevertheless, the President's approval of Director Hoover's 1938 plan for joint FBI-military domestic intelligence was a substantial exercise of independent presidential power.

The precise nature of FBI authority to investigate "subversion" became confusing in 1938-1939. Despite the references in Director Hoover's 1938 memorandum to "subversion," Attorney General Cummings cited only the President's interest in the "so-called espionage situation."[77] Cummings' successor, Attorney General Frank Murphy, appears to have abandoned the term "subversive activities."[78] Moreover, when Director Hoover provided Attorney General Murphy a copy of his 1938 plan, he described it (without mentioning "subversion") as a program "intended to ascertain the identity of persons engaged in espionage, counter-espionage, and sabotage of a nature not within the specific provision of prevailing statues."[79]

Moreover, a shift away from the authority of the appropriations provision, which was linked to the State Department's request, became necessary in 1939 when the FBI resisted an attempt by the State Department to coordinate domestic intelligence investigations. Director Hoover urged Attorney General Frank Murphy in March 1939 to discuss the situation with the President and persuade him to "take appropriate action with reference to other governmental agencies, including the State

Department, which are attempting to literally chisel into this type of work. . . ." The Director acknowledged that the FBI required "the specific authorization of the State Department" where the subject of an investigation "enjoys any diplomatic status," but he knew of "no instance in connection with the handling of the espionage work in which the State Department has had any occasion to be in any manner or degree dissatisfied with or apprehensive of the action taken by Bureau agents."[80]

Director Hoover was also concerned that the State Department would allow other Federal investigative agencies, including the Secret Service and other Treasury Department units, to conduct domestic intelligence investigations.[81] The FBI cited the following example in communications to the Attorney General in 1939:

On the West coast recently a representative of the Alcohol Tax Unit of the Treasury Department endeavored to induce a Corps Area Intelligence Officer of the War Department to utilize the services of that agency in the handling of all investigations involving espionage, counter espionage, and sabotage. . . .

A case was recently brought to the Bureau's attention in which a complaint involving potential espionage in a middle western State was referred through routine channels of a Treasury Department investigative agency and displayed in such a manner before reference ultimately in Washington to the office of Military Intelligence and then to the Federal Bureau of Investigation, that a period of some six weeks elapsed. . . .[82]

During a recent investigation . . . an attorney and Commander of the American Legion Post . . . disclosed that a Committee of that Post of the American Legion is conducting an investigation relating to un American activities on behalf of the Operator in Charge of the Secret Service, New York City.[83]

Consequently, at the FBI Director's request, the Justice Department asked the Secret Service, the Bureau of Internal Revenue, the Narcotics Bureau, the Customs Service, the Coast Guard, and the Post Office Department to instruct their personnel that information "relating to espionage and subversive activities" should be promptly forwarded to the FBI.[84]

The Justice Department letter did not solve the problem, mainly because of the State Department's continued intervention. Director Hoover advised Attorney General Frank Murphy "that the Treasury Department and the State Department were reluctant to concede jurisdiction" to the FBI and that a conference had been held in the office of an Assistant Secretary of State "at which time subtle protests against the handling of cases of this type in the Justice Department were uttered." Hoover protested this "continual bickering" among Departments, especially "in view of the serious world conditions which are hourly growing more alarming."[85]

Two months later the problem remained unresolved. Assistant Secretary of State George S. Messersmith took on the role of "coordinator" of a committee composed of representatives of the War, Navy, Treasury, Post Office, and Justice Departments. The FBI Director learned that under the proposed procedures, any agency receiving information would refer it to the State Department which, after analysis, would transit the data to that agency which it believed should conduct the substantive investigation. FBI and Justice Department officials prepared a memorandum for possible presentation to the President, pointing out the disadvantages of this procedure:

The inter-departmental committee by its operations of necessity causes delay, which may be fatal to a successful investigation. It also results in a duplication of investigative effort . . . because of the lack of knowledge of one agency that another agency is working upon the same investigation. The State Department coordinator is not in a position to evaluate properly the respective investigative ability of the representatives of particular departments in a manner comparable to that which the men actually in charge of an investigative agency may evaluate the proper merit of his own men.[86]

Endorsing this view, Attorney General Murphy wrote the President to urge abandonment of this interdepartmental committee and "a concentration of investigation of all espionage, counterespionage, and sabotage matters" in the FBI, the G-2 section of the War Department, and the Office of Naval Intelligence. The directors of these agencies would "function as a committee for the purpose of coordinating the activities of their subordinates." To buttress his recommendation, the Attorney General pointed out that the FBI and military intelligence:

> "...have not only gathered a tremendous reservoir of information concerning foreign agencies operating in the United States, but have also perfected methods of investigation and have developed channels for the exchange of information, which are both efficient and so mobile and elastic as to permit prompt expansion in the event of an emergency."

Murphy stressed that the FBI was "a highly skilled investigative force supported by the resources of an exceedingly efficient, well equipped, and adequately manned technical laboratory and identification division." This identification data related "to more than ten million persons, including a very large number of individuals of foreign extraction." The Attorney General added, "As a result of an exchange of data between the Departments of Justice, War and Navy, comprehensive indices have been prepared."[87]

President Roosevelt agreed to the Attorney General's proposal and sent a confidential directive drafted by FBI and Justice Department officials to the heads of the relevant departments. This June 1939 directive was the closet thing to a formal charter for the FBI and military domestic intelligence: It read as follows:

> *It is my desire that the investigation of all espionage, counterespionage, and sabotage maters be controlled and handled by the Federal Bureau of Investigation of the Department of Justice, the Military Intelligence Division of the War Department, and the Office of Naval Intelligence in the Navy Department. The Directors of these three agencies are to function as a committee to coordinate their activities.*

No investigations should be conducted by an investigative agency of the Government into matters involving actually *or potentially* any espionage, counterespionage, or sabotage, except by the three agencies mentioned above.

I shall be glad if you will instruct the heads of all other investigative agencies than the three named, to refer immediately to the nearest office of the Federal Bureau of Investigation any data, information, or material that may come to their notice bearing directly *or indirectly* on espionage, counterespionage, or sabotage. [88] (Emphasis added.)

The legal implications of this directive are clouded by its failure to use the term "subversive activities" and its references instead to *potential* espionage or sabotage and to information bearing *indirectly* on espionage or sabotage. This language may have been an effort by the Justice Department and the FBI to deal with the problem of legal authority posed by the break with the State Department. Since the FBI no longer wanted to base its domestic intelligence investigations on State Department requests, some other way had to be fond to retain a semblance of congressional authorization. Yet the scope of the FBI's assignment made this a troublesome point. In 1936, President Roosevelt had wanted intelligence about Communist and Fascist activities generally, not just data bearing on potential espionage or sabotage; and the 1938 plan provided for the FBI to investigative "activities of either a subversive or a so-called intelligence type."[89] There is no indication that the President's June 1939 directive had the intent or effect of limiting domestic intelligence to the investigation of violations of law.

Consistent with the FBI Director's earlier desires, these arrangements were kept secret until September 1939 when war broke out in Europe. At that time Director Hoover decided that secrecy created more problems that it solved, especially with regard to the activities of local law enforcement. He learned that the New York City Police Department had "created a special sabotage squad of fifty detectives . . . and that this squad will be augmented in the rather near future to comprise 150 men." There had been "considerable publicity" with the result that private citizens were likely to transmit information concerning sabotage "to the New York City Police Department rather than the FBI." Calling this development to the attention of the Attorney General, the Director strongly urged that the President "issue a statement or request addressed to all police officials in the United States: asking them to turn over to the FBI "any information obtained pertaining to espionage, counterespionage, sabotage, and neutrality regulations."[90]

A document to this effect was immediately drafted in the Attorney General's office and dispatched by messenger to the White House with a note from the Attorney General suggesting that it be issued in the form of "a public statement."[91] In recording his discussions that day with the Attorney General's assistant, Alexander Holtzoff, FBI official E. A. Tamm referred to the statement as "an Executive Order." Tamm also talked with the Attorney General regarding "the order":

Mr. Murphy stated that when he was preparing this he tried to make it as strong as possible. He requested that I relay this to Mr. Hoover as soon as possible and stated he knew the Director would be very glad to hear this. Mr. Murphy stated he prepared this one on the basis of the memorandum, which the Director forwarded to him.[92]

The President's statement (or order or Executive Order) read as follows:

> The Attorney General has been requested by me to instruct the Federal Bureau of Investigation of the Department of Justice to take charge of investigative work in matters relating to espionage, sabotage, and violations of the neutrality regulations.
>
> This task must be conducted in a comprehensive and effective manner on a national basis, and all information must be carefully sifted out and correlated in order to avoid confusion and irresponsibility.
>
> To this end I request all police officers, sheriffs, and other law enforcement officers in the United States promptly to turn over to the nearest representative of the Federal Bureau of Investigation any information obtained by them relating to espionage, counterespionage, sabotage, subversive activities and violations of the neutrality laws.[93]

The statement was widely reported in the press, along with the following remarks by Attorney General Murphy at a news conference held the same day:

Foreign agents and those engaged in espionage will no longer find this country a happy hunting ground for their activities. There will be no repetition of the confusion and laxity and indifference of twenty years ago.

We have opened many new FBI offices throughout the land. Our men are well prepared and well trained. At the same time, if you want to this work done in a reasonable and responsible way it must not turn into a witch-hunt. We must do no wrong to any man.

Your government asks you to cooperate with it. You can turn in any information to the nearest local representative of the Federal Bureau of Investigation.[94]

Three weeks later Murphy reiterated that the government would "not act on the basis of hysteria." He added, "Twenty years ago inhuman and cruel things were done in the name of Justice; sometimes vigilantes and others took over the work. We do not want such things done today, for the work has now been localized in the FBI."[95]

Two days after issuing the FBI statement, President Roosevelt proclaimed a national emergency "in connection with and to the extent necessary for the proper observance, safeguarding, and enforcing of the neutrality of the United States and the strengthening of our national defense within the limits of peacetime authorizations." The proclamation added, "Specific direction and authorizations will be given from time to time for carrying out these two purposes."[96]

Thereupon, he issued an Executive Order directing the Attorney General to "increase the personnel of the Federal Bureau of Investigation, Department of Justice, in such number, not exceeding 150, as he shall find necessary for the proper performance of the additional duties imposed upon the Department of Justice in connection with the national emergency."[97] President Roosevelt told a press conference that the purpose of this order expanding the government's investigative personnel was to protect the country against "some of the things that happened" before World War I:

> There was sabotage; there was a great deal of propaganda by both belligerents, and a good many definite plans laid in this country by foreign governments to try to sway American public opinion.

. . . It is to guard against that, and against the spread by any foreign nation of propaganda in this country, which would tend to be subversive—I believe that is the world—of our form of government.[98]

President Roosevelt never formally authorized the FBI or military intelligence to conduct domestic intelligence investigations of "subversive activities," except for his oral instruction in 1936 and 1938. His written directives were limited to investigations of espionage, sabotage, and violations of the neutrality regulations. Nevertheless, the President clearly knew of and approved informally the broad investigations of "subversive activities" carried out by the FBI.

President Roosevelt did use the term "subversive activities" in a directive to Attorney General Robert Jackson on wiretapping in 1940. This directive referred to the activities of other nations "engaged in the organization of propaganda of so-called 'fifth columns'" and in "preparation for sabotage." The Attorney General was directed to authorize wiretapping "of persons suspected of subversive activities against the Government of the United States, including suspected spies." The President also instructed that such wiretaps be limited "insofar as possible to aliens."[99]

With respect to investigations generally, however, the confusion as to precisely what President Roosevelt authorized is indicated by Attorney General Francis Biddle's description of FBI jurisdiction in 1942 and by a new Presidential statement in 1943. Biddle issued a lengthy order defining the duties of the various parts of the Justice Department in September 1942. The pertinent section relating to the FBI stated that it had a duty to "investigative" criminal offenses against the United States and to act as a "clearing house" for the handling of "espionage, sabotage, and other subversive matters."[100] This latter "clearing-house" function was characterized as a duty to "carry out" the President's directive of September 6, 1939.

Four months prior, President Roosevelt renewed his public appeal for "police cooperation" and added a request that "patriotic organizations" cooperate with the FBI. This statement describes his September 1939 order as granting "investigative" authority to the FBI and not simply a "clearing-house" function. However, the President defined that authority as limited to "espionage, sabotage, and violations of the neutrality regulations" without any mention of "subversion."[101]

The statement was consistent with Attorney General Biddle's internal directive later in 1943 that the Justice Department's "proper function" was "investigating the activities of persons who may have violated the law."[102]

A similar problem is involved with the authority for "counterespionage" operations by the FBI and military intelligence. President Roosevelt's confidential order of June 1939 explicitly authorized the FBI and military intelligence to handle counterespionage matters, and the 1938 plan used the terms "counter-espionage" and "counter-intelligence." However, none of the President's public directives formally authorized counterespionage measures going beyond investigation; and the Justice Department's regulations made no reference to this responsibility.

Presidential Directive

Directive of the President of the United States
June 26, 1939:

"It is my desire that the investigation of all espionage, counterespionage, and sabotage matters be controlled and handled by the Federal Bureau of Investigation of the Department of Justice, the Military Intelligence Division of the War Department, and the Office of Naval Intelligence of the Navy Department. The directors of these three agencies are to function as a committee to coordinate their activities.

"No investigations should be conducted by any investigating agency of the Government into matters involving actually or potentially any espionage, counterespionage, or sabotage, except by the three agencies mentioned above.

"I shall be glad if you will instruct the heads of all other investigating agencies that the three named, to refer immediately to the nearest office of the Federal Bureau of Investigation any data, information, or material that may come to their notice bearing directly or indirectly on espionage, counterespionage, or sabotage."

Letters To/From ONI

H.G. Dohrman to Ellis

369 South Pacific Avenue
Pittsburgh, Penna.
April seventh 1934

My dear Captain Ellis:-

Have been much disquieted lately by the news constantly trickling in revealing the very widespread scope of existent radical activities.

My own impression is that the calling of the strike at the works of the New York Shipbuilding and Drydock Co., was a tactical error, for thereby it focused the attention of the nation upon the danger to the nation of the interruption of our belated shipbuilding program. Some master mind among the radicals must have been asleep for they well know that strikes called in a half-dozen or more plants fabricating essential elements of naval construction will as effectually block progress towards the completion of the ships, as will a single prominent strike.

Deem it unfortunate that it was publicly noted that the modernization of two ships of the battleship squadron was advisedly postponed.

I write with the full knowledge of the fact that no emergency requires the return to active duty as such officers as myself and that therefore no compensation is either asked or expected.

For something over one year, while attached to the Bureau of Ordnance, worked under the late Commander A.L. Norton, on a very extensive program of anti-radical work, directed towards uncovering such movements, issuing advance warnings of all those likely to interrupt the continuous flow of navy material, or to be destructive to life and property.

My understanding, through my old time friend the late Vice-Admiral Niblack, was to the effect that Intelligence was kept advised of our movements as made or proposed. My number was "7 – 6".

We were able at that time to command, without expense, the services of the intelligence divisions of several of our greatest corporations, of men prominent alike in civil life and the clergy.

It is not purpose to convey to you the impression that the excellence of that service, and numerous commendatory letters and verbal statements, indicated that it was distinctly serviceable, can be repeated.

Wide and continued travel was necessary and much personal, as well as departmental, expense was incurred. Like almost every other man in business have suffered reverses that prohibit personal expenditures of that nature; however, my desire to be of service to the Navy is as ardent as it has been these forty-odd years.

The basis of that war time interchange of information was based on the inviolability of all such information, which was received, digested and the important portions forwarded where needed. Such Navy information as it was not incompatible with the public interests to reveal was passed along and information from private conversations between Captain Norton and myself and sources were never mentioned.

This afternoon, in the course of a two hour conversation with the executive head of the greatest of these private intelligence organizations, he expressed a willingness to renew in somewhat the same form the old relations. As a matter of fact this man and myself have almost weekly conversations and exchange information upon such subjects, for I still keep in touch with several of the best of our former men. One in particular visits constantly every place of consequence on the Mississippi and all of its tributaries, covering the entire Middle West, inclusive of the extreme northern and southern portions thereof. I am confident that he will gladly report conditions exactly as he finds them, and I may say that such reports as he may make can be absolutely relied upon. Have known him well for thirty-five years, he is professionally highly competent and his judgment sound.

If the idea appeals to you believe I can secure for you the cooperation of at least three of the nation's greatest industrial intelligence organizations, whose services will not cost the Bureau a penny. My own duty would be to act in the capacity of a screen, removing all non-essential information before forwarding the result to you.

I shall be glad to contribute as much time as possible and postage, unless it is in the end the latter should become burdensome, for these days we have to carefully scrutinize even such relatively small items as postage.

In the manner above suggested it will be feasible to cover, in a fairly thorough manner, radical activities promising future potential harm to the Navy, over the most prominent of the centers devoted to the fabrication of steel and to the kindred industries that often are found in steel districts.

In any event am offering the above for your thought; if the idea does not seem either sound or practicable to you, do not hesitate for a moment to say so.

It may be proper to add that in, to me, a highly expensive adventure into the soft coal industry, as president of an operating company kept the Tri-State Operators so fully advised of every movement of the military strikers, that violence and loss of life in our district was almost negligible throughout the strike period of 1922 and 1923.

I fully understand that it is often impossible for a Bureau Chief to do officially what he would like to do personally, even though no cost be attached to the Bureau. I know that much even if we didn't have a General McCord in that day.

Believe me to be with warmest regards and best wishes.

Cordially,

H. G. Dohrman

Ellis to Dohrman

Op 16 B 2
Apr 12, 1934

My dear Dohrman:

I am very grateful indeed to receive your extremely interesting letter of April 7th in regard to radical activities in the shipbuilding and steel industries.

Naturally this office is very much interested in receiving information along the lines you suggest and I assure you that your generous and patriotic offer to devote your time and effort without compensation to securing such information is greatly appreciated.

If you can arrange to keep in touch with the private intelligence organizations which you mention and secure a flow of information regarding the current activities of radical groups, I shall be very glad to provide for the matter of postage.

Thanking you for your communication and with assurance of my personal regards.

Very sincerely,

/s/ Hayne Ellis
Rear Admiral, U.S.N.,
Director of Naval Intelligence

Dohrman to Ellis

April twentieth 1934

My dear Admiral

Thank you for your cordial letter of the 18th, I sincerely hope that your ten days leave will prove to be both pleasant and beneficial.

Am now able to definitely say that we will have the hearty cooperation of the following:-

    The Aluminum Company of America,
    The Carnegie Steel Corporation,
    The Jone and Laughlin Steel Corporation,
        and
    The National Steel Corporation

The first and fourth at present time have no special intelligence service of their own, but do have excellent police organizations together with an unofficial but usually effective inside organization.

These concerns have plants in almost every important manufacturing district of the nation and information will be received from all of them.

Other sources previously mentioned, and some only considered but not yet mentioned, will materially add to the area covered and the efficiency of the service. When all arrangements have been completed, you will be duly advised.

If a list can be procured from C&R Ordnance and Aeronautics giving only the plants holding Navy contracts, the material under fabrication being impossible to obtain elsewhere, we will do our best to advise all such plants in advance of visits from agitators, etc. Plants making material that can be secured from numerous other plants of like type need not be included in such lists. The material being fabricated or the amounts of the several contracts are immaterial: our sole aim will be to insure, if possible, the uninterrupted flow of Navy material.

So far all former members of our old wartime organization who have been approached and had the situation explained to them, have agreed to go along with us.

With sincere good wishes,

Cordially,

/s/ H.G. Dohrman

Dohrman to Ellis

April twenty seventh, 1934

My dear Admiral:-

Supplementing my informal report of progress made as of the twentieth, am glad to be able to advise you that negotiations have been closed with the following:

> New York Central Ry. Lines
> The Pennsylvania Railroad
> The Westinghouse Electric & Mfg. Co., and,
> D.W. Sowers.

The latter is the executive head of a very efficient Buffalo (N.Y.) organization, maintained at private expense and not for profit, whose business it has been for approximately twenty years to combat radicalism. I know by experience in cooperating with it in the past how very efficient it has been. Mr. Sowers is president of a large manufacturing concern there that bears his name., and he had promised us cordial and prompt cooperation. His card files contain the names of some 4,000 actual and semi-radicals.

When our intelligence clearing house once gets going in good shape, we hope that it will be of value to you.

You will note that we gave covered, with the exception of the New England, Southern and far Western states, the heart of the nation's manufacturing, and through one of my old men, to whom previous reference has been made, a considerable portion of the South will likewise be covered.

As you will appreciate, it is something of a task to coordinate these varied sources of information, and to put the information received into shape for instant dissemination.

The time is certainly ripe for action. There were no evening papers here today, one paper had it's large windows smashed with bricks, etc. A strike of the folders.

In each case those cooperating with us have been advised, in advance, that the sources of information would not be revealed, and that each participant would receive only the information appertaining or useful to them. Some of those interested with us have excellent organizations already, others possess the nucleus. As often hapens the organization that needs it most has the poorest present service of information.

With best wishes and regards,

Cordially,

H.G. Dohrman

Dohrman to Ellis

April thirtieth 1934

My Dear Admiral:-

The enclosure[103] will illustrate the method of gleaning information adopted. You already know the institutions whose intelligence service has been placed at our disposal and with whom we now arranging inter-communicating services.

If you have two or three hundred of the green second sheets, like the enclosure, can use them to advantage. The green gives quick identification in our files.

The enclosure represents the 18 plants employing almost 17,000 men, the plants being distributed throughout the states enumerated, and all, as you have doubtless already gathered from the keyed numbers, being those of a single concern.

The other concerns are as large or larger, though their interests are not so widely scattered.

While all operations for the present are being conducted from the local Carnegie Steel offices, the probabilities are that the several concerns, later, will provide a separate office, as the work so far gives promise of assuming a considerable volume.

Conditions are not good here; four local theatres were bombed here last night due to the rivalry of two unions, one anti-AFL. A street car strike is brewing, the truck drivers and garage attendants seem likely to "go out," so there is the devil to pay generally around here.

With best wishes and regards,

Cordially,

/s/ H.G. Dohrman

Hoover to Ellis

Division of Investigation
U.S. Department of Justice
Washington, D.C.

May 21, 1934

Rear Admiral Hayne Ellis
Director, Naval Intelligence
Navy Department
Washington, D.C.

Dear Sir:

I am in receipt of information from the Pittsburgh Office of this Division to the effect that it has been learned from a reliable source there that one Horatio Garrott Dohrman is active in that vicinity in soliciting funds and organizing a unit for the alleged purpose of investigating communistic and other subversive activities. It is reported that Dohrman has represented himself as a former Lieutenant Commander in the Navy, in view of which it is believed that this information may be of interest to you.

Very truly yours,

/s/ J. E. Hoover
Director

Presidential Directive Of September 6, 1939

The attorney general has been requested by me to instruct the Federal Bureau of Investigation of the Department of Justice to take charge of investigative work in matters relating to espionage, sabotage, and violations of neutrality regulations.

This task must be conducted in a comprehensive and effective manner on a national basis, and all information must be carefully sifted out and correlated in order to avoid confusion and irresponsibility.

To this end I request all police officers, sheriffs, and all other law enforcement officers in the United States promptly to turn over to the nearest representative of the Federal Bureau of Investigation any information obtained by them relating to espionage, counterespionage, sabotage, subversive activities and violations of the neutrality law.

Police Cooperation

On September 6, 1939, I issued a directive providing that the Federal Bureau of Investigation of the Department of Justice should take charge of investigative work in matters relating to espionage, sabotage, and violations of the neutrality regulations, pointing out that the investigations must be conducted in a comprehensive manner, on a national basis, and all information carefully sifted out and correlated in order to avoid confusion and irresponsibility. I then requested all police officers, sheriffs, and other law enforcement officers in the United States, promptly to turn over to the nearest representatives of the Federal Bureau of Investigation any such information.

I am again calling the attention of all enforcement officers to the request that they report all such information promptly to the nearest field representative of the Federal Bureau of Investigation, which is charged with the responsibility of correlating this material and referring matters which are under the jurisdiction of any other Federal agency with responsibilities in this field to the appropriate agency.

I suggest that all patriotic organizations and individuals likewise report all such information relating to espionage and related matters to the Federal Bureau of Investigation in the same manner.

I am confident that all law enforcement officers, who are now rendering such invaluable assistance toward the success of the internal safety of our country, will cooperate in this matter.

(Signed) Franklin D. Roosevelt

The Scope Of FBI Domestic Intelligence

A central feature of the FBI domestic intelligence program authorized by President Roosevelt was its broad investigative scope. The breadth of intelligence gathering most clearly demonstrates why the program could not have been based on any reasonable interpretation of the power to investigative violations of law. The investigations were built upon a theory of "subversive infiltration" which remained an essential part of domestic intelligence thereafter. This theory persisted over the decades in the same way the Roosevelt directives continued in effect as the basis for legal authority. Moreover, there was a direct link between the policy of investigating "subversive" influence and the reliance on inherent executive power. The purpose of such investigations was not to assist in the enforcement of criminal laws, but rather to supply the President and other executive officials with information believed to be of value for making decisions and developing governmental policies. The "pure intelligence" function was precisely what President Roosevelt meant when he asked for "a broad picture" of the impact of Communism and Fascism on American life.

A second purpose for broad domestic intelligence investigations was to compile an extensive body of information for use in the event of an emergency or actual war. This information would supply the basis for taking preventive measures against groups or individuals disposed to interfere with the national defense effort. If such interference might take the form of sabotage or other illegal disruptions of defense production and military discipline the collection of preventive intelligence was related to law enforcement. But the relationship was often remote and highly speculative, based on political affiliations and group membership rather than any tangible evidence of preparation to commit criminal acts. As the likelihood of American involvement in the war moved closer, preventive intelligence investigations focused on whether individuals should be placed on a Custodial Detention List for possible arrest in case of war. This program was developed joint by the FBI and a special Justice Department unit in 1940-1941.

These two objectives–"pure intelligence" and preventive intelligence—were closely related to one another. Investigations designed to produce information about subversive infiltration also identified individuals thought potentially dangerous to the country's security. Likewise, investigations of persons alleged to be security threats contributed to the overall domestic intelligence picture.

Internal FBI instructions described the scope of surveillance in detail. On September 2, 1939, all FBI field offices were ordered to review their files and secure information from "reliable contacts" in order to prepare reports on "persons of German, Italian, and Communist sympathies," as well as other persons "whose interest may be directed primarily to the interest of some other nation than the United States." Such information included "a list of subscribers" and officers of all German and Italian language newspapers in the United States, language newspapers published by the Communist Party or "its affiliated organizations," and both foreign and English language newspapers "of pronounced or notorious Nationalistic sympathies." FBI offices were also instructed to identify members of all German and Italian societies, "whether they be of a fraternal character or of some other nature," and of "any other organization, regardless of nationality, which might have produced Nationalistic tendencies."[104]

In October 1939 the FBI was investigating the Communist Party and the German American Bund, using such techniques as "the employment of informants," "research into publications," "the soliciting and obtaining of assistance and information from political émigrés, and organizations which have for their purpose the maintenance of files of information bearing upon this type of study and inquiry," and "the attendance of mass meetings and public demonstrations." The compilation of information on other organizations and groups "expressing nationalist leanings" continued pursuant to the September 1939 instructions. In addition, the FBI was conducting "confidential inquiries" regarding "the various so-called radical and fascist organizations in the United States" for the purpose of identifying their "leading personnel, purposes and aims, and the part they are likely to play at a time of national crisis."[105]

In November 1939, the FBI began preparing a list of specific individuals "on whom information is available indicating strongly that (their) presence at liberty in this country in time of war or national emergency would constitute a menace to the public peace and safety of the United States Government." The list comprised persons "with strong Nazi tendencies" and "with strong Communist tendencies." The citizenship status of each individual was determined, and cards prepared summarizing the reasons for placing him on the list.[106]

FBI field offices were instructed to obtain information on such persons from "public and private records, confidential sources of information, newspaper morgues, public libraries, employment records, school records, et cetera." FBI agents were to keep the purpose of their inquiries "entirely confidential" and to reply to questions by stating as a cover that the investigation was being made in connection with "the Registration Act requiring agents of foreign principals to register with the State Department." FBI headquarters supervisors divided the list into two categories:[107]

Class #1. Those to be apprehended and interned immediately upon the outbreak of hostilities between the government of the United States and the Government they service, support, or owe allegiance to.

Class #2. Those who should be watched carefully at and subsequent to the outbreak of hostilities because their previous activities indicate the possibility but not the probability that they will act in a manner adverse to the best interests of the Government of the United States.[108]

This program was described as a "custodial detention" list in June 1940, and field offices were again instructed to furnish information on persons possessing "Communist, Fascist, Nazi or other nationalistic background."[109]

The primary subjects of FBI intelligence surveillance under this program in mid-1940 were active Communists (including Communist candidates for public offices, party officers and organizations, speakers at Communist rallies, writers of Communist books or articles, individuals "attending Communistic meetings where revolutionary preachings are given," Communists in strategic operations "or holding any position of potential influence" and Communist agitators who participate "in meetings or demonstrations accompanied by violence"), all members of the German-American Bund and similar organizations, Italian Fascist organizations and American Fascist groups such as "Silver Shirts, Ku Klux Klan, White Camelia, and similar organizations."[110] Director Hoover summarized these "subversive activities" in a memorandum to the Justice Department:

> *The holding of official positions in organizations such as the German American Bund and Communist groups; the distribution of literature and propaganda favorable to a foreign power and opposed to the American way of life; agitators who are adherents of foreign ideologies who have for their purpose the stirring up of internal strike (sic), class hatreds and the development of activities which in time of war would be a serious handicap in a program of internal security and national defense....*[111]

Director Hoover claimed publicly in 1940 that advocates of foreign "isms" had "succeeded in boring into every phase of American life, masquerading behind front organizations."[112] Intelligence about "front" groups was transmitted to the White House. For example, in 1937 the Attorney General had sent an FBI report on a proposed pilgrimage to Washington to urge passage of legislation to benefit American youth. The report stated that the American Youth Congress, which sponsored the pilgrimage, was understood to be strongly Communistic.[113] Later reports in 1937 described the Communist Party's role in plans by the Workers Alliance for nationwide demonstrations protesting the plight of the unemployed, as well as the Alliance's plans to lobby Congress in support of the federal relief systems.[114]

FBI investigations and reports (which went into Justice Department and FBI permanent files) covered entirely lawful domestic political activities. For example, one local group checked by the Bureau was called the League for Fair Play, which furnished "speakers to Rotary and Kiwanis Clubs and to schools and colleges." The FBI reported in 1941 that:

> " ...the organization was formed in 1937, apparently by two Ministers and a businessman for the purpose of further fair play, tolerance, adherence to the Constitution, democracy, liberty, justice, understanding and good will among all creeds, races and classes of the United States."

A synopsis of the report stated, "No indications of Communist activities."[115] In 1944 the FBI prepared a more extensive intelligence report on an active political group, the Independent Voters of Illinois, apparently because it was the target of Communist "infiltration." The Independent Voters group was reported to have been formed:

> "...for the purpose of developing neighborhood political units to help in the re election of President Roosevelt and the election of progressive congressmen. Apparently, IVI endorsed or aided democrats for the most part, although it was stated to be "independent." It does not appear that it entered its own candidates or that it endorsed any Communists. IVI sought to help elect those candidates who would favor fighting inflation, oppose race and class discrimination, favor international cooperation, support a "full employment program," oppose Fascism, etc."[116]

Thus, the Bureau gathered data about left-liberal groups in its search for subversive "influence." At the opposite end of the political spectrum, the activities of numerous right-wing groups like the Christian Front and Christian Mobilizers (followers of Father Coughlin), the American Destiny Party, the American Nationalist Party, and even the less extreme "America First" movement were reported by the FBI. [117]

The Bureau even looked into a Bronx, New York, child center which was "apparently dominated and run" by Communists to determine whether it was being used as a "front" for carrying out the Communist Program.[118]

One example of the nature of continuing intelligence investigations is the FBI's reports on the NAACP. The Washington, D.C. Field Office opened the case in 1941 because of a request from the Navy Department for an investigation of protests against racial discrimination in the Navy by "fifteen colored mess attendants." FBI agents used an informant to determine the NAACP's "connections with the Communist party and other Communist controlled organizations."[119]

FBI headquarter sent a request to the Oklahoma City field Office in August 1941 for an investigation of "Communist Party domination" of the NAACP in connection with the development of "Nationalistic Tendency Charts." The field office report concluded, on the basis of an informant's reports, "that there is a strong tendency for the NAACP to steer clear of Communistic activities. Nevertheless, there is a strong movement on the part of the Communists to attempt to dominate this group through an infiltration of communistic doctrines. Consequently, the activities of the NAACP will be closely observed and scrutinized in the future.[120]

FBI informants subsequently reported on NAACP conferences at Hampton, Virginia, in the fall of 1941 at Los Angeles in the summer of 1942. These investigations were conducted "to follow the activities of the NAACP and determine further the advancement of the Communist group has made into that organization."[121] Similar reports came to headquarters from field offices in Richmond, Virginia; Springfield and Chicago, Illinois; Boston, Massachusetts; Oklahoma City, Oklahoma; Indianapolis, Indiana; Savannah, Georgia; and Louisville, Kentucky, in 1942-1943. Informants were used to report on efforts "to place before the NAACP certain policies or ideas which ...may be favorable to the Communist Party."[122] An informant attended an NAACP convention in South Carolina in June 1943 and reported on his conversations with NAACP counsel Thurgood Marshall. The informant believed that Marshall was "a loyal American" and "would not permit anything radical to be done."[123]

Informants for the Oklahoma City Field Office reported on Communist efforts to "infiltrate" the NAACP and advised that the Communist Party would "be active" at a forthcoming NAACP conference.[124] On the other hand, an informant for the Chicago office reported "no evidence that there is any Communist infiltration in the Chicago branch."[125] And informants for the Detroit office advised that there were "numerous contacts by the CP members and NAACP members, some collaboration on issues which affect negroes, presence of CP members at NAACP meetings, interest of CP in NAACP, but no evidence of CP control."[126]

FBI investigation of the NAACP reflected in these and other reports to headquarters produced massive information in Bureau files about the organization, its members, their legitimate activities to oppose racial discrimination, and internal disputes with some of the chapters. One thirty-five page report contained the names of approximately 250 individuals and groups, all indexed in a table of contents.[127] The reports and their summaries contained little if any information about specific activities or planned activities in violation of federal law.

The scope of the information compiled through these investigations of alleged Communist "infiltration" is indicated by FBI estimate that by 1944 "almost 1,000,000 people knowingly or unknowingly had been drawn into Communist-Front activity."[128]

CI Between the World Wars Bibliography

Ahern, James F. *Police in Trouble*. New York: Hawthorn Books, 1972.

Allen, Frederick Lewis. *The Big Change: America Transforms Itself*. New York: Harper, 1952.

Allen, Frederick Lewis. *Since Yesterday: The Nineteen Thirties in America*. New York: Harper, 1940.

Bailey, Geoffrey. *The Conspirators*. New York: Harper and Row, 1960.

Belknap, Michael R. "The Mechanics of Repression: J. Edgar Hoover, the Bureau of Investigation and the Radicals 1917-1925." *Crime and Social Justice 7* (Spring-Summer 1977): 49-58.

Bentley, Eric, ed. *Thirty Years of Treason: Excerpts from Hearings before the House Committee on Un-American Activities, 1938-1968*. New York: Viking Press, 1972.

Berkman, Alexander. *Prison Memoirs of an Anarchists*. New York: Mother Earth, 1912.

Berle, Adolf Augustus. *Navigating the Rapids, 1918-1971: From the Papers of Adolf A. Berle*. New York: Harcourt Brace Jovanovich, 1973.

Blackstock, Paul W. *The Secret Road to World War II: Soviet versus Western Intelligence 1921-1939*. Chicago, Quadrangle, 1969.

Blackstock, Paul W. *The Strategy of Subversion: Manipulating the Politics of Other Nations*. Chicago: Quadrangle Books, 1964.

Blackstock, Paul W., and Scaf, Frank L. *Intelligence, Espionage, Counterespionage and Covert Operations: A Guide to Information Sources*. Detroit: Gale Research Co. 1978.

Bohlen, Charles E. *Witness to History*, 1929-1969. New York: W.W. Norton, 1973.

Brook-Shepherd, Gordon. *The Storm Petrels: The Flight of the First Soviet Defectors 1928-1938*. New York: Harcourt Brace Jovanovich, 1978.

Coben, Stanley. *A. Mitchell Palmer: Politician*. New York: Columbia University Press, 1963.

Dorwart, Jeffrey M. *Conflict of Duty: The U.S. Navy's Intelligence Dilemma, 1919-1945*. Annapolis, MD: Naval Institute Press, 1983.

Deacon, Richard. *Kempei Tai: A History of the Japanese Secret Service*. New York: Beaufort, 1983.

FitzGibbob, Constantine. *Secret Intelligence in the Twentieth Century (Cryptologia)*. London: Hart-Davis, MacGibbon, 1976.

Flicke, Wilhelm F. War *Secrets in the Ether*. 2 Vols. Vol. I (parts 1 & 2): to World War II; Vol. II (part 3) : World War II. Laguna Hills, Calif.: Aegean Books, 1977.

Friedman, William F. and Mendelsohn, Charles J. *The Zimmerman Telegram of January 16, 1917 and its Cryptographic Background*. Laguna Hills, California. Aegean Park Press, 1976.

George, Willis D. *Surreptitious Entry*. New York: Appleton-Century, 1946.

Hall, W. Reginald & Peaslee, Amos J. *Three Wars with Germany*. Edited and illustrated by Joseph P. Sims. New York: G. P. Putnam's Sons, 1944. Henry, Fred. "Japanese Espionage and Our Psychology for Failure." *U.S. Naval Institute Proceedings 69* (May 1943): 639-641.

Hynd, Alan. *Betrayal from the East: The Inside Story of Japanese Spies in America*. New York: McBride, 1943.

Kahn, David. "The Annotated The American Black Chamber." *Cryptologia 9:1* (1985): 1-37.

Kahn, David. "A New Source for Historians: Yardley's Seized Manuscript." *Cryptologia 6:2* (1982) 115-118.

Kruh, Louis. "Stimson, the Black Chamber, and the 'Gentlemen's Mail' Quote." *Cryptologia 12:2* (1988) 65-89.

May, Ernest K. *The World War and American Isolation, 1914-1917.* Cambridge: Harvard University Press, 1956.

Murray, Robert K. *The Red Scare: A Study in National Hysteria, 1919-1920.* Minneapolis: University of Minnesota Press, 1955.

Nicolai, Walther. *The German Secret Service: German Military Intelligence during World War I.* London: Stanley Paul, 1924.

Rintelen, Franz von Kleist. *The Dark Invader: Wartime Reminiscences of a German Naval Intelligence Officer (Sabotage against the United States)* London: Lovat, Dickson, 1933.

Rowan, Richard W. *Secret Agents Against America.* New York: Doubleday, Doran, 1939.

Rowan, Richard W. *Spies and the Next War.* Garden City, NY: Doubleday, 1934.

Seth, Ronald. *Encyclopedia of Espionage.* London: New English Library, 1972.

Strong, Kenneth. *Men of Intelligence: A Study of the Roles and Decisions of Chiefs of Intelligence From World War I to the Present Day.* London: Cassell, 1970.

U.S. Army Security Agency. *Historical Background of the Signal Security Agency, Vol. III. The Peace 1919-1939.* Washington, DC: Army Security Agency, 1946.

U.S. Army Security Agency. *History of Codes and Ciphers in the U.S. During the Period Between the Wars. Part I. 1919-1929.* Laguna Hills, CA: Aegean Park Press, 1979.

U.S. Army Security Agency. *The Origins and Development of the Army Security Agency, 1917-1947.* Laguna Hills, CA: Aegean Park Press, 1978.

Williams, David. "The Bureau of Investigation and Its Critics, 1919-1921: The Origins of Federal Political Surveillance." *Journal of American History 68* (1981): 560-579.

Williams, David. "Failed Reforms: FBI Political Surveillance, 1924-1936." *First Principles 7:1* (1981): 1-4.

Yardley, Herbert Osborne. *The American Black Chamber.* The Bobbs-Merrill Company Indianapolis, 1931.

IMPORTANT DATES AND COUNTERINTELLIGENCE EVENTS
THE PERIOD BETWEEN THE WORLD WARS, 1920-1939

Year	Date	Event
1920	1 January	The "Red Raids," also known as the "Palmer Red Raids," and the "Slacker Raids" initiated.
1921	16 January	Public backlash against the "Palmer" raids prompted a Senate investigation.
	6 June	Army establishes Signal Intelligence Service (later renamed the Signal Security Agency (1 June 1943) and 4 Nov 1952 became NSA.
	19 May	Emergency Quota Act restricts immigration to 3% of 1910 census.
	23 December	President Harding pardons Eugene Debs and others convicted under the Sedition Act of 1918 and other measures designed to curb dissent during World War I.
1924	26 May	National Origins Act places strict quotas on European immigration and bars all immigration from Asia.
	1 July	Japanese condemn immigration humiliation in "Hate America" rallies.
	10 May	J. Edgar Hoover is appointed head of Bureau of Investigation.
1928	4 June	Supreme Courts upholds Olmstead Case that use of wiretap evidence in a federal court did not by itself violate constitutional guarantees in the 4th and 5th Amendments against unreasonable searches and seizures and self-incrimination.
1929	29 October	Secretary of State withdraws funding from the "Black Chamber," effectively abolishing the office.
1933	30 January	Hitler is appointed as the German Chancellor.
	7 June	Congress authorizes use of subpoena power in sabotage cases.
	16 November	US establishes diplomatic relations with the Soviet Union.
	27 August	Corp. R. Osman court-martialed for violating Espionage Act. Sentenced to two years hard labor and fined $10,000. President Roosevelt orders new trial in 1934. He was acquitted on 21 May.
1934	15 December	Japan asks France, England, and U.S. for removal of diplomatic status from Army and Navy language officers in Tokyo as one is suspected of espionage. U.S. grants request.

IMPORTANT DATES AND COUNTERINTELLIGENCE EVENTS

THE PERIOD BETWEEN THE WORLD WARS, 1920-1939

1936	12 December	German pro-Nazi Bund societies formed as "Amerika-deutscher Volkbund," ostensibly devoted to social and athletic pursuits.
	2 July	H.T. Thompson tried on charges of selling U.S. naval information to Lt. Comdr. Miyazaki, Japanese Spy.
	15 July	John Semer Farnsworth, ex-U.S. naval officer, held on charges of selling confidential naval book to Japanese. Found guilty and sentenced to prison.
1938	26 May	Dies Committee established to investigate un-American activities.
	19 August	President Roosevelt, in reaction to Turrou incident, says he favors larger appropriations for military intelligence services to expand counterespionage activities in the U.S. However, he made it clear he would not sanction espionage by American agents abroad.
	16 October	Ernst Kuhrig and Heinrich Schackow, German citizens, arrested on espionage charges in the Canal Zone. Both sentenced to two years in prison in January 1939.
1939	26 June	Interception of Soviet communication between New York and Moscow that would be the subject of the VENONA project begins.
	17 April	Counterintelligence Branch established in Army's Military Intelligence Division.
	15 June	Mixed Claims Commission finds Germany guilty of both the Black Tom and Kingsland explosions but Germany never pays the $55 million damage award.
	26 June	Presidential Directive gives investigations of all espionage, sabotage and counterespionage to FBI, Military Intelligence Division and Office of Naval Intelligence.
	1 September	World War II begins as Germany invades Poland.
	2 September	Journalist Don Levine escorts Whittaker Chambers to Asst. Secretary of State Adolph Berle's home where Chambers reveals intelligence activities of Alger and Donald Hiss.
	4 September	French intelligence informs American Ambassador Bullitt in Paris that Alger and Donald Hiss are Soviet agents.
	6 September	Presidential Directive gives FBI the sole responsibility for investigating espionage, counterespionage and sabotage.

American Revolution
End Notes

1. This article was written by Frank J. Rafalko, Chief Community Training Branch, National Counterintelligence Center.

2. Thomas Hutchinson came from a prominent New England family. In 1737, despite his family's admonishment to him about going into politics, he was elected to the Massachusetts House of Representative. He later served as Chief Justice of the colony and then royal governor.

3. Francis Bernard was the nephew of Lord Barrington, the secretary of state for war in London. Barrington arranged for Bernard to be appointed as royal governor of New Jersey, but after two years Bernard move to Massachusetts to become royal governor there. He was recalled to London in 1769.

4. Dr. Benjamin Church.

5. A.J. Langguth, Patriots The Men Who Started the American Revolution, Simon and Schuster, New York, 1988, p. 311.

6. Edmund R. Thompson, ed., Secret New England Spies of the American Revolution, The David Atlee Phillips New England Chapter, Association of Former Intelligence Officers, Kennebunk, Maine, 1991, p. 17.

7. Allen French, General Gage's Informers, Greenwood Press, New York, 1968, p166-167.

8. Capt. James Wallace.

9. Godfrey Wainwood or Wenwood, Letter from Washington to the President of Congress, October 5, 1775.

10. Letter from George Washington to the President of Congress, October 5, 1775.

11. The 28th article of war provided that anyone caught communicating with the enemy should suffer such punishment as a court martial might direct. Unfortunately for those who favored hanging Dr. Church, article 51 stated that such punishment was limited to thirty-nine lashes, or a fine of two months' pay, and/or cashiering from the service.

12. Letter from George Washington to Governor Jonathan Trumball, November 15, 1775 in which Washington inserted the resolve of Congress he received from John Hancock regarding Church.

13. This article was written by Frank J. Rafalko, Chief, Community Training Branch, National Counterintelligence Center.

14. Col. Jacobus Swartwout (d.1826), commander of the 2d Dutchess County Regiment of Minute Men.

15. Johnathan Fowler.

16. James Kip.

17. This article was written by Dan Lovelace, National Counterintelligence Center.

18. Carl Van Doren's description of Benedict Arnold in his Secret History of the American Revolution.

19. This article is copyrighted by Eric Evans Rafalko and used with his permission.

20. Secret New England Spies of the American Revolution, ed. by Edmund R. Thompson (The David Atlee Phillips New England Chapter, Association of Former Intelligence Officers, Kennebunk, Maine, 1991, p. 73.

21. Revolutionary Diplomatic Correspondence of the United States, ed. by Francis Wharton, U.S. Department of State, 6 vols., Washington, Government Printing Office, 1889, pp. 78-80.

22. Silas Deane to the Secret Committee of Congress, August 18, 1776, in The Deane Papers, ed. Charles Isham, 5 vols, New York Historical Society Collections, Vols. XIX-XXIII, New York, 1886-1891, XIX, p. 206.

23. Bemis, Samuel F., The Diplomacy of the American Revolution, New York, D. Appleton Co., 1935, pp. 44-45.

24. Dr. Edward Bancroft to the Most Honorable Marquis of Carmarthen, September 17, 1784, Samuel F. Bemis,

British Secret Service and the French-American Alliance, American Historical Review, XXIX, No. 3 (April, 1924), p. 493.

25. There was no organization within the government known as the British Secret Service. Intelligence collection was conducted by major figures within the Foreign Ministry or military for their own purposes. In this respect, Eden was probably in charge of a small group of intelligence collectors for Lord Suffolk.

26. Dr. Edward Bancroft to the Most Honorable Marquis of Carmarthen, September 17, 1784, op. cit., p. 493.

27. Secret New England Spies of the American Revolution, ed. Edmund R. Thompson, op.cit., p. 80.

28. Jacob Bankson was one of Washington's spies.

29. Thomas Shanks, formerly an ensign of the Tenth Pennsylvania Regiment. He had been cashiered Oct. 12, 1777, for stealing shoes.

30. The board voted 10 to 4 that he was a spy and 8 to 6 that he ought to suffer death.

31. Elijah Hunter, assistant commissary of forage, at Bedford, N.Y.

32. Elijah Hunter. In the draft he is designated "H——."

33. Lieut. Gen. Frederick Haldimand, Governor of Canada.

34. This article was written by Frank J. Rafalko, Chief, Community Training Branch, National Counterintelligence Center.

35. Smith obtained this information which he communicated to Eden in "Information obtained by Lt. Col. Smith during the six weeks of his intercourse with Capt. Hyson, in February and March 1777," Mar 27-28, 1777, Stephens's Facsimiles of Manuscripts in European Archives relating to America, 1773-1783, no. 670.

36. William Eden to George III, Oct 20, 1777, Stevens, op cit., no. 275.

Civil War
End Notes

1. Dr. Harold R. Relyea, Analyst in American National Government, Government and General Research Division, Congressional Research Center, Library of Congress, for the Select Committee on Intelligence and printed in *Supplemental Reports on Intelligence Activities, Book VI, Final Report of the Select Committee to Study Governmental Operations with respect to Intelligence Activities*, United States Senate, 1976.

2. George Fort Milton. *Abraham Lincoln and the Fifth Column.* New York, the Vanguard Press, 1942, p.48.

3. Frederick Bancroft. *The Life of Williams H. Seward (Vol.2).* New York, Harper and Brothers, 1900, p. 260.

4. *Ibid.*, pp. 261-262.

5. See Richardson, *op cit.* (Vol.7), pp.3303-3305.

6. The correspondence of this panel and lists of those released at its direction may be found in Fred C. Ainsworth and Joseph W. Kirkley, comps. *The War of the Rebellion: A Compilation of the Official Records of the Union and Confederate Armies,* Series II (Vol.2). Washington, U.S. Govt. Print. Off., 1897.

7. Milton, *op. cit.,* p. 49.

8. See John W. Headley, *Confederate Operations in Canada and New York.* New York and Washington, The Neale Publishing Company, 1906; also of related interest is James D. Bulloch, *The Secret Service of the Confederate States in Europe*, New York, Thomas Yoseloff, 1956; originally published 1884.

9. Milton, *loc. cit.*

10. *Ibid.,* pp.50-51.

11. This article was written by Louise Sayre, National Security Agency.

12. Allan Pinkerton, *The Spy of the Rebellion*, New York, G.W. Carleton and Company, 1883, pp. 247-248.

13. *Ibid*, pp. 429-430.

14. Dr. Harold R. Relyea, Analyst in American National Government, Government and General Research Division, Congressional Research Center, Library of Congress, for the Select Committee on Intelligence and printed in *Supplemental Reports on Intelligence Activities, Book VI, Final Report of the Select Committee to Study Governmental Operations with respect to Intelligence Activities*, United States Senate, 1976.

15. See L.C. Baker, *History of the United States Secret Service*, Philadelphia, King and Baird, 1868, pp. 15-20: Jacob Mogelever, *Death to Traitors:* The Story of General Lafayette C. Baker, *Lincoln's Forgotten Secret Service Chief.* New York, Doubleday and Company, 1960, pp-22-48.

16. Baker, *op. cit.*, pp. 45-72: Mogelever, *op. cit.* pp. 48-62.

17. Baker. *op. cit.*, pp. 72-84: Mogelever, *op. cit.*, pp. 68-72.

18. Mogelever, *op. cit.*, p. 73.

19. See Baker, *op. cit.*, pp. 85-101.

20. *Ibid.*, pp. 102-111: Mogelever, *op. cit.*, pp. 74-79.

21. Mogelever, op. *cit.*, p. 79.

22. See *Ibid.*, pp. 79-81.

23. *Ibid.*, p. 84.

24. See Mogelever, *op. cit.*, pp. 86-88.

25. *Ibid.*, p. 89.

26. Wilfred E. Binkley. *President and Congress.* New York, Alfred A. Knopf, 1947, p. 126.

27. Letter to Albert G. Hodges (April 4, 1864) in Roy P. Baslet, ed. *The Collected Works of Abraham Lincoln* (Vol. 8). New Brunswick, Rutgers University Press, 1953, p. 281.

28. Rossiter, *op. cit.*, p. 229.

29. Mogelever, *op. cit.*, p. 91.

30. *Ibid.*, pp. 95. 169.

31. *Ibid.*, p. 111.

32. *Ibid.*, pp. 169-170.

33. *Ibid.*, p. 109.

34. *Ibid.*, p. 242; also see Baker, op. cit., pp. 174-178.

35. *Ibid.*, p. 241.

36. *Ibid.*, p. 164.

37. See *Ibid.*, pp. 101-107, 139-140.

38. See *Ibid.*, p. 108.

39. See *Ibid.*, pp. 107-108.

40. See Baker, *op. cit.*, pp. 195-203.

41. Mogelever, *op. cit.*, p. 214; the District of Columbia had only one cavalry unit during the civil war but counted the First and Second Regiment Infantry, serving from 1861 until 1865, and several short-lived infantry battalions and militia companies which were hastily organized in 1861 and mustered out by the end of the year.

42. *Ibid.*, pp. 215-216.

43. *Ibid.*, p. 220.

44. *Ibid.*, p. 221.

45. See Baker, *op. cit.*, pp. 241-253; Mogelever, *op. cit.*, pp. 245-248.

46. Generally see Mogelever, *op. cit.*, pp. 213-241.

47. Baker's own account of his bureau's activities and his troops' adventures is thin and, compared with the Mogelever account which relies on Baker's correspondence and the letters and diaries of relatives, fails to convey the questionable nature of their operations or their possible illegality; see Baker, *op. cit.*, pp. 147-198, 230-241, 253-261, 329-378, 384-452.

48. Mogelever, *op. cit.*, p. 249; in 1863 (12 Stat. 713 at 726) Congress authorized the Secretary of the Treasury to appoint three revenue agents". . . to aid in the prevention, detection, and punishment of frauds upon the revenue." These were the small beginnings of the Treasury Department's intelligence organization and the only designated investigative force available to the Secretary at the time of the Baker inquiry.

49. See Mogelever, *op. cit.*, p. 252.

50. Generally, see *Ibid.*, pp. 252-278; Baker, *op. cit.*, pp. 261-287.

51. Generally, see Baker, *op. cit.*, pp. 452-476; Mogelever, op. cit., pp. 278-292; John W. Headley, *Confederate Operations in Canada and New York*, New York and Washington, The Neale Publishing Company, 1906, pp. 211-382.

52. Mogelever, *op. cit.*, 291-292.

53. See *Ibid.*, p. 337.

54. *Ibid.*, p. 339.

55. Generally, see Baker, *op. cit.*, pp. 476-567; Mogelever, *op. cit.*, 342-385.

56. Mogelever, *op. cit.*, p. 386.

57. Generally, see Baker, *op. cit.*, pp. 582-693; Mogelever, *op. cit.*, pp. 385-419.

58. Dr. Harold R. Relyea, Analyst in American National Government, Government and General Research Division, Congressional Research Center, Library of Congress, for the Select Committee on Intelligence and printed in *Supplemental Reports on Intelligence Activities, Book VI, Final Report of the Select Committee to Study Governmental Operations with respect to Intelligence Activities*, United States Senate, 1976.

59. G.R. Tredway, *Democratic Opposition to the Lincoln Administration in Indiana*. Indianapolis, Indiana Historical Bureau, 1973, pp. 209-210.

60. *Ibid.*, p. 216.

61. Milton, *op cit.*, pp. 76-77.

62. Tredway, *op cit.*, p. 217.

63. *Ibid.* p.216: also see William Dudley Foulke. *Life of Oliver P. Morgan* (Vol.1). Indianapolis-Kansas City, The Bowen-Merrill Company, 1899, pp.405-407; also, for a view of Carrington's spies reporting on each other and otherwise over-ingratiating themselves with unsuspecting rebels, see Tredway, op. cit., pp. 216-217.

64. Tredway, *op cit.*, p. 218.

Post Civil War End Notes

1. This article was written by S/A Wayne Goldstein, Naval Criminal Investigative Service.

2. Jeffrey M. Dorwart, *The Office of Naval Intelligence, The Birth of America's First Intelligence Agency, 1865 1918*, 1979, p. 6.

3. Ibid, pp. 10-11.

4. Thomas F. Troy, *Donovan and the CIA: A History of the Establishment of the CIA*, Frederick, MD, 1981, p. 8.

5. Ibid. p. 120.

6. 38 Stat 770. Enabling legislation was also passed three days later to provide for raising volunteer forces as needed "in time of actual or threatened war." See: Stat 347-51.

7. Memo Chief of Staff for TAG, 3 Mar 1914. This crippling restriction against crossing the border was not lifted until after General Pershing's Punitive Expedition had entered Mexican territory in 1916.

8. 38 Stat 514-16.

9. See "Report of the Signal Officer," *War Department Annual Reports, 1913*, I, p. 781.

10. The latter item had recently received its first boost since 1903, in the meager form of an increase from $10,000 to $11,000 for FY 1915.

11. Memo, Chief of War College Division for Chief of Staff, 3 May 1915.

12. *Ibid.*

13. A German sabotage campaign at impeding the flow of munitions and supplies from America to the Allied powers was in full swing at this time. See: Henry Landau, *The Enemy Within*, New York, 1937.

14. Maj. Gen. Otto L. Nelson, Jr., *National Security and the General Staff*, Washington, 1946, pp. 145-147.

15. Telegram Squire to AG for McClernaud, 14 December 1912.

16. Memorandum from Col. Biddle to Col. Hughes, 9 February 1914, and Memorandum from Col. Biddle to Chief of Staff, 27 April 1914.

17. Memorandum from Brig. Gen. Macomb for Chief of Staff, 3 August 1914. Nevertheless, Lt. Col. George O. Squier, the American Military Attache in London, was allowed to visit the British Army in France as an official military observer from 16 November 1914 to 2 January 1915.

18. Memorandum from Brig. Gen. Charles G. Treat, Acting Chief of War College Division, to Chief of Staff, 14 November 1916.

19. War Division memorandum 14 November 1916.

20. Letter, Chief, Military Mission, Paris to Chief, War College Division, 29 December 1916.

21. James Morton Callahan, *American Foreign Policy in Mexican Relations*, New York, 1932, pp. 562-63.

22. "Report of the Chief of Staff," *War Department Annual Reports, 1916*, I, p. 187.

23. From August 1911 to July 1914, Maj. Ryan had been an associate professor of modern languages at the United States Military Academy. He was replaced as Expedition Intelligence officer by Capt. (later Lt. Col.) W.O. Reed, 6th Cav, on 30 April 1916.

24. Van Deman, R.H. (Maj. Gen.), Memorandum, 8 April 1949.

25. "Report of the Chief of Staff," *War Department Annual Reports, 1916*, I, p. 201.

26. Letter, Pershing to Commanding General Southern Department, 27 March 1916, subject: Preliminary Report of Punitive Expedition.

27. Capt. Nicholas N. Campanole, "Report Covering Operations of United States Punitive Expedition, Intelligence Section, 15 March 1916-5 February 1917."

28. Capt. (later Col.) Campanole succeeded Capt. W.O. Reed as Expedition Intelligence Officer, effective 10 October 1916, and then remained in that capacity until the withdrawal of the force from Mexico on 5 February 1917.
28. Harry Aubrey Toulmin, *With Pershing in Mexico*, Harrisburg, 1935, pp. 85-88. This turned out to be the last time that the US Army employed a regular Indian Scout unit in its field operations.

29. Van Deman memorandum, 8 April 1949.

30. *Ibid.*

31. Comment, Brig. Gen. H.H. Macomb for Chief of Staff, 21 June 1916, attached to Van Deman "Historical Sketch."

32. Three years earlier, in compliance with a formal request from Secretary of War Stimson, the General Staff had prepared a full report on "The Organization of the Land Forces of the United States," which recommended several specific military reforms regarding the effective mobilization of American manpower. As soon as Woodrow Wilson became President in 1912, however, this so-called "Stimson Plan" was pigeonholed. See: "Report of the Secretary of War," *War Department Annual Reports*, 1912, pp. 69-128.

33. "Report of the Chief of Staff," *War Department Annual Reports, 1916*, p. 155.

34. "Report of the Secretary of War," *War Department Annual Reports, 1915*, pp. 22-23. This plan was generally known as the "Continental Army Plan."

35. Memo from Chief, War College Division for Chief of Staff, 11 December 1916.

36. Written by Charles H, Harris and Louis R. Sadler. This article appeared in The Americas, Volume XXXIX, July 1982, Number 1. Used with the permission of the authors.

37. *Mexican Rebel: Pascual Orozco and the Mexican Revolution, 1910 1915* (Lincoln, 1967).

38. Robert Ryall Miller, *Arms Across the Border: United States Aid to Juarez During the French Intervention in Mexico* (Philadelphia, 1973), pp.7, 32, 38.

39. Francisco Almada's *La rebelion de Tomochi* (Chihuahua, 1938) is the standard source for the insurrection. Also see the U.S. v Victor L. Ochoa, District Court, El Paso, FRC-FW, No. 893 and District Court, El Paso, nos. 4,8,7,6,5,1009, 1024, all in FRC-FW. See also Yolanda Guaderrama Alexander, "Las Palomas: Years of Turmoil, 1893-1917" (Graduate Seminar Paper, Department of History, New Mexico State University, 1974), pp. 7-16.

40. U.S. v. Leocardio B. Trevino et al., U.S. Commissioner, El Paso, FRC-FW, no. 83, and District Court, El Paso, FRC-FW, No. 1361. See also U.S. Commissioner, El Paso, FRC-FW, nos. 100, 156, 88, 117, 101. Additional details are available in National Archives, Numerical and Minor Files of the Department of State, Microcopy M-862, roll 429, file nos. 5026 and 5028; and Richard Estrada, Border Revolution: The Mexican Revolution in the Ciudad Juarez/El Paso area, 1906-1915," (unpublished M.A. thesis, University of Texas, at El Paso, 1975), pp. 38-44.

41. Charles H. Harris III and Louis R. Sadler, "The 1911 Reyes Conspiracy: The Texas Side," *Southwestern Historical Quarterly* (April, 1980), pp 325-348.

42. For a study of United States arms policy see Harold Eugene Holcombe, "United States Arms Control and the Mexican Revolution, 1910-1924," (unpublished Ph.D. dissertation, University of Alabama, 1968), pp.26-33. The Madero government's use of the British Foreign Office in persuading Taft to ban the exportation of munitions to the Orozquitas can be found in: Lord Codry telegram to the British Ambassador in Washington James Bryce, March 12, 1912; Cowdry to Bryce, March 13, 1912; Cowdry to Enrique Creel, March 12, 1912; and Foreign Office minute of March 13, 1912, all in Foreign Office 115/1683, British Public Record Office, Kew Gardens, London. See also Peter Calvert, *The Mexican Revolution, 1910 1914: The Diplomacy of Anglo American Conflict* (Cambridge, 1968), pp. 108-109.

43. Ironically, the Rangers, whose strength had been more than doubled (15-43) in October, 1911 at federal expense to pacify the Texas border had been reduced to their former numbers by late January, 1912, because the border appeared peaceful. Senate Document no. 404, 62nd Cong., 2nd sess. (Washington, 1912). During the Orozco rebellion, after first being ordered not to assist Federal officials in the enforcement of the neutrality laws, they generally worked closely with the Bureau of Investigation. See Texas Governor O.B. Colquitt to Adjutant General Henry Hutchings, February 2, 1912, Walter Prescott Webb Papers, vol. 18, Barker Texas History Center, University of Texas at Austin. Also see

Monthly Returns Company A, March, April and June, 1912 and Company B, February, May and June, 1912, Texas Ranger Archive, Texas State Library, Austin, Texas.

44. The key word in the statement is blatant. As is well known, the British Secret Intelligence Service operated on a rather large scale in the United States during both World War I and II; however, they were rather more discreet. See for example, H. Montgomery Hyde, *Room 3603: The Story of the British Intelligence Center in New York during World War II* (New York, 1963) and William Stephenson's somewhat sensationalized *A Man Called Intrepid: The Secret War* (New York, 1976).

45. H.A. Thompson to S.W. Finch, April 21, 1912, National Archives, Federal Bureau of Investigation (hereafter cited as BI), Record Group 65, microcopy, no number, roll 1; See also Edward Tyrell to Chief, U.S. Secret Service, September 26, 1912, National Archives, Microcopy no. 3, 157, Record Group 87, Records of the U.S. Secret Service, Daily Reports of Agents, 1875 through 1936, Daily Report, March 1, 1912, BI, roll 2.

46. F.H. Lancaster report, March 1, 1912, BI, roll 2.

47. Testimony of James G. McNary, Vice-President, First National Bank of El Paso, who stated that $500,000 was involved, *Revolutions in Mexico: Hearings Before a Subcommittee of the Committee on Foreign Relations, United States Senate*. 62nd Cong., 2nd sess. (Washington, 1913), 169; Felix Sommerfeld who should have known gave the figure as being between $600,000 and $700,000, Ibid., 437. Two stories, emanating from officials of the Huerta government in 1913, cite Llorente's expenditure as being $283,943 and another account states that $150,000 was spent. See *El Paso Morning Times*, June 3, and July 21, 1913.

48. See the Sommerfeld file. Military Intelligence Division (hereafter cited as MID), National Archives, Record Group 165, Records of the War Department General and Special Staffs, MID, 9140-1754; Sommerfeld's testimony in *Revolutions in Mexico*, pp. 387-447. Also see Michael C. Meyer, "Villa, Sommerfeld, Columbus y los alemanes." *Historia Mexicana* 28 (April-June 1979), pp. 546-566.

49. I.J. Bush, *Gringo Doctor* (Caldwell, Idaho, 1939), pp. 183-186, 226; William H. Beezley, *Insurgent Governor: Abraham Gonzalez and the Mexican Revolution in Chihuahua* (Lincoln, 1973), pp. 33-69.

50. L.E. Ross reports, March 1 and 9, 1912, BI, roll 2.

51. Lancaster reports, March 1 and 9, 1912, roll 2 and March 4, 5, 6, 8, 1912, roll 1; Ross report, March 19, 1912, roll 1; Thompson to Finch, March 3, 1912, roll 1; Thompson, April 19, 1912, BI roll 1; C.D. Hebert to Finch, April 29, 1912, roll 1; Hebert reports, May 5, 8, 14, 15, 1912, roll 2 all in BI; For example, see the Thiel Agency's reports, entitled "Revolutionary Information," March 4, 5, 6, 8, 16, 22, 23, 24, 26, 27, 28, 29, April 2, 4, 8, 10, 22, and 28, BI, roll 1. For the Thiel Agency's reports to the Mexico Northwestern, see Revolutionary Information," October 22, 1912, John H. McNeely Collection, Box 13, Packet "Misc. 1912-1914," Records of the Mexico Northwestern Railway, Archives, University of Texas at El Paso. For the Thiel Agency's reports to the Mexican government, see Isidro Fabela et al., (eds.) *Documentos historicos de la Revolucion Mexicana*, 27 vols. (Mexico 1964-1973) (hereafter cited as DHRM) VII, pp. 371-375, 391-394, 416-418.

52. Lancaster to Finch, "Personal and Confidential," March 23, 1912, BI, roll 1.

53. Sanche de Gramont, *The Secret War: The Story of International Espionage Since World War II* (New York, 1962), pp. 149-150.

54. Thompson report, June 21, 1912, BI, roll 1; E.M. Blanford report, April 7, 1913, roll 3, both in BI; Manuel Cuesta to Secretario de Relaciones Exteriores, March 9, 1912, *DHRM*, VII, 183; Enrique de la Sierra to same, February 24, 1913, *Ibid.*, XIV, pp. 78-79.

55. Lancaster reports, March 13, 18, 22, 1912; Ross report, April 24, 1912; Hawkins reports, April 17, 18, 24, 1912; Thiel Agency report, March 27, 1912; and Thompson report, April 19, 1912, all in BI roll 1.

56. Ross reports, March 19, 20, 23, April 5, 23, 1912, roll 1; Hebert report, May 8, 1912, roll 2, all in BI.

57. M.L. Gresh report, October 22, 1912, roll 2; J.W. Vann report, October 28, 1912, roll 3; C.E. Breniman reports, October 25 and 30, November 3, 4, 24, 1912, roll 3, all in BI. Ross's reports to Llorente, dated October 18 and 19, November 1912, are in the Enrique C. Llorente Papers, Manuscripts Division, New York Public Library.

58. Inspector of Consulates to Secretario de Relaciones Exteriores, May 14, 1913, *DHRM*, XIV, pp. 229-230; See also Abraham Molina to Jose Maria Maytorena, April 22, 1913, *Ibid.*, XIV, 190; Jose Maria Maytorena to Abraham Molina, May 8, 1913, *Ibid.*, XIV, 221.

59. U.S. v. Victor L. Ochoa, District Court, El Paso, FRC-FW, No. 893 and Almada, *La rebelion de Tomochi*, pp. 127-128, 133. The best summary of his revolutionary career is found in the *El Paso Times*, September 20, 1921.

60. R.L. Barnes reports, June 21-25, 1912, BI, roll 2.

61. Zork Hardware Company Records, Archives, University of Texas at El Paso. In 1912, the firm's name was Krakauer, Zork and Moye's Sucs., Inc. The Company was one of the largest hardware dealers in the Southwest, with assets exceeding $1,100,000. Although the 1912 account books do not indicate to whom the sales of arms and ammunitions were made, they clearly show that a sizable percentage of the firm's sales for the year were munitions.

62. *Revolution in Mexico*, 124.

63. U.S. v. Robert Krakauer, Castulo Herra, Pascual Arellano, Adolph Krakauer, Victor L. Ochoa, S. Dominguez, G. Gutierrez, Francisco Navarro, Julius Krakauer, District Court, El Paso, FRC-FW, no. 1626. See also U.S. v. Sabino Guaderrama, Avelino Guarderrama, Longino Gonzalez, Isabel Larrazola, District Court, El Paso, FRC-FW, no. 1629.

64. U.S. v. Shelton-Payne Arms Co., Douglas Hardware Co., W. H. Shelton, John Henry Payne, W.F. Fisher, District Court, Phoenix, FRC-LN, no. c-676; U.S. v. L.D. McCartney, Shelton-Payne Arms Co., W.H. Shelton, John Henry Payne, J.N. Gonzalez, District Court, Phoenix, FRC-LN, no. C-677; U.S. v. Krakauer, Zork & Moye, Julius Krakauer, L.D. McCartney, District Court, Phoenix, FRC-LN, no. C-679.

65. See cases in footnote 28.

66. U.S. v. Arnulfo-Chavez, U.S. Commissioner, El Paso, no. 1081, District Court, El Paso, no. 1590, both in FRC-FW. The Guaderrama clan in El Paso exemplified this type of entrepreneur. For information concerning their activity during this period see, U.S. v. Sabino Guaderrama, Isabel Rangel, Jose Cerros, U.S. Commissioner, El Paso, no. 1135; U.S. v. Castulo Herrera, Sabino Guaderrama, Avelino Guaderrama, U.S. Commissioner, El Paso, no. 1070; U.S. v. Sabino Guaderrama, Avelino Guaderrama, Longino Gonzalez, Isabel Larrazola, District Court, El Paso, no. 1629, all in FRC-FW. The Guaderrama were still going strong in 1915, being involved, among other things, in the Huerta conspiracy. See U.S. v. Sabino Guaderrama, U.S. Commissioner, El Paso, no. 1376, and U.S. v. Victoriano Huerta et al., District Court, San Antonio, no. 2185, both in FRC-FW.

67. See, for instance, the following cases in U.S. District Court, El Paso, FRC-FW: U.S. v. James McKay, no. 1555; U.S. v. John Thomas, no. 1552; U.S. v. Peter S. Aikin, no. 1553, U.S. v. Francisco M.F. Najera, no. 1560; U.S. v. Allen L. Rogers, no. 1551; U.S. v. Alfredo Guerro, no. 1554; U.S. v. Francisca Molina, no. 1575; U.S. v. Petra Ochoa, no. 1593; U.S. v. Josefina Santa Cruz, no. 1602; U.S. v. Maria Solis, no. 1603.

68. U.S. v. Fred Freepartner, W.E. Mason, Joe de Lauter, Lou Mullady, Enrique Esparza, Agustin Gallo, U.S. Commissioner, El Paso, nos. 1066 and 1067, District Court, El Paso, no. 1598, both in FRC-FW.

69. U.S. v. John Dickson, U.S. Commissioner, El Paso, no. 1097, District Court, El Paso, no. 1598, both in FRC-FW.

70. Testimony of Felix Sommerfeld, *Revolution in Mexico*, pp 427-431; El Paso *Herald*, August 22-23, 1912; El Paso *Morning Times*, July 2, 25, 1912.

71. Ross reports, May 18-22, 1912; Thompson reports, May 21-23, October 3, 18, 21, 1921; Hebert report, May 22, 1912; Harris reports, May 25, 28, 29, June 6, 7, 10, 14, October 13, 18, 1912, all in BI, roll 2; Harris reports, October 27 and 30, November 3, 4, 6, 1912; Gresh report, October 31, 1912; Breniman report, November 13, 1912; Blanford report, November 14, 1912; Harris to A. Bruce Bielaski, November 20, 1912, all in BI, roll 3; U.S. v. Ignacio Salvador Rojas Vertiz, Frank Borbon, T.C. Cabney, Pascual Orozco, Jr., Gonzalo C. Enrile, U.S. Commissioner, El Paso, FRC-FW, no. 1089 and District Court, El Paso, FRC-FW, nos. 1628, 1633.

72. U.S. v. Ignacio Lopez, Salvador Rojas Vertiz, Frank Borbon, T.C. Cabney, Pascual Orozco, Jr., Gonzalo Enrile, District Court, El Paso, FRC-FW, no. 1628.

73. Thompson report, June 7, 1912; Barnes report, June 8, 1912; Ross reports, June 8 and 10, 1912, all in BI, roll 2; U.S. v. Castulo Herrera, Ignacio Gutierrez, Eduardo Ochoa, Jesus de la Torre, Ignacio Nunez, U.S. Commissioner, District of New Mexico, Federal Records Center, Denver (hereafter cited as FRC-D), No. 1161, District Court, Santa Fe, FRC-D, no. 85; U.S. v. Ignacio Nunez and Jesus de la Torre, U.S. Commissioner, District of New Mexico, FRC-D, nos. 1024 and 1604, District Court, Santa Fe, FRC-D, no.

1654; U.S. v. Ignacio Gutierrez, U.S. Commissioner, District of New Mexico, FRC-D, no. 1251.

74. U.S. v. Lazaro Alanis (Jose) Ines Salazar, Roque Gomez, Concepcion Tovar, Marcial Andujos, U.S. Commissioner, District of New Mexico, FRC-D, nos. 1158 and 1268, U.S. Commissioner, El Paso, FRC-FW, nos. 1158 and 1167, District Court, Santa Fe, FRC-D, no. 84; Thompson reports, August 12 and 14, 1912, BI, roll 2; Ross report, August 14, 1912, BI. roll 2; Barnes report, August 16, 1912, BI roll 2, El Paso *Morning Times*, August 13, 1912.

75. Testimony of Manuel L. Lujan, *Revolutions in Mexico*, pp 296-297; Dispatches from the U.S. Military Attaché, Capt. W.A. Burnside, July 24, 1912, MID 5761-532 and July 24, 1912, MID 5384-16.

76. Francisco I. Madero to Enrique Llorente, May 30, 1912, *DHRM*, VII, 422.

77. Charpentier's testimony in *Revolutions in Mexico*, pp. 447-451, 505-528; McDonald's testimony, *Ibid.*, pp. 680-683; Mahoney's testimony, *Ibid.*, pp. 683-686.

78. Charpentier, Mahoney, and McDonald were tried and acquitted in 1912. See U.S. v. E.L. Charpentier, D.J. Mahoney, Robert McDonald, A Monahan (sic-J.H. Noonan), District Court, El Paso, FRC-FW, no. 1607; Llorente's case was continued until April 14, 1916, when it was dismissed. See U.S. v. Enrique C. Llorente, R.H.G. McDonald, D.J. Mahoney, J.H. Noonan, E.L. Charpentier, District Court, El Paso, FRC-FW, no. 1650. As an example to the permutations that occurred among border characters, in 1914 Victor L. Ochoa was enlisting men for the Carrancistas, and one of those he enlisted was R.H.G. McDonald. See U.S. v. Victor L. Ochoa, Fred Mendenhall, R.H.G. McDonald, Agustin Pantoja, Ramon Gutierrez, District Court, El Paso, FRC-FW, no. 1810; U.S. v. E.L. Holmdahl, Victor L. Ochoa, Tandy Sanford, Fred Mendenhall, U.S. Commissioner, El Paso, FRC-FW, no. 1363; U.S. v. Victor L. Ochoa, Tandy Sanford, John Sanford, Fred Mendenhall, Rafael Diaz, R.H.G. McDonald, Jose Orozco, Francisco Rojas, Vicente Carreon, U.S. Commissioner, El Paso, FRC-FW, no. 1359.

79. Ernest Knable, Assistant Attorney General to Secretary of State, May 15, 1912, National Archives, Record group 60, Department of Justice (hereafter cited as DJ), file no. 90755-1557; Also see Wickersham to Charles Boynton, May 16, 1912, DJ, 90755-1562 and May 20, 1912, DJ 90755-1565; Charles Boytin to Wickersham, May 17, 1912, DJ, 90755-1564 and June 8, 1912, DJ, 90755-1590; Not until it was obvious that Orozco had lost did the U.S. government begin putting pressure on Llorente. See Huntington Wilson to Wickersham, June 24, 1912, Records of the Department of State Relating to the Internal Affairs of Mexico, 1910-1929, National Archives Microfilm Publications, Microcopy no. 274, file no. 812.00/4246; Wickersham to Boynton, June 27, 1912, DJ, 90755-1605 and J.A. Fowler to Secretary of State, June 28, 1912, DJ, 90755-1605; Thompson reports, November 6, 7, and 3o, 1912, BI, roll 3.

80. U.S. v. Luis Diaz de Leon, U.S. Commissioner, El Paso, no. 1036 and District Court, El Paso, no. 1563; U.S. v. Canuto Leyva, District Court, El Paso, no. 1617; U.S. v. Rutilio Rodriguez, District Court, El Paso, no. 1618; U.S. v. Victor Ochoa, District Court, El Paso, no. 1625; U.S. v. Jesus Quintana et al., U.S. Commissioner, El Paso, no. 1037; U.S. v. J. Saldivar, District Court, El Paso, no. 1569, all in FRC-FW.

81. El Paso *Morning Times*, June 24, 1912.

82. Ross reports, July 6 and September 8, 11, 1912, roll 3; Harris reports, July 29, August 2, 7, October 31, 1912, roll 3; R.L. Barnes report, September 28, 1912, roll 2, all in BI.

83. Walter Mills, *The Road to War*, Boston, 1935, p. 147.

84. Captain Franz Rintelen von Kleist, *The Dark Invader: Wartime Reminiscences of a German Intelligence Officer*, New York, 1933, pp. 57-60. This book should be treated with great circumspection as it contains much swashbuckling daring-do as believable information.

85. Reinhard R. Doerries, *Imperial Challenge, Ambassador Count Bernstorff and German American Relations, 1908 1917*, Chapel Hill, 1989, p. XV.

86. Copyrighted by Eric Rafalko. Used with his permission.

87. Colonel Allison Ind, A Short History of Espionage, New York, David McKay Company, Inc. 1963, p. 155.

88. The article is from an interview with Robert L. Bannerman, who served in the Office of Security, Department of State from 1936 to 1947, becoming director in the latter year.

89. Heinrich von Eckhardt.

90. Joan M. Jensen, *Military Surveillance of Civilians in American*, Morristown, New Jersey, General Learning Press, 1975, p. 5.

91. Joan M. Jensen, *The Price of Vigilance*, Chicago, Ill, Rand McNally, 1968, p. 12.

92. Jensen, Military Surveillance, *op cit*., pp. 4-5.

93. 41st Cong., Sess. III, Ch. 14.

94. Max Lowenthal, *The Federal Bureau of Investigation*, New York, Harcourt Brace Jovanovich, 1950, pp. 10-13.

95. 28 U.S.C. 533 (3).

96. Jensen, *The Price of Vigilence* 15; Homer Cummings and Carl McFarland, *Federal Justice*, New York, McMillian Co., 1937, pp. 415-416.

97. Cummings and McFarland, *op. cit*., p. 416.

98. 33 U.S. Statute at Large 1214.

99. 39 U.S. Statute at Large 889.

100. Cir. Ltr, Bruce Bielaski to all Special Agents and Local Officers, Bureau of Investigation, 22 Mar 1917.

101. French Strother, *Fighting Germany's Spies*, New York, 1918. P. 394.

102. History of MID. P. 1042.

103. Letter from McAdoo to Gregory, 2 June 1917.

104. Letter from McAdoo to President Wilson, 2 June 1917.

105. Letter from Gregory to President Wilson, 14 Jun 1917.

106. Joan M. Jensen, The Price of Vigilence, *op. cit*. Pp. 118-119.

107. FBI Intelligence Division, *An Analysis of FBI Domestic Security Intelligence Investigations: Authority, Official Attitudes and Activities in Historical Perspective*, 10/28/75.

108. Memorandum of F.X. O'Donnell, 10/24/38.

109. Jensen, *op. cit*., pp. 102-103.

110. Act of June 15, 1917, Title I, Section 3.

111. The Supreme Court upheld such convictions in Schenck v. U.S., U.S. 47 (1919) and Abrams v. U.S., 250 U.S. 616 (1919).

112. Zechariah Chafee, *Free Speech in the United States*, Cambridge, Harvard University Press, 1941, p. 69.

113. Homer Cummings and Carl McFarland, Federal Justice, *op. cit*., p. 247.

114. Copyrighted by Charles H. Harris III and Louis R. Sadler. Used with the permission of the authors.

115. See, for example, Allen Dulles, *The Craft of Intelligence*, Harper & Row Publishers, N.Y., 1965, pp38-39.

116. Michael C. Meyer, "The Mexican-German Conspiracy of 1915*," The Americas*, July 1966, pp-76-89; James A. Sandos, "German Involvement in Northern Mexico, 1915-1916: A New Look at the Columbus Raid, "*The Hispanic American Historical Review*, February 1970, pp 70-88; and Barbara Tuchman, *The Zimmerman Telegram*, The Viking Press Inc., N.Y., 1958, passim.

117. The only printed source which treats the Jahnke conspiracy in detail is Henry Landau, *The Enemy Within: The Inside Story of German Sabotage in America*, G.P. Putnam's Sons, N.Y., 1937, which can still be read with profit although it contains errors and is undocumented. Surprisingly, this study has generally been neglected by historians of American intelligence.

118. "Interrogation of Lothar Witzke," San Antonio, Texas, 16-18 September 1919, Volume II, Exhibit 24, and "Affidavit of Alfred Edward Woodley Mason," Cairo, Egypt, 15 February 1929, Volume II, Exhibit 625, Mixed Claims Commission (MCC), United States and Germany, Federal Records Center, East Point, Ga.

119. Landau, *op cit*, pp 77-84 and 114.

120. "Affidavit of Admiral Sir W. Reginald Hall," former chief of British Naval Intelligence, 28 December 1926, with annexed copies of 327 German cablegrams intercepted by the British government during World War I, Volume VII, Exhibit 320, MCC, United States and Germany, Federal Records Center, East Point, Ga.

121. Major R.L. Barnes to Colonel Garrison, 9 April 1919, National Archives, Record Group 165, Records of the War Department General and Special Staffs, Military Intelligence Division (MID), 51-45.

122. Testimony of Altendorf in "U.S. War Department Record of the Court Martial of Lothar Witzke," Volume VIII, Exhibit 321, MCC, United States and Germany, Federal Records Center, East Point, Ga.

123. William Gleaves to Captain R. Davila, 1 August 1915, Venustiano Carranza Archives, Centro de Estudios de Historia de Mexico, Departmento Cultural de Condumex, S.A., Mexico City, Mex.; and "Affidavit of Alfred Edward Woodley Mason," *op cit*. Also, see Gleaves file, MID, 10541-546.

124. Testimony of Altendorf and Gleaves, "U.S. War Department Record of the Court Martial of Lothar Witzke," *op cit*.

125. Testimony of Butcher, Ibid.

126. "Affidavit of Alfred Edward Woodley Mason," *op cit*.; Testimony of Gleaves, "U.S. War Department Record of the Court Martial of Lothar Witzke," *op cit*.; and Guy L. Fake Affidavit, 18 August 1924, Volume II, Exhibit 10, MCC, United States and Germany, Federal Records Center, East Point, Ga.

127. Testimony of Gleaves, Altendorf, Nuenhoffer and Major R.M. Campbell, "U.S. War Department Record of the Court Martial of Lothar Witzke." *op cit*.

128. Testimony of Altendorf and Major R.M. Campbell, "U.S. Department of Record of the Court Martial of Lothar Witzke," *op cit*.; and Van Deman to intelligence officer, Western Department, 17 January 1918, MID, 10541-268.

129. Testimony of Altendorf, "US War Department Record of the Court Martial of Lothar Witzke," *op cit*; and Altendorf Report, undated, in MID, 10541-268.

130. See Chapman's cipher telegram to Butcher, 26 January 1918, in National Archives, Record Group 84, Records of the Foreign Service Posts of the Department of State, Nogales, Sonora, Mex., Consulate Files, 1918, File Number 820.

131. Special Border Report, 4 February 1918, Nogales, Ariz., MID, 10541-268.

132. Ibid.

133. Percy Altendorf, "My Trip to Mexico," and Butcher Report, undated, both in MID, 10541-268. See also the file on Calles, MID, 8536-297.

134. Butcher Report, *op cit*.

135. *Ibid*.; and Testimony of Charles Beatty, "U.S. War Department Record of the Court Martial of Lothar Witzke," *op cit*.

136. Testimony of Butcher, "U.S. War Department Record of the Court Martial of Lothar Witzke," *op cit*.; and Butcher Report, op cit. and Special Border Report, Nogales, Ariz., 2 February 1918, both in MID 10541-268.

137. Testimony of Butcher, "U.S. Was Department Record of the Court Martial of Lothar Witzke," *op cit*.

138. The best account of the decrypting of the telegram is the testimony of Manly, "U.S. War Department Record of the Court Martial of Lothar Witzke." *op cit*. See also Herbert O. Yardley, *The American Black Chamber*, Bobbs-Merrill Co. Inc., Indianapolis, Ind., 1931, pp 90-114; David Kahn, *The Codebreakers: The Story of Secret Writing*, The Macmillan Co, N.Y., 1967, pp 253-54; Yardley memorandum attached to telegram from R.L. Barnes to Milstaff, 7 August 1918, MID, 10541-268; and Major General Ralph H. Van Deman, *Memoirs*, Unpublished Manuscript, Library, US Army Intelligence Center and School, Fort. Huachuca, Ariz., pp 62-63.

139. Exhibit 13, "U.S. War Department Record of the Court Martial of Lothar Witzke," *op cit*.

140. John M. Maguire to Lieutenant Van Dusen, 11 June 1918, in MID, 10541-268.

141. Testimony of Witzke, "U.S. War Department Record of the Court Martial of Lothar Witzke," *op cit*.

142. Court-Martial Verdict, "U.S. War Department Record of the Court Martial of Lothar Witzke," *op cit*.

143. For example, see Special Border Report, Nogales, Ariz., 7 February 1918, in MID 8536-293.

144. Campbell to Van Deman, 18 March 1918, MID 10541-367.

145. Campbell to chief, Military Intelligence Branch, 4 September 1918, MID, 10541-367.

146. See Consul Chapman to Consul Lawton, 26 March and 18 April 1918, Consul Lawton to Consul McPherson, 20 April 1918, Consul Chapman to Captain Joel Lipscomb, 29 April 1918, and Consul Simpich to Consul Lawton, 3 May 1918, all found in File Number 820, 1918, Nogales Consulate File; Captain G.L. Jones to R.L. Barnes, 14 May 1918, MID 8536-314; and Captain H.S. Dickey to chief, MID, 28 August 1918, MID 51-45.

147. The correspondence can be found in Department of State File Number 150. 636/31, National Archives; Nogales Consulate File 820, 1918; and Colonel Marlborough Churchill to A. Caminetti, 14 August 1918, MID, 51-45.

148. A detailed statement of this controversy can be found in Joan M. Jensen, *The Price of Vigilance*, Rand McNally & Co., Chicago, Ill., 1968, pp 118-29; and William R. Corson, *The Armies of Ignorance: The Rise of the American Intelligence Empire*, Dial Press/James Wade Books, N.Y., 1977, pp 52-63.

149. Acting judge advocate general to the adjutant general, 17 January 1921, Volume II, Exhibit 157, MCC, United States and Germany, Federal Records Center, East Point, Ga.; and Gregory to Wilson, 25 November 1918, MID, 10541-268. See also Edmund M. Morgan, "Court-Martial Jurisdiction Over Non-Military Persons Under the Articles of War," *Minnesota Law Review*, January 1920, pp76-116. Morgan, however, has one serious error in the article-that Witzke died in prison (p 80). For Wilson's commutation of Witzke's sentence, see enclosure in the "U.S. War Department Record of the Court-Martial of Lothar Witzke," *op cit*.

150. Captain Frank P. Stretton to director of Military Intelligence, 2 October 1919, Major R.B. Woodruff to same, 26 January 1920 and MID Memorandum, 25 May 1921, all in MID, 10541-268; and interrogation of Witzke, 16-18 September 1919, Volume II, Exhibit 24, MCC, United States and Germany, Federal Records Center, E. Pt., Ga.

151. German Embassy Memorandum to the Department of State, September 1923, in MID, 10541-268; *The Washington Post*, 21 November 1923; Landau, *op cit.*, pp 183-85. Also see Admiral Sir Reginald Hall and Amos J. Peaslee, *Three Wars With Germany*, G.P. Putnam's Sons, N.Y., 1944, p 110; and Report Number 590, 11 October 1935, MID, 10541-268.

152. Colonel Edward Davis to director of Military Intelligence, 18 June and 30 July 1920; Davis to military attaché, Mexico City, Mex., 13 August 1920, all in MID, 10541-367; and Ladislas Farago, *The Game of the Foxes: The Untold Story of German Espionage in the United States and Great Britain During World War II*, David McKay Co. Inc., N.Y. 1971, pp 654-58 and 622. Surprisingly Farago does not mention Jahnke's espionage career during World War I.

153. Alvaro Obregón, *Ocho mil kilómetros en campaña*. Third Edition, Fondo de Cultura Económica, Mexico City, Mex., 1960, pp 199 and 207; and Major R.L. Barnes to director of Military Intelligence, 6 November 1918, MID, 9685-129.

154. Gleaves file, MID, 10541-546; and Guy L Fake Affidavit, *op cit*.

155. See the voluminous Altendorf file, MID, 51-45. The last entry, referring to his activities in Havana is Lieutenant Colonel V.W. Cooper to Major J.C. Schwenck, 5 November 1928.

156. Act of October 16, 1918.

157. Confidential Memorandum to all Special Agents and Employees, 8/12/19.

158. Coben, *A Mitchell Palmer*, New York, Columbia University Press, 1963, pp. 130, 207.

159. Coben, *op. cit.*, pp. 210, 215-216; see also *Preston's Aliens and Dissenters*, chs, 7-8; Chafee, *Free Speech in the United States*, ch 5.; Robert K. Murray, *Red Scare: A Study in National Hysteria*, Minneapolis, University of Minnesota Press, 1955.

160. Preston, *op. cit.*, p. 221.

161. Confidential Memorandum, 8/12/19.

162. Memorandum from Burke to Caminetti, 11/19/19, cited in Preston, *Aliens and Dissenters*, pp. 216-217.

163. Memorandum from Hoover to Caminetti, 12/17/19, cited in Coben, *A. Mitchell Palmer*, p. 223.

164. Memorandum from Hoover to Caminetti, 1/22/20, cited in Preston, *op. cit.*, p. 219.

165. Memorandum from Hoover to Caminetti, 3/16/20, cited in Preston, p. 219.

166. Memorandum from Hoover to Caminetti, 2/2/20; 4/6/20, cited in Preston, p. 224.

167. Preston, *op. cit.*, p. 222.

168. Memorandum from Hoover to Caminetti, 3/16/20, cited in Preston, p. 223.

169. Preston, *op. cit.*, pp. 223-224; see Louis F. Post, *The Deportations Delirium of Nineteen Twenty*, Chicago, Kerr, 1923.

CI Between The War
End Notes

1. Japanese.

2. Memorandum from Chief, MI4 to G-2 Exec., 28 July 1923.

3. Federal troops were dispatched to West Virginia during both 1920 and 1921, for the purpose of preserving order in coal mining districts. See: S. Doc., 263, 67th Cong., 2d sess., "Federal Aid in Domestic Disturbances 1903-1922," 18 September 1922.

4. Lecture delivered by Director of Military Intelligence at Conference of Department and Division Commanders," 12 January 1920, quoted in MID 10560-367-4.

5. Letter, Acting Director, MID to Department of Justice, 11 August 1920.

6. "Political Spy System in U.S.," *New York Call*, 16 August 1920.

7. See MID 10560-272, 30 June 1921.

8. See MID 10560-60, 28 January 1920, and Memorandum 1st. Lt. G.L. Harding for Gen. Churchill, 13 March 1920.

9. Memorandum from Chief, MI4 for Gen. Churchill, 23 March 1920.

10. See Files 62-375-13X, 15 and 22, dated respectively 4, 18, and 20 January 1921. Records of the FBI. Department of Justice.

11. File 62-375-15, 18 January 1921. Records of the FBI.

12. Letter, TAG to Third Corps Area, 9 June 1922, AG 322.999 (3-26-21).

13. See "Emergency Plan White, War Department Basic 1940." File 382 Reg. No. 53. DRB, TAG.

14. Letter, TAG to Corps Area Commanders, 6 December 1922, AG 322.999 (3-26-21).

15. MID 271-A-9-117, 16 October 1922.

16. *Ibid.*

17. MID 271-A-9-58, 16 January 1923; MID 271-A-69, 30 June 1923.

18. Memorandum, Assistant Chief of Staff G-2 for TAG, 30 January 1923. Lt. Long eventually received an official reprimand for his part in this affair.

19. Memorandum, Assistant Chief of Staff G-2 for TAG, 19 February 1923.

20. Letter, CG Ninth Corps Area to CO's all Posts, Camps and Stations, 20 December 1922.

21. MID 2710A-9-209, incl. 4, 12 March 1923.

22. Letter from Assistant Chief of Staff G-2 Hawaiian Department to Assistant Chief of Staff G-2, War Department General Staff, 16 February 1924.

23. Letter G-2 Executive to Assistant Chief of Staff G-2 Hawaiian Department, 6 March 1924.

24. MID 10560-731, 8 September 1924.

25. Memorandum, Acting Assistant Chief of Staff G-2 for Chief of Staff, 8 March 1924.

26. Col. Reeves had succeeded Col. (later Brig. Gen.) W.K. Naylor as Assistant Chief of Staff G-2, effective 1 July 1924. He continued to serve in that capacity until 1 May 1927, when he was relieved by Brig. Gen. (later Maj. Gen.) Stanley Ford.

27. Memorandum, Acting Assistant Chief of Staff G-2 for Chief of Staff, 2 April 1925.

28. MID 248-20-372, 383, and 392.

29. Gen. Smith served as Assistant Chief of Staff G-2 at the War Department General Staff from 3 January 1931 to 25 May 1933. His successor was Brig. Gen. (later Maj. Gen.) Harry S. Knight, who served from 22 December 1934 to 25 November 1935.

30. Memorandum, Assistant Chief of Staff G-2 for Chief of Staff, 19 February 1931.

31. Memorandum, Assistant Chief of Staff for Chief of Staff, 9 June 1932.

32. See Benjamin Gitlow, *The Whole of Their Lives*, New York, 1948, pp. 226-30; *Congressional Record*, 31 August 1949, pp. 12529-32. The latter document contains conclusive statements on this subject made to Howard Rushmore of the New York *Journal American* by bonus marcher John T. Pace, self-admitted Communist leader of the BEF.

33. Superintendent of the Metropolitan Police Department, D.C. during the initial bonus march was Brig. Gen. Pelham D. Glassford, USA-Ret, USMA Class of 1904.

34. Letter, Special Agent M.H. Purvus, Chicago, Illinois, to Director, Division of Investigation, 28 May 1932.

35. It should be recalled that this first BEF march on Washington was actually the forerunner of several other marches of the same general nature. While some of the later marches did turn out to be of major concern to the MID officials, the BEF affair was by far the largest and the only one requiring the use of Federal troops for eviction purposes.

36. Letter, CG First Corps Area to TAG, 6 January 1938; Memorandum, Assistant Chief of Staff G-2 for Chief of Staff, 5 April 1938.

37. Letter, G-2 Exec to Assistant Chief of Staff G-2 Ninth Corps Area, 21 August 1934.

38. Memorandum, Ch Opns Br to G-2 Exec, June 1936.

39. Letter TAG to CG Panama Canal Department, 12 March 1934.

40. OCS Memorandum dated 2 August 1935. Maj. Taylor had been in charge of the original counterintelligence group formed in MID during World War I to investigate War Department civilian employees. Following his demobilization, he had served in the New York City Police Department and retired as a police captain.

41. Memorandum, Assistant Chief of Staff G-2 for Chief of Staff, 8 June 1938. Responsibility for espionage planning was transferred from the Counterintelligence Branch to the Intelligence Branch in May 1941.

42. These censorship instructions were derived mainly from an AEF booklet that had been published in 1918. See *History of Military Censorship*, CSGID 314.7, 30 October 1942.

43. Letter, Brig. Gen. John T. Bissell, USA-Ret, to OCMH, 16 July 1954.

44. Memorandum, Assistant Chief of Staff G-2 for Chief of Staff, 1 December 1939.

45. MID 383.4, CFCP, 6 October 1940.

46. Memorandum, Assistant Chief of Staff G-2 for Chief of Staff, 28 August 1941. Twelve copies of this plan were also sent to the Director of Naval Intelligence for distribution to the 12 Naval Districts organized within the continental limits of the United States.

47. Letter J. E. Hoover to John J. McCloy, 16 November 1940; Ralph Budd to SW, 12 September 1940.

48. White House Memorandum to Cabinet members, 17 March 1941.

49. Following the outbreak of war in Europe, President Roosevelt first proclaimed a national emergency with certain specified limits, on 8 September 1939, and then, on 27 May 1941, declared that the Nation was confronted with an "unlimited national emergency." See *Federal Register*, IV, (July-Sept 1939), p. 3851 and VI (May 1941), p. 2617.

50. Alpheus Thomas Mason, *Harlan Fiske Stone: Pillar of the Law*, New York, Viking, 1956, pp. 149-151.

51. Memorandum from Attorney General Stone to J. Edgar Hoover, 5/13/24, cited in Mason, *op. cit.*, p. 151.

52. Mason, op. cit., pp. 150-152; Donald Johnson, The Challenge to American Freedoms: World War I and the Rise of the American Civil Liberties Union, University of Kentucky Press, 1963, P. 174.

53. Mason, op. cit., p. 113. See charges of Illegal Practices of the Justice Department, Hearings before the Senate Committee on the Judiciary, 66th Cong. 3rd Sess, (1921).

54. Johnson, *The Challenge to American Freedoms*, pp. 174-175.

55. Baldwin v. Franks, 120 U.S. 678.

56. Memorandum from Earl J. Davis to the Attorney General, 6/10/24, cited in Preston, *op. cit.*, pp. 241-242.

57. Memorandum from Roger Baldwin, 8/7/24, cited in Preston, *op. cit.*, p. 243.
58. Memorandum from Hoover to the Attorney General, 12/13/24.
59. Memorandum from Hoover to Ridgeley, 5/14/25.
60. Memorandum from Colonel Reeves, Office of the Chief of Staff, to Hoover, 9/29/25.
61. Memorandum from Hoover to Colonel Reeves, 10/7/25.
62. U.S. Senate Committee on Education and Labor, Industrial Espionage, 75th Cong, 2d Sess. (1937), cited in Jerold Auerbach, *Labor and Liberty: The LaFollette Committee and the New Deal*, Indianapolis, Bobbs-Merrill, 1966, p. 98.
63. Jensen, *Military Surveillance*, pp. 23-24.
64. Memorandum of telephone call between J. Edgar Hoover and Congressman Fish, January 19, 1931.
65. Memorandum from Hoover to the Attorney General, 1/2/32.
66. Memorandum from Hoover to Field Offices, 9/5/36.
67. Memorandum from E.A. Tamm to Hoover, 8/28/36.
68. Hoover memorandum, 8/24/36.
69. Memorandum from Hoover to Tamm, 9/10/36.
70. Letter from Cummings to the President, 10/20/38.
71. 28 U.S.C. 533(3).
72. Hoover memorandum, enclosed with letter from Cummings to the President, 10/20/38.
73. Hoover memorandum, enclosed with letter from Cummings to the President, 10/20/38.
74. Hoover memorandum, enclosed with letter from Cummings to the President, 10/20/38.
75. Confidential memorandum, by J. Edgar Hoover, 11/7/38.
76. Hoover memorandum, enclosed with letter from Cummings to the President, 10/20/38.
77. Letter from Cummings to the President, 10/20/38.
78. On 2/7/39, the Assistant to the Attorney General wrote letters to the Secret Service, the Bureau of Internal revenue, the Narcotics Bureau, the Customs Service, the Coast Guard, and the Postal Inspection service stating that the FBI and military intelligence had "undertaken activities to investigate matters relating to espionage and subversive activities." (Letter from J. B. Keenan, Assistant to the Attorney General, to F. J. Wilson, Chief, Secret Service, 2/7/39.) a letter from attorney General Murphy to the Secretary of the Treasury shortly thereafter also referred to "subversive activities." (Letter from Attorney General Murphy to the Secretary of the Treasury, 2/16/39.) However, a similar letter two days later referred only to matters "involving espionage, counterespionage, and sabotage," without mentioning "subversive activities." (Letter from Attorney General Murphy to the Secretary of the Treasury, 2/18/39.) Attorney General Murphy had abandoned this reference, although there is no record of any reasons for doing so.
79. Memorandum from J. Edgar Hoover to Attorney General Murphy, 3/16/39.
80. Memorandum from Hoover to Murphy, 3/16/39.
81. Memorandum from J. Edgar Hoover to Alexander Holtzoff, Special Assistant to the Attorney General, 1/18/39.
82. Memorandum from Hoover to Murphy, 3/16/39.
83. Memorandum from Hoover to the Acting Assistant to the Attorney General, 5/5/39.
84. Letter of J. B. Keenan, Assistant to the Attorney General, 2/7/39. (Compare the similar letter from Attorney General Murphy, omitting the term "subversive activities," at p. 401, note 93.)
85. Memorandum from Hoover to the Attorney General, 3/16/39.
86. Memorandum from E. A. Tamm to Hoover, 5/31/39.
87. Letter from Murphy to the President, 6/17/39.
88. Confidential Memorandum of the President, 6/26/39. President Roosevelt also dictated a separate additional memorandum for Secretary Hull which read, in part,

"This does not mean that the intelligence work of the State Department should cease in any way. It should be carried on as heretofore but the directors of the three agencies should be constantly kept in touch by the State Department with the work it is doing." (Memorandum from the President to the Secretary of State, 6/26/39.)

89. Hoover memorandum, enclosed with letter from Cummings to the President, 10/20/38.

90. Memorandum from Hoover to the Attorney General, 9/6/39.

91. Letter from Murphy to the President, 9/6/39.

92. E. A. Tamm, Memoranda for the File, 9/6/39, 11:34 a.m., 12:47 p.m., 2:30 p.m., 6:20 p.m. This memorandum indicates Tamm was told that the President's statement would declare that the FBI was authorized to investigate "subversive activities." There is no explanation for the disparity between this message and the President's actual statement.

93. Statement of the President, 9/6/39.

94. New York Times, 9/7/39, p. 8, col. 1.

95. New York Times, 10/1/39, p. 38, col. 3.

96. Proclamation, 9/8/39, 54 Stat. 2643.

97. Executive Order No. 8247, 9/8/39, cited in letter from Attorney General Murphy to the President, 9/12/39, Roosevelt Library, Official File 14-b, Box 14.

98. 1939 Public Papers of Franklin D. Roosevelt, pp. 495-496.

99. Confidential memorandum from President Roosevelt to Attorney General Jackson, 5/21/40. In May 1941 the Secretary of War and the Secretary of the Navy urged "a broadening of the investigative responsibility of the Federal Bureau of Investigation in the fields of subversive control of labor." (Memorandum from the Secretary of War and the Secretary of the Navy to the President, 5/29/41.) The President replied that he was sending their letter to the Attorney General with my General approval. (Memorandum from President Roosevelt to the Secretaries of War and Navy, 6/4/41.) Attorney General Biddle's response cited investigations under the recently enacted Smith Act. (Memorandum from Attorney General Biddle to the President, 6/23/41.)

100. Attorney General's Order No. 3732, 9/25/42.

101. Statement of the President on "Police Cooperation," 1/8/43. A note in the President's handwriting added that the FBI was to receive information "relating to espionage and related matters."

102. Memorandum from Attorney General Biddle to Assistant Attorney General Hugh Cox and FBI Director Hoover, 7/16/43.

103. The enclosure is not provided as it did not add anything of CI significance.

104. Memorandum from Hoover to Field Offices, 9/2/39.

105. Memorandum from Clyde Tolson to Hoover, 10/30/39.

106. Memorandum for E. A. Tamm, 11/9/39.

107. Memorandum from Hoover to Field Offices, 12/6/39.

108. Memorandum for E. A. Tamm, 12/2/39.

109. Memorandum from Hoover to Field Offices, 6/15/40.

110. Memorandum for the Director, 8/19/40.

111. Memorandum from Hoover to M. F. McGuire, the Assistant to the Attorney General, 8/21/40.

112. *Proceedings of the Federal State Conference on Law Enforcement Problems of National Defense*, 8/5-6/40.

113. Letter from Attorney General Cummings to the President (and enclosure), 1/30/37. (FDR Library.)

114. Letter from Attorney general Cummings to the President (and enclosure), 8/13/37. (FDR Library.)

115. Report of New York City Field Office, 10/22/41, summarized in Justice Department memorandum from s. Brodie to Assistant Attorney General Quinn, 10/10/47.

116. Report of Chicago Field Office, 12/29/44, summarized in Justice Department memorandum from S. Brodie to Assistant Attorney General Quinn, 10/9/47.

117. Justice Department memorandum re Christian Front, 10/28/41.

118. Report of New York City Field Office, 9/7/45, summarized in Justice Department memorandum from s. Brodie to Assistant Attorney general Quinn, 10/9/47.

119. Report of Washington, D.C. Field Office, 3/11/41.

120. Report of Oklahoma City Field Office, 9/19/41.

121. Report of Los Angeles field Office, 7/27/42; report of Norfolk, Virginia Field Office, 4/18/42.

122. Report of Louisville, Kentucky Field Office, 2/13/43.

123. Report of Savannah, Georgia Field Office, 9/9/43.

124. Report of Oklahoma City Field Office, 10/29/43.

125. Report of Chicago Field Office, 11/24/43.

126. Report of Detroit Field Office, 1/15/44.

127. Report of Detroit Field Office, 1/15/44.

128. Whithead, *The FBI Story*, p. 329.

www.ingramcontent.com/pod-product-compliance
Lightning Source LLC
Chambersburg PA
CBHW080440170426
43195CB00017B/2839